THE CITIZEN'S HANDBOOK

THE CITIZEN'S HANDBOOK

Compiled by T. J. Stiles

BERKLEY BOOKS, NEW YORK

THE CITIZEN'S HANDBOOK

A Berkley Book / published by arrangement with
the compiler

PRINTING HISTORY
Berkley mass market edition / August 1993
Berkley trade paperback edition / September 1994

ISBN: 0-425-14387-2

BERKLEY®
Berkley Books are published by The Berkley Publishing Group,
200 Madison Avenue, New York, New York 10016.
BERKLEY and the "B" design
are trademarks belonging to Berkley Publishing Corporation.

PRINTED IN THE UNITED STATES OF AMERICA

10 9 8 7 6 5 4 3 2 1

CONTENTS

INTRODUCTION

America, it has often been said, is a nation built on law. One of the most remarkable things the founders did, as they tried to build a new nation, was to create one basic body of law to define the powers, limits, and operations of the national government: the Constitution. Other nations in the past had been democracies, but none had such a sweeping, carefully crafted fundamental law; even today, Britain has no equivalent. In the Constitution, the founders transformed the democratic, libertarian ideals of the Revolution into a practical system of government. Since it went into effect in 1789, almost every aspect of American public life has flowed from it, or has been tested against it.

If any consistent theme unites the documents and speeches in this book, it is the continuing power of our original ideals. Unlike most nations—in the eighteenth century or today—the United States is a country built by immigrants descended from a vast array of peoples, races, and religions. We are a diverse nation held together by the same ideals expressed by the people who won the American Revolution—equality, personal liberty, democratic government—and by the Constitution they created to guarantee them. Each generation has returned to the Constitution, to writings such as Tom Paine's *Common Sense* and the Declaration of Independence (all of which are here in this volume), and has found fresh meaning in the principles expressed there.

The remaining entries in this volume, however, do more than simply restate the Constitution and its principles. As Americans have returned to the founding documents for inspiration, they have fought bitterly over the true meaning of those words. Laws and ideals, after all, emerge from politics—often dirty, nasty, and even (as in the Civil War) bloody. The Constitutional Convention of 1787 itself was no lovefest: It was an often rough debate between men who shared the same ideals, but interpreted them in ways that benefited themselves most. The delegates from small states believed in the majority-rule principle of democracy, for example, but they did not want to be drowned out by the states with large populations. Slaveowners believed in personal liberty, but did not believe it included African Americans—slave *or* free man. As remarkable a founding document as the Constitution is, it is a product of political compromise between what would be called "special interests" today.

This blend of idealism and practicality—praised by Benjamin Franklin in an entry in this book—continues to be an important theme in American politics and government. One of the most important speeches in early American history is George Washington's Farewell Address, also found here. Washington's address is remembered best for two warnings, one of which Americans followed for over a century and another that was immediately ignored. Washington condemned alliances with foreign powers—an injunction followed until World War I—but he also warned against the divisiveness of party politics. Americans then and now admired Washington's high idealism and sense of public duty, but citizens in a democracy inevitably organize into parties, according to their beliefs and interests. From the earliest days to the 1990s, critics have warned that partisan political bickering will destroy the nation; but somehow we have managed to muddle through, Constitution and ideals intact.

The workings of politics, however, in battles between opposing interests and opposing beliefs, have changed the way we view the Constitution and our founding ideals. Most of the great conflicts in American history—over slavery and equal rights for women and African Americans, to name a few—have been fought between groups that believed they were protecting the true meaning of our Constitutional principles. The entries in this book show us how these principles were remade and expanded by the great figures who fought those political battles—and who found fresh meaning in our original ideals.

In these pages, we hear from Frederick Douglass, condemning slavery in terms that would have been familiar to slaveowning Thomas Jefferson when he battled against British rule. We read Abraham Lincoln's great speeches, which call forth the memory of the Revolution to redefine the meaning of liberty in the midst of the Civil War. We hear from Susan B. Anthony, arguing that the rights of women are implicit within the Constitution, that what was needed was for Americans to realize the true essence of what we claimed to believe. Leaders like these pushed back the frontier of prejudice, slowly building a generous, open understanding of who an American is, and what he or she is entitled to. In Martin Luther King, Jr.'s "I Have a Dream" speech and President Lyndon B. Johnson's "We Shall Overcome" address, this process culminated in the triumph of the civil rights movement, as both the American people and the federal government recognized the right of everyone to equal dignity under the law.

Not all conflicts in American history, unfortunately, have had such heartening results. One group of Americans—the original group—suffered such destruction at the hands of the majority that it has yet to recover. Two items in this volume represent the history of the conflict between the immigrant Americans and the native Indians. The first is from an address to Congress by Andrew Jackson, an old Indian fighter himself who presided over the catastrophic, forced removal of five Indian nations from Georgia and the Gulf states to what is now Oklahoma in the 1830s. Jackson's address described the logic of conquest which was brutally applied to the Native Americans throughout the nineteenth century: Since white Americans were more numerous, more advanced, and stronger, they had the right to do what they wanted to the Indians. The essay that follows it, by Chief Joseph of the Nez Percés tribe, eloquently answers that logic with a powerful description of the Indians' dignified efforts to maintain their traditional existence in their ancestral homelands.

American government, of course, has been concerned with more than the divisions between the peoples on our shores. In the twentieth century the United States emerged as one of the most powerful nations the world has ever seen, and it has been drawn into conflicts and alliances overseas (despite the early warnings of George Washington). As in domestic politics, the American approach to international politics has been a mix of lofty principles and practical concern for protecting our interests. In this book, we see how Franklin D. Roosevelt and Harry S Truman defined America's goals in the two greatest international conflicts of the century—the Second World War and the Cold War—with just this blend of idealism and self-interest. The United States entered both struggles out of fear for our survival (as seen in Roosevelt's "Day of Infamy" address and Truman's doctrine of containing communist expansion), but we viewed these struggles in terms of basic rights, much as we envision the United States itself. Both Roosevelt's "Four Freedoms" address and Truman's speech put forward the ideals where our foreign policy was ultimately directed. This combination of realism and idealism continues to shape our foreign policy today.

The twentieth century has also brought unexpected challenges at home, challenges that have led to great changes in our vision of what government should do. When Franklin D. Roosevelt was elected in 1932, in the midst of the Great Depression, he responded with the New Deal—a burst of activity, of dramatic new legislation that expressed the view that the national government needed to act to improve the lot of its suffering citizens. His first inaugural address captured this spirit, filling Americans with confidence that Washington would respond to the economic crisis.

A few decades later, a revered old general, President Dwight D. Eisenhower, took advantage of his farewell address to warn Americans of the dangers of the Cold War. With an acute understanding that few in government shared, he warned that the demands of an immense military establishment to oppose the Soviet Union were distorting our economy and government. An immense "military-industrial complex" had arisen, he noted, and it posed almost as great a threat to our traditional notion of free and limited government as any foreign enemy. Little was done in response to Eisenhower's warning, but his address was a clarion call alerting us to a sweeping change in our society.

No book this size can contain anything but a small sample of the words that have built our notion of what America means, but the sample here speaks to the most important changes that have come about in the last two centuries or so. It also speaks to the astonishing durability of our founding ideals and laws. We owe a remarkable debt to our founding fathers. They lived in a very different time and world than we do now—a world with far fewer people, far less advanced science, where transportation was slow and horizons close at hand. But they set forth a set of principles that transcended their own times and circumstances, and they established laws and a political tradition that allowed those principles to live and grow.

We also owe a tremendous debt to those who have found fresh meaning in those same ideals. From Frederick Douglass to Martin Luther King, Jr., from Abraham Lincoln to Franklin D. Roosevelt, we have had leaders who fought the limitations and injustices of their times within the great framework of the Constitution. The great rebels of our history might have fought to overthrow the whole system of government; the great presidents might have trampled the limits of the Constitution to accomplish what they wanted. Instead, they picked up the tremendous legacy of the founders and infused their principles with new life, expanded them to new limits. Thanks to them, the American Revolution has never quite ended.

—T. J. Stiles

—1—

COMMON SENSE

Thomas Paine

January, 1776

In 1774, an Englishman named Thomas Paine moved to Philadelphia, where he soon established himself with the help of Benjamin Franklin. As the American Revolution erupted, he took over as editor of the *Philadelphia Magazine* while he developed the case for American independence. Influenced by such men as Franklin and Benjamin Rush, Paine composed a powerful series of pamphlets entitled *The American Crisis*, which he published over the course of the war. General George Washington was so taken by the first one that he had it read aloud to his troops in December, 1775.

Shortly after, on January 10, 1776, Paine published his most influential pamphlet of all: *Common Sense*. Written in straightforward, compelling language, *Common Sense* made a powerful case for outright independence from England (an issue that was still hotly debated in the rebellious colonies). Paine drew on both the Bible and natural reason to attack the very idea of monarchical government, and he argued that the American people would prosper as an independent nation.

Common Sense became an immediate bestseller; tens of thousands of copies were sold within weeks of publication.

Paine's eloquent and forceful arguments propelled independence to the center of public debate. Seven months later, the Continental Congress voted in favor of the Declaration of Independence. *Common Sense* proved to be one of the most influential and enduring statements of the Revolution's democratic ideals and of the colonists' grievances against Britain.

The excerpt that follows omits Paine's scriptural arguments and the details of his proposals for a government charter and a navy.

COMMON SENSE

OF THE ORIGIN AND DESIGN OF GOVERNMENT IN GENERAL. WITH CONCISE REMARKS ON THE ENGLISH CONSTITUTION.

Some writers have so confounded society with government, as to leave little or no distinction between them; whereas they are not only different, but have different origins. Society is produced by our wants, and government by our wickedness; the former promotes our happiness *positively* by uniting our affections, the latter *negatively* by restraining our vices. The one encourages intercourse, the other creates distinctions. The first is a patron, the last a punisher.

Society in every state is a blessing, but government even in its best state is but a necessary evil; in its worst state an intolerable one; for when we suffer, or are exposed to the same miseries *by a government*, which we might expect in a country *without government*, our calamities is heightened by reflecting that we furnish the means by which we suffer. Government, like dress, is the badge of lost innocence; the palaces of kings are built on the ruins of the bowers of paradise. For were the impulses of conscience clear, uniform, and irresistibly obeyed, man would need no other lawgiver; but that not being the case, he finds it necessary to surrender up a part of his property to furnish means for the protection of the rest; and this he is induced to do by the same prudence which in every other case advises him out of two evils to choose the least. *Wherefore,* security being the true design and end of government, it unanswerably follows that whatever *form* thereof appears most likely to ensure it to us, with the least expence and greatest benefit, is preferable to all others.

In order to gain a clear and just idea of the design and end of government, let us suppose a small number of persons settled in some sequestered part of the earth, unconnected with the rest, they will then represent the first peopling of any country, or of the world. In this state of natural liberty, society will be their first thought. A thousand motives will excite them thereto, the strength of one man is so unequal to his wants, and his mind so unfitted for perpetual solitude, that he is soon obliged to seek assistance and relief of another, who in his turn requires the same. Four or five united would be able to raise a tolerable dwelling in the midst of a wilderness, but *one* man might labour out the common period of life without accomplishing any thing; when he had felled his timber he could not remove it, nor erect it after it was removed; hunger in the mean time would urge him from his work, and every different want call him a different way. Disease, nay even misfortune would be death, for though neither might be mortal, yet either would disable him from living, and reduce him to a state in which he might rather be said to perish than to die.

Thus necessity, like a gravitating power, would soon form our newly arrived emigrants into society, the reciprocal blessings of which, would supercede, and render the obligations of law and government unnecessary while they remained perfectly just to each other; but as nothing but heaven is impregnable to vice, it will unavoidably happen, that in proportion as they surmount the first difficulties of emigration, which bound them together in a common cause, they will begin to relax in their duty and attachment to each other; and this remissness, will point out the necessity, of establishing some form of government to supply the defect of moral virtue.

Some convenient tree will afford them a State-House, under the branches of which, the whole colony may assemble to deliberate on public matters. It is more than probable that their first laws will have the title only of REGULATIONS, and be enforced by no other penalty than public disesteem. In this first parliament every man, by natural right will have a seat.

But as the colony increases, the public concerns will increase likewise, and the distance at which the members may be separated, will render it too inconvenient for all of them to meet on every occasion as at first, when their number was small, their habitations near, and the public concerns few and trifling. This will point out the convenience of their consenting to leave the legislative part to be managed by a select number chosen from the whole body, who are supposed to have the same concerns at stake which those have who appointed them, and who will act in the same manner as the whole body would act were they present. If the colony continue increasing, it will become necessary to augment the number of the representatives, and that the interest of every part of the colony may be attended to, it will be found best to divide the whole into convenient parts, each part sending its proper number; and that the *elected* might never form to themselves an interest separate from the *electors*, prudence will point out the propriety of having elections often; because as the *elected* might by that means return and mix again with the general body of the *electors* in a few months, their fidelity to the public will be secured by the prudent reflexion of not making a rod for themselves. And as this frequent interchange will establish a common interest with every part of the community, they will mutually and naturally support each other, and on this (not on the unmeaning name of king) depends the *strength of government, and the happiness of the governed.*

Here then is the origin and rise of government; namely, a mode rendered necessary by the inability of moral virtue to govern the world; here too is the design and end of government, viz. freedom and security. And however our eyes may be dazzled with snow, or our ears deceived by sound; however prejudice may warp our wills, or interest darken our understanding, the simple voice of nature and of reason will say, it is right.

I draw my idea of the form of government from a principle in nature, which no art can overturn, viz. that the more simple any thing is, the less liable it is to be disordered, and the easier repaired when disordered; and with this maxim in view, I offer a few remarks on the so much boasted constitution of England. That it was noble for the dark and slavish times in which it was erected is granted. When the world was over-run with tyranny the least remove therefrom was a glorious rescue. But that it is imperfect, subject to convulsions, and incapable of producing what it seems to promise, is easily demonstrated.

Absolute governments (tho' the disgrace of human nature) have this advantage with them, that they are simple; if the people suffer, they know the head from which their suffering springs, know likewise the remedy, and are not bewildered by a variety of causes and cures. But the constitution of England is so exceedingly complex, that the nation may suffer for years together without being able to discover in which part the fault lies, some will say in one and some in another, and every political physician will advise a different medicine.

I know it is difficult to get over local or long standing prejudices, yet if we will suffer ourselves to examine the component parts of the English constitution, we shall find them to be the base remains of two ancient tyrannies, compounded with some new republican materials.

First.–The remains of monarchical tyranny in the person of the king.

Secondly.–The remains of aristocratical tyranny in the persons of the peers.

Thirdly.–The new republican materials, in the persons of the commons, on whose virtue depends the freedom of England.

The two first, by being hereditary, are independent of the people; wherefore in a *constitutional sense* they contribute nothing towards the freedom of the state.

To say that the constitution of England is a *union* of three powers reciprocally *checking* each other, is farcical, either the words have no meaning, or they are flat contradictions.

To say that the commons is a check upon the king, presupposes two things.

First.–That the king is not to be trusted without being looked after, or in other words, that a thirst for absolute power is the natural disease of monarchy.

Secondly.–That the commons, by being appointed for that purpose, are either wiser or more worthy of confidence than the crown.

But as the same constitution which gives the commons a power to check the king by withholding the supplies, gives afterwards the king a power to check the commons, by empowering him to reject their other bills; it again supposes that the king is wiser than those whom it has already supposed to be wiser than him. A mere absurdity!

There is something exceedingly ridiculous in the composition of monarchy; it first excludes a man from the means of information, yet empowers him to act in cases where the highest judgment is required. The state of a king shuts him from the world, yet the business of a king requires him to know it thoroughly; wherefore the different parts, unnaturally opposing and destroying each other, prove the whole character to be absurd and useless.

Some writers have explained the English constitution thus; the king, say they, is one, the people another; the peers are an house in behalf of the king; the commons in behalf of the people; but this hath all the distinctions of an house divided against itself; and though the expressions be pleasantly arranged, yet when examined they appear idle and ambiguous; and it will always happen, that the nicest construction that words are capable of, when applied to the description of some thing which either cannot exist, or is too incomprehensible to be within the compass of description, will be words of sound only, and though they may amuse the ear, they cannot inform the mind, for this explanation includes a previous question, viz. *How came the king by a power which the people are afraid to trust, and always obliged to check?* Such a power could not be the gift of a wise people, neither can any power, *which needs checking*, be from God; yet the provision, which the constitution makes, supposes such a power to exist.

But the provision is unequal to the task; the means either cannot or will not accomplish the end, and the whole affair is a *felo de se*; for as the greater weight will always carry up the less, and as all the wheels of a machine are put in motion by one, it only remains to know which power in the constitution has the most weight, for that will govern; and though the others, or a part of them, may clog, or, as the phrase is, check the rapidity of its motion, yet so long as they cannot stop it, their endeavours will be ineffectual; the first moving power will at last have its way, and what it wants in speed is supplied by time.

That the crown is this overbearing part in the English constitution needs not be mentioned, and that it derives its whole consequence merely from being the giver of places and pensions is self-evident, wherefore, though we have been wise enough to shut and lock a door against absolute monarchy, we at the same time have been foolish enough to put the crown in possession of the key.

The prejudice of Englishmen, in favour of their own government by king, lords, and commons, arises as much or more from national pride than reason. Individuals are undoubtedly safer in England than in some other countries, but the *will* of the king is as much the *law* of the land in Britain as in France, with this difference, that instead of proceeding directly from his mouth, it is handed to the people under the most formidable shape of an act of parliament. For the fate of Charles the First, hath only made kings more subtle—not more just.

Wherefore, laying aside all national pride and prejudice in favour of modes and forms, the plain truth is, that *it is wholly owing to the constitution of the people, and not to the constitution of the government* that the crown is not as oppressive in England as in Turkey.

An inquiry into the *constitutional errors* in the English form of government is at this time highly necessary; for as we are never in a proper condition of doing justice to others, while we continue under the influence of some leading partiality, so neither are we capable of doing it to ourselves while we remain fettered by any obstinate prejudice. And as a man, who is attached to a prostitute, is unfitted to choose or judge of a wife, so any prepossession in favour of a rotten constitution of government will disable us from discerning a good one.

OF MONARCHY AND HEREDITARY SUCCESSION.

Mankind being originally equals in the order of creation, the equality could only be destroyed by some subsequent circumstance; the distinctions of rich, and poor, may in a great measure be accounted for, and that without having recourse to the harsh, ill-sounding names of oppression and avarice. Oppression is often the *consequence*, but seldom or never the *means* of riches; and though avarice will preserve a man from being necessitously poor, it generally makes him too timorous to be wealthy.

But there is another and greater distinction for which no truly natural or religious reason can be assigned, and that is, the distinction of men into KINGS and SUBJECTS. Male and female are the distinctions of nature, good and bad the distinctions of heaven; but how a race of men came into the world so exalted above the rest, and distinguished like some new species, is worth enquiring into, and whether they are the means of happiness or of misery to mankind.

In the early ages of the world, according to the scripture chronology, there were no kings; the consequence of which was there were no wars; it is the pride of kings which throw mankind into confusion. Holland without a king hath enjoyed more peace for this last century than any of the monarchial governments in Europe. Antiquity favors the same remark; for the quiet and rural lives of the first patriarchs hath a happy something in them, which vanishes away when we come to the history of Jewish royalty. . . .

To the evil of monarchy we have added that of hereditary succession; and as the first is a degredation and lessening of ourselves, so the second, claimed as a matter of right, is an insult and an imposition on posterity. For all men being originally equals, no *one* by *birth* could have a right to set up his own family in perpetual preference to all others for ever, and though himself might deserve *some* decent degree of honors of his contemporaries, yet his descendants might be far too unworthy to inherit them. One of the strongest *natural* proofs of the folly of hereditary right in kings, is, that nature disapproves it, otherwise she would not so frequently turn it into ridicule by giving mankind an *ass for a lion.*

Secondly, as no man at first could possess any other public honors than were bestowed upon him, so the givers of those honors could have no power to give away the right of posterity, and though they might say 'We choose you for *our* head,' they could not, without manifest injustice to their children, say 'that your children and your children's children shall reign over *ours* for ever.' Because such an unwise, unjust, unnatural compact might (perhaps) in the next succession put them under the government of a rogue or a fool. Most wise men, in their private sentiments, have ever treated hereditary right with contempt; yet it is one of those evils, which when once established is not easily removed; many submit from fear, others from superstition, and the more powerful part shares with the king the plunder of the rest.

This is supposing the present race of kings in the world to have had an honourable origin; whereas it is more than probable, that could we take off the dark covering of antiquity, and trace them to their first rise, that we should find the first of them nothing better than the principal ruffian of some restless gang, whose savage manners or pre-eminence in subtilty obtained him the title of chief among plunderers; and who by increasing in power, and extending his depredations, over-awed the quiet and defenceless to purchase their safety by frequent contributions. Yet his electors could have no idea of giving hereditary right to his descendants, because such a perpetual exclusion of themselves was incompatible with the free and unrestrained principles they professed to live by. Wherefore, hereditary succession in the early ages of monarchy could not take place as a matter of claim, but as something casual or complimental; but as few or no records were extant in those days, and traditionary history stuffed with fables, it was very easy, after the lapse of a few generations, to trump up some superstitious tale, conveniently timed, Mahomet like, to cram hereditary right down the throats of the vulgar. Perhaps the disorders which threatened, or seemed to threaten on the decease of a leader and the choice of a new one (for elections among ruffians could not be very orderly) induced many at first to favor hereditary pretentions; by which means it happened, as it hath happened since, that what at first was submitted to as a convenience, was afterwards claimed as a right.

England, since the conquest, hath known some few good monarchs, but groaned beneath a much larger number of bad ones, yet no man in his senses can say that their claim under William the Conqueror is a very honorable one. A French bastard landing with an armed banditti, and establishing himself king of England against the consent of the natives, is in plain terms a very paltry rascally original.—It certainly hath no divinity in it. However, it is needless to spend much time in exposing the folly of hereditary right, if there are any so weak as to believe it, let them promiscuously worship the ass and lion, and welcome. I shall neither copy their humility, nor disturb their devotion.

Yet I should be glad to ask how they suppose kings came at first? The question admits but of three answers, viz. either by lot, by election, or by usurpation. If the first king was taken by lot, it establishes a precedent for the next, which excludes hereditary succession. Saul was by lot yet the succession was not hereditary, neither does it appear from that transaction there was any intention it ever should. If the first king of any country was by election, that likewise establishes a precedent for the next; for to say, that the *right* of all future generations is taken away, by the act of the first electors, in their choice not only of a king, but of a family of kings for ever, hath no parallel in or out of scripture but the doctrine of original sin, which supposes the free will of all men lost in Adam; and from such comparison, and it will admit of no other, hereditary succession can derive no glory. For as in Adam all sinned, and as in the first electors all men obeyed; as in the one all mankind were subjected to Satan, and in the other to Sovereignty; as our innocence was lost in the first, and our authority in the last; and as both disable us from re-assuming some former state and privilege, it unanswerably follows that original sin and hereditary succession are parallels. Dishonourable rank!

Inglorious connexion! Yet the most subtile sophist cannot produce a juster simile.

As to usurpation, no man will be so hardy as to defend it; and that William the Conqueror was an usurper is a fact not to be contradicted. The plain truth is, that the antiquity of English monarchy will not bear looking into.

But it is not so much the absurdity as the evil of hereditary succession which concerns mankind. Did it ensure a race of good and wise men it would have the seal of divine authority, but as it opens a door to the *foolish*, the *wicked*, and the *improper*, it hath in it the nature of oppression. Men who look upon themselves born to reign, and others to obey, soon grow insolent; selected from the rest of mankind their minds are early poisoned by importance; and the world they act in differs so materially from the world at large, that they have but little opportunity of knowing its true interests, and when they succeed to the government are frequently the most ignorant and unfit of any throughout the dominions.

Another evil which attends hereditary succession is, that the throne is subject to be possessed by a minor at any age; all which time the regency, acting under the cover of a king, have every opportunity and inducement to betray their trust. The same national misfortune happens, when a king worn out with age and infirmity, enters the last stage of human weakness. In both these cases the public becomes a prey to every miscreant, who can tamper successfully with the follies either of age or infancy.

The most plausible plea, which hath ever been offered in favour of hereditary succession, is, that it preserves a nation from civil wars; and were this true, it would be weighty; whereas, it is the most barefaced falsity ever imposed upon mankind. The whole history of England disowns the fact. Thirty kings and two minors have reigned in that distracted kingdom since the conquest, in which time there have been (including the Revolution) no less than eight civil wars and nineteen rebellions. Wherefore instead of making for peace, it makes against it, and destroys the very foundation it seems to stand on.

The contest for monarchy and succession, between the houses of York and Lancaster, laid England in a scene of blood for many years. Twelve pitched battles, besides skirmishes and sieges, were fought between Henry and Edward. Twice was Henry prisoner to Edward, who in his turn was prisoner to Henry. And so uncertain is the fate of war and the temper of a nation, when nothing but personal matters are the ground of a quarrel, that Henry was taken in triumph from a prison to a palace, and Edward obliged to fly from a palace to a foreign land; yet, as sudden transitions of temper are seldom lasting, Henry in his turn was driven from the throne, and Edward recalled to succeed him. The parliament always following the strongest side.

This contest began in the reign of Henry the Sixth, and was not entirely extinguished till Henry the Seventh, in whom the families were united. Including a period of 67 years, viz. from 1422 to 1489.

In short, monarchy and succession have laid (not this or that kingdom only) but the world in blood and ashes. 'Tis a form of government which the word of God bears testimony against, and blood will attend it.

If we inquire into the business of a king, we shall find that in some countries they have none; and after sauntering away their lives without pleasure to themselves or advantage to the nation, withdraw from the scene, and leave their successors to tread the same idle round. In absolute monarchies the whole weight of business civil and military, lies on the king; the children of Israel in their request for a king, urged this plea 'that he may judge us, and go out before us and fight our battles.' But in countries where he is neither a judge nor a general, as in E—d, a man would be puzzled to know what *is* his business.

The nearer any government approaches to a republic the less business there is for a king. It is somewhat difficult to find a proper name for the government of E—. Sir William Meredith calls it a republic; but in its present state it is unworthy of the name, because the corrupt influence of the crown, by having all the places in its disposal, hath so effectually swallowed up the power, and eaten out the virtue of the house of commons (the republican part in the constitution) that the government of England is nearly as monarchical as that of France or Spain. Men fall out with names without understanding them. For it is the republican and not the monarchical part of the constitution of England which Englishmen glory in, viz. the liberty of choosing an house of commons from out of their own body—and it is easy to see that when the republican virtue fails, slavery ensues. Why is the constitution of E—d sickly, but because monarchy hath poisoned the republic, the crown hath engrossed the commons?

In England a k— hath little more to do than to make war and give away places; which in plain terms, is to impoverish the nation and set it together by the ears. A pretty business indeed for a man to be allowed eight hundred thousand sterling a year for, and worshipped into the bargain! Of more worth is one honest man to society, and in the sight of God, than all the crowned ruffians that ever lived.

THOUGHTS ON THE PRESENT STATE OF AMERICAN AFFAIRS.

In the following pages I offer nothing more than simple facts, plain arguments, and common sense; and have no other preliminaries to settle with the reader, than that he will divest himself of prejudice and prepossession, and suffer his reason and his feelings to determine for themselves; that he will put *on*, or rather that he will not put *off*, the true character of a man, and generously enlarge his views beyond the present day.

Volumes have been written on the subject of the struggle between England and America. Men of all ranks have embarked in the controversy, from different motives, and with various designs; but all have been ineffectual, and the period of debate is closed. Arms, as the last resource, decide the contest; the appeal was the choice of the king, and the continent hath accepted the challenge. . . .

The sun never shined on a cause of greater worth. 'Tis not the affair of a city, a country, a province, or a kingdom, but of a continent—of at least one eighth part of the habitable globe. 'Tis not the concern of a day, a year, or an age; posterity are virtually involved in the contest, and will be more or less affected, even to the end of time, by the proceedings now. Now is the seed time of continental union, faith and honor. The least fracture now will be like a name engraved with the point of a pin on the tender rind of a young oak; the wound will enlarge with the tree, and posterity read it in full grown characters.

By referring the matter from argument to arms, a new æra for politics is struck; a new method of thinking hath arisen. All plans, proposals, &c. prior to the nineteenth of April, *i. e.* to the commencement of hostilities, are like the almanacks of the last year;

which, though proper then, are superceded and useless now. Whatever was advanced by the advocates on either side of the question then, terminated in one and the same point, viz. a union with Great Britain; the only difference between the parties was the method of effecting it; the one proposing force, the other friendship; but it hath so far happened that the first hath failed, and the second hath withdrawn her influence.

As much hath been said of the advantages of reconciliation, which, like an agreeable dream, hath passed away and left us as we were, it is but right, that we should examine the contrary side of the argument, and inquire into some of the many material injuries which these colonies sustain, and always will sustain, by being connected with, and dependant on Great Britain. To examine that connexion and dependance, on the principles of nature and common sense, to see what we have to trust to, if separated, and what we are to expect, if dependant.

I have heard it asserted by some, that as America hath flourished under her former connexion with Great-Britain, that the same connexion is necessary towards her future happiness, and will always have the same effect. Nothing can be more fallacious than this kind of argument. We may as well assert, that because a child has thrived upon milk, that it is never to have meat; or that the first twenty years of our lives is to become a precedent for the next twenty. But even this is admitting more than is true, for I answer roundly, that America would have flourished as much, and probably much more, had no European power had any thing to do with her. The commerce by which she hath enriched herself are the necessaries of life, and will always have a market while eating is the custom of Europe.

But she has protected us, say some. That she hath engrossed us is true, and defended the continent at our expence as well as her own is admitted, and she would have defended Turkey from the same motive, viz. the sake of trade and dominion.

Alas, we have been long led away by ancient prejudices, and made large sacrifices to superstition. We have boasted the protection of Great-Britain, without considering, that her motive was *interest*, not *attachment*; that she did not protect us from *our enemies* on *our account*, but from *her enemies* on *her own account*, from those who had no quarrel with us on any *other account*, and who will always be our enemies on the *same account*. Let Britain wave her pretensions to the continent, or the continent throw off the dependance, and we should be at peace with France and Spain were they at war with Britain. The miseries of Hanover last war ought to warn us against connexions.

It hath lately been asserted in parliament, that the colonies have no relation to each other but through the parent country, *i. e.* that Pennsylvania and the Jerseys, and so on for the rest, are sister colonies by the way of England; this is certainly a very roundabout way of proving relationship, but it is the nearest and only true way of proving enemyship, if I may so call it. France and Spain never were, nor perhaps ever will be our enemies as *Americans*, but as our being the *subjects of Great Britain.*

But Britain is the parent country, say some. Then the more shame upon her conduct. Even brutes do not devour their young, nor savages make war upon their families; wherefore the assertion, if true, turns to her reproach; but it happens not to be true, or only partly so, and the phrase *parent* or *mother country* hath been jesuitically adopted by the — and his parasites, with a low papistical design of gaining an unfair bias on the credulous weakness of our minds. Europe, and not England, is the parent country of America. This new world hath been the asylum for the persecuted lovers of civil and religious liberty from *every part* of Europe. Hither have they fled, not from the tender embraces of the mother, but from the cruelty of the monster; and it is so far true of England, that the same tyranny which drove the first emigrants from home, pursues their descendants still.

In this extensive quarter of the globe, we forget the narrow limits of three hundred and sixty miles (the extent of England) and carry our friendship on a larger scale; we claim brotherhood with eve-European christian, and triumph in the generosity of the sentiment.

It is pleasant to observe by what regular gradations we surmount the force of local prejudice, as we enlarge our acquaintance with the world. A man born in any town in England divided into parishes, will naturally associate most with his fellow parishioners (because their interests in many cases will be common) and distinguish him by the name of *neighbour*; if he meet him but a few miles from home, he drops the narrow idea of a street, and salutes him by the name of *townsman*; if he travels out of the county, and meet him in any other, he forgets the minor divisions of street and town, and calls him *countryman*, i. e. *countyman*; but if in their foreign excursions they should associate in France or any other part of *Europe*, their local remembrance would be enlarged into that of *Englishmen.* And by a just parity of reasoning, all

Europeans meeting in America, or any other quarter of the globe, are *countrymen*; for England, Holland, Germany, or Sweden, when compared with the whole, stand in the same places on the larger scale, which the divisions of street, town, and county do on the smaller ones; distinctions too limited for continental minds. Not one third of the inhabitants, even of this province, are of English descent. Wherefore I reprobate the phrase of parent or mother country applied to England only, as being false, selfish, narrow and ungenerous.

But admitting that we were all of English descent, what does it amount to? Nothing. Britain, being now an open enemy, extinguishes every other name and title: And to say that reconciliation is our duty, is truly farcical. The first king of England, of the present line (William the Conqueror) was a Frenchman, and half the peers of England are descendants from the same country; wherefore by the same method of reasoning, England ought to be governed by France.

Much hath been said of the united strength of Britain and the colonies, that in conjunction they might bid defiance to the world. But this is mere presumption; the fate of war is uncertain, neither do the expressions mean any thing; for this continent would never suffer itself to be drained of inhabitants to support the British arms in either Asia, Africa, or Europe.

Besides, what have we to do with setting the world at defiance? Our plan is commerce, and that, well attended to, will secure us the peace and friendship of all Europe; because it is the interest of all Europe to have America a *free port*. Her trade will always be a protection, and her barrenness of gold and silver secure her from invaders.

I challenge the warmest advocate for reconciliation, to shew, a single advantage that this continent can reap, by being connected with Great Britain. I repeat the challenge, not a single advantage is derived. Our corn will fetch its price in any market in Europe, and our imported goods must be paid for buy them where we will.

But the injuries and disadvantages we sustain by that connection, are without number; and our duty to mankind at large, as well as to ourselves, instruct us to renounce the alliance: Because, any submission to, or dependance on Great Britain, tends directly to involve this continent in European wars and quarrels; and sets us at variance with nations, who would otherwise seek our friendship, and against whom, we have neither anger nor complaint. As

Europe is our market for trade, we ought to form no partial connection with any part of it. It is the true interest of America to steer clear of European contentions, which she never can do, while by her dependance on Britain, she is made the make-weight in the scale of British politics.

Europe is too thickly planted with kingdoms to be long at peace, and whenever a war breaks out between England and any foreign power, the trade of America goes to ruin, *because of her connection with Britain.* The next war may not turn out like the last, and should it not, the advocates for reconciliation now will be wishing for separation then, because, neutrality in that case, would be a safer convoy than a man of war. Every thing that is right or natural pleads for separation. The blood of the slain, the weeping voice of nature cries, 'TIS TIME TO PART. Even the distance at which the Almighty hath placed England and America, is a strong and natural proof, that the authority of the one, over the other, was never the design of Heaven. The time likewise at which the continent was discovered, adds weight to the argument, and the manner in which it was peopled encreases the force of it. The reformation was preceded by the discovery of America, as if the Almighty graciously meant to open a sanctuary to the persecuted in future years, when home should afford neither friendship nor safety.

The authority of Great-Britain over this continent, is a form of government, which sooner or later must have an end: And a serious mind can draw no true pleasure by looking forward, under the painful and positive conviction, that what he calls 'the present constitution' is merely temporary. As parents, we can have no joy, knowing that *this government* is not sufficiently lasting to ensure any thing which we may bequeath to posterity: And by a plain method of argument, as we are running the next generation into debt, we ought to do the work of it, otherwise we use them meanly and pitifully. In order to discover the line of our duty rightly, we should take our children in our hand, and fix our station a few years farther into life; that eminence will present a prospect, which a few present fears and prejudices conceal from our sight.

Though I would carefully avoid giving unnecessary offence, yet I am inclined to believe, that all those who espouse the doctrine of reconciliation, may be included within the following descriptions. Interested men, who are not to be trusted; weak men who *cannot* see; prejudiced men who *will not* see; and a certain set of moderate men, who think better of the European world than it deserves; and this last class by an ill-judged deliberation, will be the cause of more calamities to this continent than all the other three.

It is the good fortune of many to live distant from the scene of sorrow; the evil is not sufficiently brought to *their* doors to make *them* feel the precariousness with which all American property is possessed. But let our imaginations transport us for a few moments to Boston, that seat of wretchedness will teach us wisdom, and instruct us for ever to renounce a power in whom we can have no trust. The inhabitants of that unfortunate city, who but a few months ago were in ease and affluence, have now no other alternative than to stay and starve, or turn out to beg. Endangered by the fire of their friends if they continue within the city, and plundered by the soldiery if they leave it. In their present condition they are prisoners without the hope of redemption, and in a general attack for their relief, they would be exposed to the fury of both armies.

Men of passive tempers look somewhat lightly over the offences of Britain, and, still hoping for the best, are apt to call out, '*Come we shall be friends again for all this.*' But examine the passions and feelings of mankind. Bring the doctrine of reconciliation to the touchstone of nature, and then tell me, whether you can hereafter love, honour, and faithfully serve the power that hath carried fire and sword into your land? If you cannot do all these, then are you only deceiving yourselves, and by your delay bringing ruin upon posterity. Your future connection with Britain, whom you can neither love nor honour, will be forced and unnatural, and being formed only on the plan of present convenience, will in a little time fall into a relapse more wretched than the first. But if you say, you can still pass the violations over, then I ask, Hath your house been burnt? Hath your property been destroyed before your face? Are your wife and children destitute of a bed to lie on, or bread to live on? Have you lost a parent or a child by their hands, and yourself the ruined and wretched survivor? If you have not, then are you not a judge of those who have. But if you have, and can still shake hands with the murderers, then are you unworthy the name of husband, father, friend, or lover, and whatever may be your rank or title in life, you have the heart of a coward, and the spirit of a sycophant.

This is not inflaming or exaggerating matters, but trying them by those feelings and affections which nature justifies, and without which, we should be incapable of discharging the social duties of life, or enjoying the felicities of it. I mean not to exhibit horror for the purpose of provoking revenge, but to awaken us from fatal and unmanly slumbers, that we may pursue determinately some fixed object. It is not in the power of Britain or of Europe to conquer America, if she do not conquer herself by *delay* and *timidity*. The present winter is worth an age if rightly employed, but if lost or neglected, the whole continent will partake of the misfortune; and there is no punishment which that man will not deserve, be he who, or what, or where he will, that may be the means of sacrificing a season so precious and useful.

It is repugnant to reason, to the universal order of things, to all examples from the former ages, to suppose, that this continent can longer remain subject to any external power. The most sanguine in Britain does not think so. The utmost stretch of human wisdom cannot, at this time compass a plan short of separation, which can promise the continent even a year's security. Reconciliation is now a falacious dream. Nature hath deserted the connexion, and Art cannot supply her place. For, as Milton wisely expresses, 'never can true reconcilement grow where wounds of deadly hate have pierced so deep.'

Every quiet method for peace hath been ineffectual. Our prayers have been rejected with disdain; and only tended to convince us, that nothing flatters vanity, or confirms obstinancy in Kings more than repeated petitioning—and nothing hath contributed more than that very measure to make the Kings of Europe absolute: Witness Denmark and Sweden. Wherefore since nothing but blows will do, for God's sake, let us come to a final separation, and not leave the next generation to be cutting throats, under the violated unmeaning names of parent and child.

To say, they will never attempt it again is idle and visionary, we thought so at the repeal of the stamp-act, yet a year or two undeceived us; as well we may suppose that nations, which have been once defeated, will never renew the quarrel.

As to government matters, it is not in the power of Britain to do this continent justice: The business of it will soon be too weighty, and intricate, to be managed with any tolerable degree of convenience, by a power, so distant from us, and so very ignorant of us; for if they cannot conquer us, they cannot govern us. To be always running three or four thousand miles with a tale or a petition, waiting four or five months for an answer, which when obtained requires five or six more to explain it in, will in a few years be looked upon as folly and childishness—There was a time when it was proper, and there is a proper time for it to cease.

Small islands not capable of protecting themselves, are the proper objects for kingdoms to take under their care; but there is something very absurd, in supposing a continent to be perpetually governed by an island. In no instance hath nature made the satellite larger than its primary planet, and as England and America, with respect to each other, reverses the common order of nature, it is evident they belong to different systems: England to Europe, America to itself.

I am not induced by motives of pride, party, or resentment to espouse the doctrine of separation and independance; I am clearly, positively, and conscientiously persuaded that it is the true interest of this continent to be so; that every thing short of *that* is mere patchwork, that it can afford no lasting felicity,—that it is leaving the sword to our children, and shrinking back at a time, when, a little more, a little farther, would have rendered this continent the glory of the earth.

As Britain hath not manifested the least inclination towards a compromise, we may be assured that no terms can be obtained worthy the acceptance of the continent, or any ways equal to the expence of blood and treasure we have been already put to.

The object contended for, ought always to bear some just proportion to the expence. The removal of N—, or the whole detestable junto, is a matter unworthy the millions we have expended. A temporary stoppage of trade, was an inconvenience, which would have sufficiently ballanced the repeal of all the acts complained of, had such repeals been obtained; but if the whole continent must take up arms, if every man must be a soldier, it is scarcely worth our while to fight against a contemptible ministry only. Dearly, dearly, do we pay for the repeal of the acts, if that is all we fight for; for in a just estimation, it is as great a folly to pay a Bunker-hill price for law, as for land. As I have always considered the independancy of this continent, as an event, which sooner or later must arrive, so from the late rapid progress of the continent to maturity, the event could not be far off. Wherefore, on the breaking out of hostilities, it was not worth the while to have disputed a matter, which time would have finally redressed, unless we meant to be in earnest; otherwise, it is like wasting an estate on a suit at law, to regulate the trespasses of a tenant, whose lease is just expiring. No man was a warmer wisher for reconciliation than myself, before the fatal nineteenth of April 1775, but the moment the event of that day was made known, I rejected the hardened, sullen tempered Pharoah of — for ever; and disdain the wretch, that with the pretended title of FATHER OF HIS PEOPLE can unfeelingly hear of their slaughter, and composedly sleep with their blood upon his soul.

But admitting that matters were now made up, what would be the event? I answer, the ruin of the continent. And that for several reasons.

First. The powers of governing still remaining in the hands of the k—, he will have a negative over the whole legislation of this continent. And as he hath shewn himself such an inveterate enemy to liberty, and discovered such a thirst for arbitrary power; is he, or is he not, a proper man to say to these colonies, '*You shall make no laws but what I please*.' And is there any inhabitants in America so ignorant, as not to know, that according to what is called the *present constitution*, that this continent can make no laws but what the king gives leave to; and is there any man so unwise, as not to see, that (considering what has happened) he will suffer no Law to be made here, but such as suit his purpose. We may be as effectually enslaved by the want of laws in America, as by submitting to laws made for us in England. After matters are made up (as it is called) can there be any doubt but the whole power of the crown will be exerted, to keep this continent as low and humble as possible? Instead of going forward we shall go backward, or be perpetually quarrelling or ridiculously petitioning.—We are already greater than the king wishes us to be, and will he not hereafter endeavour to make us less? To bring the matter to one point. Is the power who is jealous of our prosperity, a proper power to govern us? Whoever says *No* to this question is an *independant*, for independancy means no more, than, whether we shall make our own laws, or, whether the—, the greatest enemy this continent hath, or can have, shall tell us '*there shall be no laws but such as I like*.'

But the k— you will say has a negative in England; the people there can make no laws without his consent. In point of right and good order, there is something very ridiculous, that a youth of twenty-one (which hath often happened) shall say to several millions of people, older and wiser than himself, I forbid this or that act of yours to be law. But in this place I decline this sort of reply, tho' I will never cease to expose the absurdity of it, and only answer, that England being the king's residence, and America not so, makes quite another case. The k—'s negative *here* is ten times more dangerous and fatal than it can be in England, for *there* he will scarcely refuse his consent to a bill for putting England into as strong a state of defence as possible, and in America he would never suffer such a bill to be passed.

America is only a secondary object in the system of British politics. England consults the good of *this* country, no farther than it answers her *own* purpose. Wherefore, her own interest leads her to suppress the growth of *ours* in every case which doth not promote her advantage, or in the least interfere with it. A pretty state we should soon be in under such a second-hand government, considering what has happened! Men do not change from enemies to friends by the alteration of a name: And in order to shew that reconciliation *now* is a dangerous doctrine, I affirm, *that it would be policy in the k— at this time, to repeal the acts for the sake of reinstating himself in the government of the provinces*; in order, that HE MAY ACCOMPLISH BY CRAFT AND SUBTILITY, IN THE LONG RUN, WHAT HE CANNOT DO BY FORCE AND VIOLENCE IN THE SHORT ONE. Reconciliation and ruin are nearly related.

Secondly, That as even the best terms, which we can expect to obtain, can amount to no more than a temporary expedient, or a kind of government by guardianship, which can last no longer than till the colonies come of age, so the general face and state of things, in the interim, will be unsettled and unpromising. Emigrants of property will not choose to come to a country whose form of government hangs but by a thread, and who is every day tottering on the brink of commotion and disturbance; and numbers of the present inhabitants would lay hold of the interval, to dispose of their effects, and quit the continent.

But the most powerful of all arguments, is, that nothing but independance, i. e. a continental form of government, can keep the peace of the continent and preserve it inviolate from civil wars. I dread the event of a reconciliation with Britain now, as it is more than probable, that it will be followed by a revolt somewhere or other, the consequences of which may be far more fatal than all the malice of Britain.

Thousands are already ruined by British barbarity; (thousands more will probably suffer the same fate.) Those men have other feelings than us who have nothing suffered. All they *now* possess is liberty, what they before enjoyed is sacrificed to its service, and having nothing more to lose, they disdain submission. Besides, the general temper of the colonies, towards a British government, will be like that of a youth, who is nearly out of his time, they will care very little about her. And a government which cannot preserve the peace, is no government at all, and in that case we pay our money for nothing; and pray what is it that Britain can do, whose power will be wholly on paper, should a civil tumult break out the very day after reconciliation? I have heard some men say, many of whom I believe spoke without thinking, that they dreaded an independance, fearing that it would produce civil wars. It is but seldom that our first thoughts are truly correct, and that is the case here; for there are ten times more to dread from a patched up connexion than from independance. I make the sufferers case my own, and I protest, that were I driven from house and home, my property destroyed, and my circumstances ruined, that as man, sensible of injuries, I could never relish the doctrine of reconciliation, or consider myself bound thereby.

The colonies have manifested such a spirit of good order and obedience to continental government, as is sufficient to make every reasonable person easy and happy on that head. No man can assign the least pretence for his fears, on any other grounds, that such as are truly childish and ridiculous, that one colony will be striving for superiority over another.

Where there are no distinctions there can be no superiority, perfect equality affords no temptation. The republics of Europe are all (and we may say always) in peace. Holland and Swisserland are without wars, foreign or domestic: Monarchical governments, it is true, are never long at rest; the crown itself is a temptation to enterprizing ruffians at *home*; and that degree of pride and insolence ever attendant on regal authority, swells into a rupture with foreign powers, in instances, where a republican government, by being formed on more natural principles, would negociate the mistake.

But where says some is the King of America? I'll tell you Friend, he reigns above, and doth not make havock of mankind like the Royal — of Britain. Yet that we may not appear to be defective even in earthly honors, let a day be solemnly set apart for proclaiming the charter; let it be brought forth placed on the divine law, the word of God; let a crown be placed thereon, by which the world may know, that so far as we approve of monarchy, that in America THE LAW IS KING. For as in absolute governments the King is law, so in free countries the law *ought* to be King; and there ought to be no other. But lest any ill use should afterwards arise, let the crown at the conclusion of the ceremony be demolished, and scattered among the people whose right it is.

A government of our own is our natural right: And when a man seriously reflects on the precariousness of human affairs, he will become convinced, that it is infinitely wiser and safer, to form a constitution of our own in a cool deliberate manner, while we have it in our power, than to trust such an interesting event to time and chance. If we omit it now, some Massenello may hereafter arise, who laying hold of popular disquietudes, may collect together the desperate and the discontented, and by assuming to themselves the powers of government, may sweep away the liberties of the continent like a deluge. Should the government of America return again into the hands of Britain, the tottering situation of things, will be a temptation for some desperate adventurer to try his fortune; and in such a case, what relief can Britain give? Ere she could hear the news the fatal business might be done, and ourselves suffering like the wretched Britons under the oppression of the Conqueror. Ye that oppose independance now, ye know not what ye do; ye are opening a door to eternal tyranny, by keeping vacant the seat of government. There are thousands and tens of thousands, who would think it glorious to expel from the continent, that barbarous and hellish power, which hath stirred up the Indians and Negroes to destroy us; the cruelty hath a double guilt, it is dealing brutally by us, and treacherously by them.

To talk of friendship with those in whom our reason forbids us to have faith, and our affections wounded through a thousand pores instruct us to detest, is madness and folly. Every day wears out the little remains of kindred between us and them, and can there be any reason to hope, that as the relationship expires, the affection will increase, or that we shall agree better, when we have ten times more and greater concerns to quarrel over than ever?

Ye that tell us of harmony and reconciliation, can ye restore to us the time that is past? Can ye give to prostitution its former innocence? Neither can ye reconcile Britain and America. The last cord now is broken, the people of England are presenting addresses against us. There are injuries which nature cannot forgive; she would cease to be nature if she did. As well can the lover forgive the ravisher of his mistress, as the continent forgive the murders of Britain. The Almighty hath implanted in us these unextinguishable feelings for good and wise purposes. They are the guardians of his image in our hearts. They distinguish us from the herd of common animals. The social compact would dissolve, and justice be extirpated the earth, or have only a casual existence were we callous to the touches of affection. The robber and the murderer, would often escape unpunished, did not the injuries which our tempers sustain, provoke us into justice.

O ye that love mankind! Ye that dare oppose, not only the tyranny, but the tyrant, stand forth! Every spot of the old world is over-run with oppression. Freedom hath been hunted round the globe. Asia, and Africa, have long expelled her.—Europe regards her like a stranger, and England hath given her warning to depart. O! receive the fugitive, and prepare in time an asylum for mankind.

OF THE PRESENT ABILITY OF AMERICA, WITH SOME MISELLANEOUS REFLEXIONS.

I have never met with a man, either in England or America, who hath not confessed his opinion, that a separation between the countries, would take place one time or other. And there is no instance in which we have shewn less judgment, than in endeavouring to describe, what we call, the ripeness or fitness of the Continent for independance.

As all men allow the measure, and vary only in their opinion of the time, let us, in order to remove mistakes, take a general survey of things and endeavour if possible, to find out the *very* time. But we need not go far, the inquiry ceases at once, for the *time hath found us*. The general concurrence, the glorious union of all things prove the fact.

It is not in numbers but in unity, that our great strength lies; yet our present numbers are sufficient to repel the force of all the world. The Continent hath, at this time, the largest body of armed and disciplined men of any power under Heaven; and is just arrived at that pitch of strength, in which no single colony is able to support itself, and the whole, when united can accomplish the matter, and either more, or, less than this, might be fatal in its effects.

The present time, likewise, is that peculiar time, which never happens to a nation but once, *viz*. the time of forming itself into a government. Most nations have let slip the opportunity, and by that means have been compelled to receive laws from their conquerors, instead of making laws for themselves. First, they had a king, and then a form of government; whereas, the articles or charter of government, should be formed first, and men delegated to execute them afterward: but from the errors of other nations, let us learn wisdom, and lay hold of the present opportunity—*To begin government at the right end.*

When William the conqueror subdued England he gave them law at the point of the sword; and until we consent that the seat of government in America, be legally and authoritatively occupied, we shall be in danger of having it filled by some fortunate ruffian, who may treat us in the same manner, and then, where will be our freedom? where our property?

As to religion, I hold it to be the indispensible duty of all government, to protect all conscientious professors thereof, and I know of no other business which government hath to do therewith. Let a man throw aside that narrowness of soul, that selfishness of principle, which the niggards of all professions are so unwilling to part with, and he will be at once delivered of his fears on that head. Suspicion is the companion of mean souls, and the bane of all good society. For myself I fully and conscientiously believe, that it is the will of the Almighty, that there should be diversity of religious opinions among us: It affords a larger field for our Christian kindness. Were we all of one way of thinking, our religious dispositions would want matter for probation; and on this liberal principle, I look on the various denominations among us, to be like children of the same family, differing only, in what is called their Christian names.

In page fifty-four,* I threw out a few thoughts on the propriety of a Continental Charter, (for I only presume to offer hints, not plans) and in this place, I take the liberty of rementioning the subject, by observing, that a charter is to be understood as a bond of solemn obligation, which the whole enters into, to support the right of every separate part, whether of religion, personal freedom, or property. A firm bargain and a right reckoning make long friends.

*[Not reproduced in this edition.]

In a former page I likewise mentioned the necessity of a large and equal representation; and there is no political matter which more deserves our attention. A small number of electors, or a small number of representatives, are equally dangerous. But if the number of the representatives be not only small, but unequal, the danger is increased. As an instance of this, I mention the following; when the Associators petition was before the House of Assembly of Pennsylvania; twenty-eight members only were present, all the Bucks county members, being eight, voted against it, and had seven of the Chester members done the same, this whole province had been governed by two counties only, and this danger it is always exposed to. The unwarrantable stretch likewise, which that house made in their last sitting, to gain an undue authority over the Delegates of that province, ought to warn the people at large, how they trust power out of their own hands. A set of instructions for the Delegates were put together, which in point of sense and business would have dis-honored a school-boy, and after being approved by a *few*, a *very few* without doors, were carried into the House, and there passed *in behalf of the whole colony*; whereas, did the whole colony know, with what ill-will that House hath entered on some necessary public measures, they would not hesitate a moment to think them unworthy of such a trust.

Immediate necessity makes many things convenient, which if continued would grow into oppressions. Expedience and right are different things. When the calamities of America required a consultation, there was no method so ready, or at that time so proper, as to appoint persons from the several Houses of Assembly for that purpose and the wisdom with which they have proceeded hath preserved this continent from ruin. But as it is more than probable that we shall never be without a CONGRESS, every well wisher to good order, must own, that the mode for choosing members of that body, deserves consideration. And I put it as a question to those, who make a study of mankind, whether *representation and election* is not too great a power for one and the same body of men to possess? When we are planning for posterity, we ought to remember that virtue is not hereditary.

It is from our enemies that we often gain excellent maxims, and are frequently surprised into reason by their mistakes. Mr Cornwall (one of the Lords of the Treasury) treated the petition of the New-York Assembly with contempt, because *that* House, he said, consisted but of twenty-six members, which trifling number, he argued, could not with decency be put for the whole. We thank him for his involuntary honesty.

TO CONCLUDE, however strange it may appear to some, or however unwilling they may be to think so, matters not, but many strong and striking reasons may be given, to shew, that nothing can settle our affairs so expeditiously as an open and determined declaration for independance. Some of which are,

First.—It is the custom of nations, when any two are at war, for some other powers, not engaged in the quarrel, to step in as mediators, and bring about the preliminaries of a peace: but while America calls herself the subject of Great Britain, no power, however well disposed she may be, can offer her mediation. Wherefore, in our present state we may quarrel on for ever.

Secondly.—It is unreasonable to suppose, that France or Spain will give us any kind of assistance, if we mean only to make use of that assistance for the purpose of repairing the breach, and strengthening the connection between Britain and America; because, those powers would be sufferers by the consequences.

Thirdly.—While we profess ourselves the subjects of Britain, we must, in the eye of foreign nations, be considered as rebels. The precedent is somewhat dangerous to *their peace*, for men to be in arms under the name of subjects; we on the spot, can solve the paradox: but to unite resistance and subjection, requires an idea much too refined for common understanding.

Fourthly.—Were a manifesto to be published, and despatched to foreign courts, setting forth the miseries we have endured, and the peaceable methods we have ineffectually used for redress; declaring, at the same time, that not being able, any longer to live happily or safely under the cruel disposition of the B—sh court, we had been driven to the necessity of breaking off all connection with her; at the same time assuring all such courts of our peaceable disposition towards them, and of our desire of entering into trade with them: Such a memorial would produce more good effects to this Continent, than if a ship were freighted with petitions to Britain.

Under our present denomination of British subjects we can neither be received nor heard abroad: The custom of all courts is against us, and will be so, until, by an independance, we take rank with other nations.

These proceedings may at first appear strange and difficult; but, like all other steps which we have already passed over, will in a little time become familiar and agreeable; and, until an independance is declared, the Continent will feel itself like a man who continues putting off some unpleasant business from day to day, yet knows it must be done, hates to set about it, wishes it over, and is continually haunted with the thoughts of its necessity.

—2—

DECLARATION OF INDEPENDENCE

July 4, 1776

Throughout the 1770s, long-standing tensions between Great Britain and its American colonies grew into anger and suspicion. The colonists resisted British taxation with the Boston Tea Party, which led the English parliament to pass the Intolerable Acts, which led in turn to a united front by the Colonies in the First Continental Congress in October, 1774. After open war broke out between Britain and the Americans on April 19, 1775, representatives from the thirteen colonies convened the Second Continental Congress in Philadelphia on May 10 of that year.

By June, 1776, the war with Britain had raged for over a year, and the split between the mother country and the American colonies had grown past the point of repair. On June 7, Richard Henry Lee of Virginia introduced a resolution for independence. After four days of debate, the Continental Congress appointed a committee of distinguished representatives—including Thomas Jefferson, John Adams, Benjamin Franklin, Roger Sherman, and Robert Livingston—to prepare a declaration of independence for the United Colonies. The committee assigned Thomas Jefferson the task of preparing the document; after going over Jefferson's draft, the group submitted the declaration to the Congress on June

28. On July 2, the Congress voted unanimously in favor of independence, and then spent the next two days editing and amending Jefferson's declaration. On July 4, 1776, the Congress unanimously passed the final version of the declaration (the New York delegation abstained, on the orders of its state legislature). After a formal edition of the Declaration of Independence was prepared on parchment on August 2, fifty-six members of the Second Continental Congress signed the document.

The Declaration of Independence has been important both as the formal beginning of the United States, and as a powerful statement of the principles of American government. By proclaiming the principles of natural rights—the idea that all citizens share rights that no government can take away—and that a government can only rule with the consent of the governed, it laid the foundations of American democracy and individual liberty.

THE UNANIMOUS DECLARATION OF THE THIRTEEN UNITED STATES OF AMERICA

When in the Course of human events, it becomes necessary for one people to dissolve the political bands which have connected them with another, and to assume among the Powers of the earth, the separate and equal station to which the Laws of Nature and of Nature's God entitle them, a decent respect to the opinions of mankind requires that they should declare the causes which impel them to the separation.

We hold these truths to be self-evident, that all men are created equal, that they are endowed by their Creator with certain unalienable Rights, that among these are Life, Liberty and the pursuit of Happiness. That to secure these rights, Governments are instituted among Men, deriving their just powers from the consent of the governed, That whenever any Form of Government becomes destructive of these ends, it is the Right of the People to alter or to abolish it, and to institute new Government, laying its foundation on such principles and organizing its powers in such form, as to them shall seem most likely to effect their Safety and Happiness. Prudence, indeed, will dictate that Governments long established should not be changed for light and transient causes; and accordingly all experience hath shown, that mankind are more disposed to suffer, while evils are sufferable, than to right themselves by abolishing the forms to which they are accustomed. But when a long train of abuses and usurpations, pursuing invariably the same Object evinces a design to reduce them under absolute Despotism, it is their right, it is their duty, to throw off such Government, and to provide new Guards for their future security.—Such has been the patient sufferance of these Colonies; and such is now the necessity which constrains them to alter their former Systems of Government. The history of the present King of Great Britain is a history of repeated injuries and usurpations, all having in direct object the establishment of an absolute Tyranny over these States. To prove this, let Facts be submitted to a candid world.

He has refused his Assent to Laws, the most wholesome and necessary for the public good.

He has forbidden his Governors to pass Laws of immediate and pressing importance, unless suspended in their operation till his Assent should be obtained; and when so suspended, he has utterly neglected to attend to them.

He has refused to pass other Laws for the accommodation of large districts of people, unless those people would relinquish the right of Representation in the Legislature, a right inestimable to them and formidable to tyrants only.

He has called together legislative bodies at places unusual, uncomfortable, and distant from the depository of their Public Records, for the sole purpose of fatiguing them into compliance with his measures.

He has dissolved Representative Houses repeatedly, for opposing with manly firmness his invasions on the rights of the people.

He has refused for a long time, after such dissolutions, to cause others to be elected; whereby the Legislative Powers, incapable of Annihilation, have returned to the People at large for their exercise; the State remaining in the mean time exposed to all the dangers of invasion from without, and convulsions within.

He has endeavoured to prevent the population of these States; for that purpose obstructing the Laws of Naturalization of Foreigners; refusing to pass others to encourage their migration hither, and raising the conditions of new Appropriations of Lands.

He has obstructed the Administration of Justice, by refusing his Assent to Laws for establishing Judiciary Powers.

He has made Judges dependent on his Will alone, for the tenure of their offices, and the amount and payment of their salaries.

He has erected a multitude of New Offices, and sent hither swarms of Officers to harass our People, and eat out their substance.

He has kept among us, in times of peace, Standing Armies without the Consent of our legislature.

He has affected to render the Military independent of and superior to the Civil Power.

He has combined with others to subject us to a jurisdiction foreign to our constitution, and unacknowledged by our laws; giving his Assent to their acts of pretended legislation:

For quartering large bodies of armed troops among us:

For protecting them, by a mock Trial, from Punishment for any Murders which they should commit on the Inhabitants of these States:

For cutting off our Trade with all parts of the world:

For imposing taxes on us without our Consent:

For depriving us in many cases, of the benefits of Trial by Jury:

For transporting us beyond Seas to be tried for pretended offences:

For abolishing the free System of English Laws in a neighbouring Province, establishing therein an Arbitrary government, and enlarging its Boundaries so as to render it at once an example and fit instrument for introducing the same absolute rule into these Colonies:

For taking away our Charters, abolishing our most valuable Laws, and altering fundamentally the Forms of our Governments:

For suspending our own Legislature, and declaring themselves invested with Power to legislate for us in all cases whatsoever.

He has abdicated Government here, by declaring us out of his Protection and waging War against us.

He has plundered our seas, ravaged our Coasts, burnt our towns, and destroyed the lives of our people.

He is at this time transporting large armies of foreign mercenaries to compleat the works of death, desolation and tyranny, already begun with circumstances of Cruelty & perfidy scarcely paralleled in the most barbarous ages, and totally unworthy the Head of a civilized nation.

He has constrained our fellow Citizens taken Captive on the high Seas to bear Arms against their Country, to become the executioners of their friends and Brethren, or to fall themselves by their Hands.

He has excited domestic insurrections amongst us, and has endeavoured to bring on the inhabitants of our frontiers, the merciless Indian Savages, whose known rule of warfare, is an undistinguished destruction of all ages, sexes and conditions.

In every stage of these Oppressions We have Petitioned for Redress in the most humble terms: Our repeated Petitions have been answered only by repeated injury. A Prince, whose character is thus marked by every act which may define a Tyrant, is unfit to be the ruler of a free People.

Nor have We been wanting in attention to our Brittish brethren. We have warned them from time to time of attempts by their legislature to extend an unwarrantable jurisdiction over us. We have reminded them of the circumstances of our emigration and settlement here. We have appealed to their native justice and magnanimity, and we have conjured them by the ties of our common kindred to disavow these usurpations, which, would inevitably interrupt our connections and correspondence. They too have been deaf to the voice of justice and of consanguinity. We must, therefore, acquiesce in the necessity, which denounces our Separation, and hold them, as we hold the rest of mankind, Enemies in War, in Peace Friends.

We, therefore, the Representatives of the united States of America, in General Congress, Assembled, appealing to the Supreme Judge of the world for the rectitude of our intentions, do, in the Name, and by Authority of the good People of these Colonies, solemnly publish and declare, That these United Colonies are, and of Right ought to be Free and Independent States; that they are Absolved from all Allegiance to the British Crown, and that all political connection between them and the State of Great Britain, is and ought to be totally dissolved; and that as Free and Independent States, they have full Power to levy War, conclude Peace, contract Alliances, establish Commerce, and to do all other Acts and Things which Independent States may of right do. And for the support of this Declaration, with a firm reliance on the Protection of Divine Providence, we mutually pledge to each other our Lives, our Fortunes and our sacred Honor.

JOHN HANCOCK.

New Hampshire—JOSIAH BARTLETT, WM. WHIPPLE, MATTHEW THORNTON.

Massachusetts Bay—SAML. ADAMS, JOHN ADAMS, ROBT. TREAT PAINE, ELBRIDGE GERRY.

Rhode Island—STEP. HOPKINS, WILLIAM ELLERY.

Connecticut—ROGER SHERMAN, SAM'EL HUNTINGTON, WM. WILLIAMS, OLIVER WOLCOTT.

New York—WM. FLOYD, PHIL. LIVINGSTON, FRANS. LEWIS, LEWIS MORRIS.

New Jersey—RICHD. STOCKTON, JNO. WITHERSPOON, FRAS. HOPKINSON, JOHN HART, ABRA. CLARK.

Pennsylvania—ROBT. MORRIS, BENJAMIN RUSH, BENJA. FRANKLIN, JOHN MORTON, GEO. CLYMER, JAS. SMITH, GEO. TAYLOR, JAMES WILSON, GEO. ROSS.

Delaware—CÆSAR RODNEY, GEO. READ, THO. M'KEAN.

Maryland—SAMUEL CHASE, WM. PACA, THOS. STONE, CHARLES CARROLL of Carrollton.

Virginia—GEORGE WYTHE, RICHARD HENRY LEE, TH. JEFFERSON, BENJA. HARRISON, THOS. NELSON, jr., FRANCIS LIGHTFOOT LEE, CARTER BRAXTON.

North Carolina—WM. HOOPER, JOSEPH HEWES, JOHN PENN.

South Carolina—EDWARD RUTLEDGE, THOS. HEYWARD, jr., THOMAS LYNCH, jr., ARTHUR MIDDLETON.

Georgia—BUTTON GWINNETT, LYMAN HALL, GEO. WALTON.

—3—

ADDRESS IN FAVOR OF THE CONSTITUTION

Benjamin Franklin

September 17, 1787

From 1781 to 1788, the national government of the United States operated according to the Articles of Confederation, the basic law of the nation until the ratification of the Constitution. The Articles established a weak central government: each state had only one vote in Congress, which had no power to enforce its will on the states. After only a few years, most Americans recognized the need for a new, more vital government structure.

From May to September, 1787, delegates from every state except Rhode Island met in the Federal Constitutional Convention in the State House in Philadelphia to draw up a new basic law for the country. Fifty-five of the leading citizens of the new nation—including Alexander Hamilton, James Madison, Charles Pinckney, Roger Sherman, and Rufus King—debated the shape of the new government as George Washington presided. No official records of the proceedings were kept, but the debate was intense as each representative sought to protect his own state's interests. In the end, the delegates arrived at compromises between the large states (led by Governor Edmund Randolph of Virginia), who wanted greater representation for bigger population, and the small states (led by William Paterson of New Jersey), who wanted equal representation for each state. Indeed, the Constitution has also been called the Great Compromise.

On September 17, 1787, the last day of the Convention, the delegates listened to a critical address by the aging Benjamin Franklin. Franklin, of course, was one of the greatest founders of the new nation, and the Convention listened with the utmost respect. Speaking in favor of the document they had created, he expressed much of the spirit of the Convention itself. Political realities and idealism, he argued, needed to be balanced, and he doubted that the Convention could create a Constitution that would do a better job than the one they had just completed. It would be foolish, he said, to hold out for a truly perfect document. After he spoke, all the members of the Convention except for Edmund Randolph, George Mason, and Elbridge Gerry signed the Constitution, and it was submitted for ratification.

ADDRESS IN FAVOR OF THE CONSTITUTION

Mr. President, I confess that I do not entirely approve of this Constitution at present, but Sir, I am not sure I shall never approve it: For having lived long, I have experienced many Instances of being oblig'd, by better Information or fuller Consideration, to change Opinions even on important Subjects, which I once thought right, but found to be otherwise. It is therefore that the older I grow the more apt I am to doubt my own Judgment, and to pay more Respect to the Judgment of others. Most Men indeed as well as most Sects in Religion, think themselves in Possession of all Truth, and that wherever others differ from them it is so far Error. Steele, a Protestant in a Dedication tells the Pope, that the only Difference between our two Churches in their Opinions of the Certainty of their Doctrine, is, the Romish Church is infallible, and the Church of England is never in the Wrong. But tho' many private Persons think almost as highly of their own Infallibility, as of that of their Sect, few express it so naturally as a certain French Lady, who in a little Dispute with her Sister, said, I don't know how it happens, Sister, but I meet with no body but myself that's *always* in the right. *Il n'y a que moi qui a toujours raison.*

In these Sentiments, Sir, I agree to this Constitution, with all its Faults, if they are such; because I think a General Government necessary for us, and there is no *Form* of Government but what may be a Blessing to the People if well administred; and I believe farther that this is likely to be well administred for a Course of Years, and can only end in Despotism as other Forms have done before it, when the People shall become so corrupted as to need

Despotic Government, being incapable of any other. I doubt too whether any other Convention we can obtain, may be able to make a better Constitution: For when you assemble a Number of Men to have the Advantage of their joint Wisdom, you inevitably assemble with those Men all their Prejudices, their Passions, their Errors of Opinion, their local Interests, and their selfish Views. From such an Assembly can a perfect Production be expected? It therefore astonishes me, Sir, to find this System approaching so near to Perfection as it does; and I think it will astonish our Enemies, who are waiting with Confidence to hear that our Councils are confounded, like those of the Builders of Babel, and that our States are on the Point of Separation, only to meet hereafter for the Purpose of cutting one anothers Throats. Thus I consent, Sir, to this Constitution because I expect no better, and because I am not sure that it is not the best. The Opinions I have had of its Errors, I sacrifice to the Public Good. I have never whisper'd a Syllable of them abroad. Within these Walls they were born, and here they shall die. If every one of us in returning to our Constituents were to report the Objections he has had to it, and use his Influence to gain Partizans in support of them, we might prevent its being generally received, and thereby lose all the salutary Effects and great Advantages resulting naturally in our favour among foreign Nations, as well as among ourselves, from our real or apparent Unanimity. Much of the Strength and Efficiency of any Government, in procuring and securing Happiness to the People depends on Opinion, on the general Opinion of the Goodness of that Government as well as of the Wisdom and Integrity of its Governors. I hope therefore that for our own Sakes, as a Part of the People, and for the sake of our Posterity, we shall act heartily and unanimously in recommending this Constitution, wherever our Influence may extend, and turn our future Thoughts and Endeavours to the Means of having it well administred.

On the whole, Sir, I cannot help expressing a Wish, that every Member of the Convention, who may still have Objections to it, would with me on this Occasion doubt a little of his own Infallibility, and to make *manifest* our *Unanimity*, put his Name to this Instrument.

—4—

THE UNITED STATES CONSTITUTION AND AMENDMENTS

Ratified June 21, 1788

After the Constitutional Convention adopted the Constitution on September 17, 1787, Congress sent it to the states for ratification. After the ninth state, New Hampshire, ratified the document on June 21, 1788, it became the basic law of the country, and it has since been amended twenty-six times.

The Constitution is the oldest written constitution of any nation in the world, and it continues to serve as a model for other countries as they establish or reorganize their governments. Both a landmark document of democratic idealism and a great political compromise between the original states, it operates on the principles of federalism and separation of powers. Federalism provides for a division of powers between the state and national governments; the national, or federal, government always takes precedence over state laws, unless expressly prohibited by the Constitution. Under the separation of powers, the legislative, judicial, and executive branches each retain unique powers and roles that prevent any one part of government from growing too strong. Part of the strength of the Constitution stems from the somewhat cynical skepticism of the framers: They feared human ambition and failings too much to entrust the government to a

President, Congress, or group of judges alone. Instead, the executive, legislative, and judicial branches restrain each other even as they must cooperate to run the nation.

The framers of the Constitution took care to create a basic document, laying out general principles that would last over time. They tried to avoid being overly specific; instead, they left the actual details of government to the laws enacted by Congress. In addition, many of the framers wanted a list of individual rights included in the Constitution. In the end, these rights—known as the Bill of Rights—were added to the Constitution as the first ten amendments, after being passed by Congress in 1789 and ratified by 1791. Though a few areas of the Constitution have become outdated (notably the sections that refer to slavery), it has proven to be one of the most durable governing documents in history.

THE CONSTITUTION OF THE UNITED STATES OF AMERICA

We the People of the United States, in Order to form a more perfect Union, establish Justice, insure domestic Tranquility, provide for the common defence, promote the general Welfare, and secure the Blessings of Liberty to ourselves and our Posterity, do ordain and establish this Constitution for the United States of America.

ARTICLE I

Section 1 All legislative Powers herein granted shall be vested in a Congress of the United States, which shall consist of a Senate and House of Representatives.

Section 2 The House of Representatives shall be composed of Members chosen every second Year by the People of the several States, and the Electors in each State shall have the Qualifications requisite for Electors of the most numerous Branch of the State Legislature.

No Person shall be a Representative who shall not have attained to the age of twenty five Years, and been seven Years a Citizen of the United States, and who shall not, when elected, be an Inhabitant of that State in which he shall be chosen.

Representatives and direct Taxes shall be apportioned among the several States which may be included within this Union, according to their respective Numbers, which shall be determined by adding to the whole Number of free Persons, including those bound to Service for a Term of Years, and excluding Indians not taxed, three fifths of all other Persons. The actual Enumeration shall be made within three Years after the first Meeting of the Congress of the United States, and within every subsequent Term of ten Years, in such Manner as they shall by Law direct. The Number of Representatives shall not exceed one for every thirty Thousand, but each State shall have at Least one Representative; and until such enumeration shall be made, the State of New Hampshire shall be entitled to chuse three, Massachusetts eight, Rhode-Island and Providence Plantations one, Connecticut five, New-York six, New Jersey four, Pennsylvania eight, Delaware one, Maryland six, Virginia ten, North Carolina five, South Carolina five, and Georgia three.

When vacancies happen in the Representation from any State, the Executive Authority thereof shall issue Writs of Election to fill such Vacancies.

The House of Representatives shall chuse their Speaker and other Officers; and shall have the sole Power of Impeachment.

Section 3 The Senate of the United States shall be composed of two Senators from each State, chosen by the Legislature thereof, for six Years; and each Senator shall have one Vote.

Immediately after they shall be assembled in Consequence of the first Election, they shall be divided as equally as may be into three Classes. The Seats of the Senators of the first Class shall be vacated at the Expiration of the second Year, of the second Class at the Expiration of the fourth Year, and of the third Class at the Expiration of the sixth Year, so that one third may be chosen every second Year; and if Vacancies happen by Resignation, or otherwise, during the Recess of the Legislature of any State, the Executive thereof may make temporary Appointments until the next Meeting of the Legislature, which shall then fill such Vacancies.

No Person shall be a Senator who shall not have attained to the Age of thirty Years, and been nine Years a Citizen of the United States, and who shall not, when elected, be an Inhabitant of that State for which he shall be chosen.

The Vice President of the United States shall be President of the Senate, but shall have no Vote, unless they be equally divided.

The Senate shall chuse their other Officers, and also a President pro tempore, in the Absence of the Vice President, or when he shall exercise the Office of President of the United States.

The Senate shall have the sole Power to try all Impeachments. When sitting for that Purpose, they shall be on Oath or Affirmation. When the President of the United States is tried the Chief Justice shall preside: And no Person shall be convicted without the Concurrence of two thirds of the Members present.

Judgment in Cases of Impeachment shall not extend further than to removal from Office, and disqualification to hold and enjoy any Office of honor, Trust or Profit under the United States: but the Party convicted shall nevertheless be liable and subject to Indictment, Trial, Judgment and Punishment, according to Law.

Section 4 The Times, Places and Manner of holding Elections for Senators and Representatives, shall be prescribed in each State by the Legislature thereof; but the Congress may at any time by Law make or alter such Regulations, except as to the Places of chusing Senators.

The Congress shall assemble at least once in every Year, and such Meeting shall be on the first Monday in December, unless they shall by Law appoint a different Day.

Section 5 Each House shall be the Judge of the Elections, Returns and Qualifications of its own Members, and a Majority of each shall constitute a Quorum to do Business; but a smaller Number may adjourn from day to day, and may be authorized to compel the Attendance of absent Members, in such Manner, and under such Penalties as each House may provide.

Each House may determine the Rules of its Proceedings, punish its Members for disorderly Behavior, and, with the Concurrence of two thirds, expel a Member.

Each House shall keep a Journal of its Proceedings, and from time to time publish the same, excepting such Parts as may in their Judgment require Secrecy; and the Yeas and Nays of the Members of either House on any question shall, at the Desire of one fifth of those Present, be entered on the Journal.

Neither House, during the Session of Congress, shall, without the Consent of the other, adjourn for more than three days, nor to any other Place than that in which the two Houses shall be sitting.

Section 6 The Senators and Representatives shall receive a Compensation for their Services, to be ascertained by Law, and paid out of the Treasury of the United States. They shall in all Cases, except Treason, Felony and Breach of the Peace, be privileged from Arrest during their Attendance at the Session of their respective Houses, and in going to and returning from the same; and for any Speech or Debate in either House, they shall not be questioned in any other Place.

No Senator or Representative shall, during the Time for which he was elected, be appointed to any civil Office under the Authority of the United States, which shall have been created, or the Emoluments whereof shall have been encreased during such time; and no Person holding any Office under the United States, shall be a Member of either House during his Continuance in Office.

Section 7 All Bills for raising Revenue shall originate in the House of Representatives; but the Senate may propose or concur with Amendments as on other Bills.

Every Bill which shall have passed the House of Representatives and the Senate, shall, before it become a Law, be presented to the President of the United States; If he approve he shall sign it, but if not he shall return it, with his Objections to that House in which it shall have originated, who shall enter the Objections at large on their Journal, and proceed to reconsider it. If after such Reconsideration two thirds of that House shall agree to pass the Bill, it shall be sent, together with the Objections, to the other House, by which it shall likewise be reconsidered, and if approved by two thirds of that House, it shall become a Law. But in all such Cases the Votes of both Houses shall be determined by Yeas and Nays, and the Names of the Persons voting for and against the Bill shall be entered on the Journal of each House respectively. If any Bill shall not be returned by the President within ten Days (Sundays excepted) after it shall have been presented to him, the Same shall be a Law, in like Manner as if he had signed it, unless the Congress by their Adjournment prevent its Return, in which Case it shall not be a Law.

Every Order, Resolution, or Vote to which the Concurrence of the Senate and House of Representatives may be necessary (except on a question of Adjournment) shall be presented to the President of the United States; and before the Same shall take Effect, shall be approved by him, or being disapproved by him, shall be repassed by two thirds of the Senate and House of Representatives, according to the Rules and Limitations prescribed in the Case of a Bill.

Section 8 The Congress shall have Power To lay and collect Taxes, Duties, Imposts and Excises, to pay the Debts and provide for the common Defence and general Welfare of the United States; but all Duties, Imposts and Excises shall be uniform throughout the United States;

To borrow Money on the credit of the United States;

To regulate Commerce with foreign Nations, and among the several States, and with the Indian Tribes;

To establish an uniform Rule of Naturalization, and uniform Laws on the subject of Bankruptcies throughout the United States;

To coin Money, regulate the Value thereof, and of foreign Coin, and fix the Standard of Weights and Measures;

To provide for the Punishment of counterfeiting the Securities and current Coin of the United States;

To establish Post Offices and post Roads;

To promote the Progress of Science and useful Arts, by securing for limited Times to Authors and Inventors the exclusive Right to their respective Writings and Discoveries;

To constitute Tribunals inferior to the supreme Court;

To define and punish Piracies and Felonies committed on the high Seas, and Offences against the Law of Nations;

To declare War, grant Letters of Marque and Reprisal, and make Rules concerning Captures on Land and Water;

To raise and support Armies, but no Appropriation of Money to that Use shall be for a longer Term than two Years;

To provide and maintain a Navy;

To make Rules for the Government and Regulation of the land and naval Forces;

To provide for calling forth the Militia to execute the Laws of the Union, suppress Insurrections and repel Invasions;

To provide for organizing, arming, and disciplining, the Militia, and for governing such Part of them as may be employed in the Service of the United States, reserving to the States respectively, the Appointment of the Officers, and the Authority of training the Militia according to the discipline prescribed by Congress;

To exercise exclusive Legislation in all Cases whatsoever, over such District (not exceeding ten Miles square) as may, by Cession of Particular States, and the Acceptance of Congress, become the

Seat of the Government of the United States, and to exercise like Authority over all Places purchased by the Consent of the Legislature of the State in which the Same shall be, for the Erection of Forts, Magazines, Arsenals, dock-Yards, and other needful Buildings;—And

To make all Laws which shall be necessary and proper for carrying into Execution the foregoing Powers, and all other Powers vested by this Constitution in the Government of the United States, or in any Department or Officer thereof.

Section 9 The Migration or Importation of such Persons as any of the States now existing shall think proper to admit, shall not be prohibited by the Congress prior to the Year one thousand eight hundred and eight, but a Tax or duty may be imposed on such Importation, not exceeding ten dollars for each Person.

The Privilege of the Writ of Habeas Corpus shall not be suspended, unless when in Cases of Rebellion or Invasion the public Safety may require it.

No Bill of Attainder or ex post facto Law shall be passed.

No Capitation, or other direct, Tax shall be laid, unless in Proportion to the Census or Enumeration herein before directed to be taken.

No Tax or Duty shall be laid on Articles exported from any State.

No Preference shall be given by any Regulation of Commerce or Revenue to the Ports of one State over those of another; nor shall Vessels bound to, or from, one State, be obliged to enter, clear or pay Duties in another.

No Money shall be drawn from the Treasury, but in Consequence of Appropriations made by Law; and a regular Statement and Account of the Receipts and Expenditures of all public Money shall be published from time to time.

No Title of Nobility shall be granted by the United States: And no Person holding any Office of Profit or Trust under them, shall, without the Consent of the Congress, accept of any present, Emolument, Office, or Title, of any kind whatever, from any King, Prince, or foreign State.

Section 10 No State shall enter into any Treaty, Alliance, or Confederation; grant Letters of Marque and Reprisal; coin Money;

emit Bills of Credit; make any Thing but gold and silver Coin a Tender in Payment of Debts; pass any Bill of Attainder, ex post facto Law, or Law impairing the Obligation of Contracts, or grant any Title of Nobility.

No State shall, without the Consent of the Congress, lay any Imposts or Duties on Imports or Exports, except what may be absolutely necessary for executing its inspection Laws: and the net Produce of all Duties and Imposts, laid by any State on Imports or Exports, shall be for the Use of the Treasury of the United States; and all such Laws shall be subject to the Revision and Controul of the Congress.

No State shall, without the Consent of Congress, lay any Duty of Tonnage, keep Troops, or Ships of War in time of Peace, enter into any Agreement or Compact with another State, or with a foreign Power, or engage in War, unless actually invaded, or in such imminent Danger as will not admit of delay.

ARTICLE II

Section 1 The executive Power shall be vested in a President of the United States of America. He shall hold his Office during the Term of four Years, and, together with the Vice President, chosen for the same Term, be elected, as follows:

Each State shall appoint, in such Manner as the Legislature thereof may direct, a Number of Electors, equal to the whole Number of Senators and Representatives to which the State may be entitled in the Congress: but no Senator or Representative, or Person holding an Office of Trust or Profit under the United States, shall be appointed an Elector.

The Electors shall meet in their respective States, and vote by Ballot for two Persons, of whom one at least shall not be an Inhabitant of the same State with themselves. And they shall make a List of all the Persons voted for, and of the Number of Votes for each; which List they shall sign and certify, and transmit sealed to the Seat of the Government of the United States, directed to the President of the Senate. The President of the Senate shall, in the Presence of the Senate and House of Representatives, open all the Certificates, and the Votes shall then be counted. The Person having the greatest Number of

Votes shall be the President, if such Number be a Majority and the whole Number of Electors appointed; and if there be more than one who have such Majority, and have an equal Number of Votes, then the House of Representatives shall immediately chuse by Ballot one of them for President; and if no Person have a Majority, then from the five highest on the List the said House shall in like Manner chuse the President. But in chusing the President, the Votes shall be taken by States, the Representation from each State having one Vote; a quorum for this Purpose shall consist of a Member or Members from two thirds of the States, and a Majority of all the States shall be necessary to a Choice. In every Case, after the Choice of the President, the Person having the greatest Number of Votes of the Electors shall be the Vice President. But if there should remain two or more who have equal Votes, the Senate shall chuse from them by Ballot the Vice President.

The Congress may determine the Time of chusing the Electors, and the Day on which they shall give their Votes; which Day shall be the same throughout the United States.

No Person except a natural born Citizen, or a Citizen of the United States, at the time of the Adoption of this Constitution, shall be eligible to the Office of President; neither shall any person be eligible to that Office who shall not have attained to the Age of thirty five Years, and been fourteen Years a Resident within the United States.

In Case of the Removal of the President from Office, or of his Death, Resignation, or Inability to discharge the Powers and Duties of the said Office, the Same shall devolve on the Vice President, and the Congress may by Law provide for the Case of Removal, Death, Resignation or Inability, both of the President and Vice President, declaring what Officer shall then act as President, and such Officer shall act accordingly, until the Disability be removed, or a President shall be elected.

The President shall, at stated Times, receive for his Services, a Compensation, which shall neither be encreased nor diminished during the Period for which he shall have been elected, and he shall not receive within that Period any other Emolument from the United States, or any of them.

Before he enter on the Execution of his Office, he shall take the following Oath or Affirmation:—"I do solemnly swear (or affirm) that I will faithfully execute the Office of President of the

United States, and will to the best of my Ability, preserve, protect and defend the Constitution of the United States.''

Section 2 The President shall be Commander in Chief of the Army and Navy of the United States, and of the Militia of the several States, when called into the actual Service of the United States; he may require the Opinion, in writing, of the principal Officer in each of the executive Departments, upon any Subject relating to the Duties of their respective Offices, and he shall have Power to grant Reprieves and Pardons for Offences against the United States, except in Cases of Impeachment.

He shall have Power, by and with the Advice and Consent of the Senate, to make Treaties, provided two thirds of the Senators present concur; and he shall nominate, and by and with the Advice and Consent of the Senate, shall appoint Ambassadors, other public Ministers and Consuls, Judges of the supreme Court, and all other Officers of the United States, whose Appointments are not herein otherwise provided for, and which shall be established by Law; but the Congress may by Law vest the Appointment of such inferior Officers, as they think proper, in the President alone, in the Courts of Law, or in the Heads of Departments.

The President shall have Power to fill up all Vacancies that may happen during the Recess of the Senate, by granting Commissions which shall expire at the End of their next Session.

Section 3 He shall from time to time give to the Congress Information of the State of the Union, and recommend to their Consideration such Measures as he shall judge necessary and expedient; he may, on extraordinary Occasions, convene both Houses, or either of them, and in Case of Disagreement between them, with Respect to the Time of Adjournment, he may adjourn them to such Time as he shall think proper; he shall receive Ambassadors and other public Ministers; he shall take Care that the Laws be faithfully executed, and shall Commission all the Officers of the United States.

Section 4 The President, Vice President and all civil Officers of the United States, shall be removed from Office on Impeachment for, and Conviction of, Treason, Bribery, or other high Crimes and Misdemeanors.

ARTICLE III

Section 1 The judicial Power of the United States, shall be vested in one supreme Court, and in such inferior Courts as the Congress may from time to time ordain and establish. The Judges, both of the supreme and inferior Courts, shall hold their Offices during good Behavior, and shall, at stated Times, receive for their Services, a Compensation, which shall not be diminished during their Continuance in Office.

Section 2 The judicial Power shall extend to all Cases, in Law and Equity, arising under this Constitution, the Laws of the United States, and Treaties made, or which shall be made, under their Authority;—to all Cases affecting Ambassadors, other public Ministers and Consuls;—to all Cases of admiralty and maritime Jurisdiction;—to Controversies to which the United States shall be a Party;—to Controversies between two or more States;—between a State and Citizens of another State;—between Citizens of different States;—between Citizens of the same State claiming Lands under Grants of different States, and between Citizens of the same State claiming Lands under Grants of different States, and between a State, or the Citizens thereof, and foreign States, Citizens or Subjects.

In all Cases affecting Ambassadors, other public Ministers and Consuls, and those in which a State shall be Part, the supreme Court shall have original Jurisdiction. In all the other Cases before mentioned, the supreme Court shall have appellate Jurisdiction, both as to Law and Fact, with such Exceptions, and under such Regulations as the Congress shall make.

The Trial of all Crimes, except in Cases of Impeachment, shall be by Jury; and such Trial shall be held in the State where the said Crimes shall have been committed; but when not committed within any State, the Trial shall be at such Place or Places as the Congress may by Law have directed.

Section 3 Treason against the United States, shall consist only in levying War against them, or in adhering to their Enemies, giving them Aid and Comfort. No Person shall be convicted of Treason unless on the Testimony of two Witnesses to the same overt Act, or on Confession in open Court.

The Congress shall have Power to declare the Punishment of Treason, but no Attainder of Treason shall work Corruption of Blood, or Forfeiture except during the Life of the Person attainted.

ARTICLE IV

Section 1 Full Faith and Credit shall be given in each State to the public Acts, Records, and judicial Proceedings of every other State. And the Congress may by general Laws prescribe the Manner in which such Acts, Records and Proceedings shall be proved, and the Effect thereof.

Section 2 The Citizens of each State shall be entitled to all Privileges and Immunities of Citizens in the several States.

A person charged in any State with Treason, Felony, or other Crime, who shall flee from Justice, and be found in another State, shall on Demand of the executive Authority of the State from which he fled, be delivered up, to be removed to the State having Jurisdiction of the Crime.

No Person held to Service or Labour in one State, under the Laws thereof, escaping into another, shall, in Consequence of any Law or Regulation therein, be discharged from such Service or Labour, but shall be delivered up on Claim of the Party to whom such Service or Labour may be due.

Section 3 New States may be admitted by the Congress into this Union; but no new State shall be formed or erected within the Jurisdiction of any other State; nor any State be formed by the Junction of two or more States, or Parts of States, without the Consent of the Legislatures of the States concerned as well as of the Congress.

The Congress shall have Power to dispose of and make all needful Rules and Regulations respecting the Territory or other Property belonging to the United States; and nothing in this Constitution shall be so construed as to Prejudice any Claims of the United States, or of any particular State.

Section 4 The United States shall guarantee to every State in this Union a Republican Form of Government, and shall protect each of them against Invasion; and on Application of the Legislature, or of the Executive (when the Legislature cannot be convened) against domestic Violence.

ARTICLE V

The Congress, whenever two thirds of both Houses shall deem it necessary, shall propose Amendments to this Constitution, or, on the Application of the Legislatures of two thirds of the several States, shall call a Convention for proposing Amendments, which, in either Case, shall be valid to all Intents and Purposes, as Part of this Constitution, when ratified by the Legislatures of three fourths of the several States, or by Conventions in three fourths thereof, as the one or the other Mode of Ratification may be proposed by the Congress; Provided that no Amendment which may be made prior to the Year One thousand eight hundred and eight shall in any Manner affect the first and fourth Clauses in the Ninth Section of the first Article; and that no State, without its Consent, shall be deprived of its equal Suffrage in the Senate.

ARTICLE VI

All Debts contracted and Engagements entered into, before the Adoption of this Constitution, shall be as valid against the United States under this Constitution, as under the Confederation.

This Constitution, and the Laws of the United States which shall be made in Pursuance thereof; and all Treaties made, or which shall be made, under the Authority of the United States, shall be the supreme Law of the Land; and the Judges in every State shall be bound thereby, any Thing in the Constitution or Laws of any State to the Contrary notwithstanding.

The Senators and Representatives before mentioned, and the Members of the several State Legislatures, and all executive and judicial Officers, both of the United States and of the several States, shall be bound by Oath or Affirmation, to support this constitution; but no religious Test shall ever be required as a Qualification to any Office or public Trust under the United States.

ARTICLE VII

The Ratification of the Conventions of nine States, shall be sufficient for the Establishment of this Constitution between the States so ratifying the Same.

AMENDMENT I

Congress shall make no law respecting an establishment of religion, or prohibiting the free exercise thereof; or abridging the freedom of speech, or of the press; or the right of the people peaceably to assemble, and to petition the Government for a redress of grievances.

AMENDMENT II

A well regulated Militia, being necessary to the security of a free State, the right of the people to keep and bear Arms, shall not be infringed.

AMENDMENT III

No soldier shall, in time of peace be quartered in any house, without the consent of the Owner, nor in time of war, but in a manner to be prescribed by law.

AMENDMENT IV

The right of the people to be secure in their persons, houses, papers, and effects, against unreasonable searches and seizures, shall not be violated, and no Warrants shall issue, but upon probable cause, supported by Oath or affirmation, and particularly describing the place to be searched, and the persons or things to be seized.

AMENDMENT V

No person shall be held to answer for a capital, or otherwise infamous crime, unless on a presentment or indictment of a Grand Jury, except in cases arising in the land or naval forces, or in the Militia, when in actual service in time of War or public danger; nor shall any person be subject for the same offence to be twice put in jeopardy of life or limb; nor shall be compelled in any criminal case to be a witness against himself, nor be deprived of life, liberty, or property, without due process of law; nor shall private property be taken for public use, without just compensation.

AMENDMENT VI

In all criminal prosecutions, the accused shall enjoy the right to a speedy and public trial, by an impartial jury of the State and district wherein the crime shall have been committed, which district shall have been previously ascertained by law, and to be informed of the nature and cause of the accusation; to be confronted with the witnesses against him; to have compulsory process for obtaining witnesses in his favor, and to have Assistance of Counsel for his defence.

AMENDMENT VII

In Suits at common law, where the value in controversy shall exceed twenty dollars, the right of trial by jury shall be preserved, and no fact tried by a jury, shall be otherwise reexamined in any Court of the United States, than according to the rules of the common law.

AMENDMENT VIII

Excessive bail shall not be required, nor excessive fines imposed, nor cruel and unusual punishments inflicted.

AMENDMENT IX

The enumeration in the Constitution, of certain rights, shall not be construed to deny or disparage others retained by the people.

AMENDMENT X

The powers not delegated to the United States by the Constitution, nor prohibited by it to the States, are reserved to the States respectively, or to the people.

AMENDMENT XI

The Judicial power of the United States shall not be construed to extend to any suit in law or equity, commenced or prosecuted against one of the United States by Citizens of another State, or by Citizens or Subjects of any Foreign State.

AMENDMENT XII

The Electors shall meet in their respective states and vote by ballot for President and Vice President, one of whom, at least, shall not be an inhabitant of the same state with themselves; they shall name in their ballots the person voted for as President, and in distinct ballots the person voted for as Vice President, and they shall make distinct lists of all persons voted for as President, and of all persons voted for as Vice President, and of the number of votes for each, which lists they shall sign and certify, and transmit sealed to the seat of the government of the United States, directed to the President of the Senate;—The President of the Senate shall, in the presence of the Senate and House of Representatives, open all the certificates and the votes shall then be counted;—The person having the greatest number of votes for President, shall be the President, if such number be a majority of the whole number of Electors appointed; and if no person have such majority, then from the persons having the highest numbers not exceeding three on the list of those voted for as President, the House of Representatives shall choose immediately, by ballot, the President. But in choosing the President, the votes shall be taken by states, the representation from each state having one vote; a quorum for this purpose shall consist of a member or members from two-thirds of the states, and a majority of all the states shall be necessary to a choice. And if the House of Representatives shall not choose a President whenever the right of choice shall devolve upon them, before the fourth day of March next following, then the Vice President shall act as President, as in the case of the death or other constitutional disability of the President.—The person having the greatest number of votes as Vice President, shall be the Vice President, if such number be a majority of the whole number of Electors appointed, and if no person have a majority, then from the two highest numbers on the list, the Senate shall choose the Vice President; a quorum for the purpose shall consist of two-thirds of the whole number of Senators, and a majority of the whole number shall be necessary to a choice. But no person constitutionally ineligible to the office of President shall be eligible to that of Vice President of the United States.

AMENDMENT XIII

Section 1 Neither slavery nor involuntary servitude, except as a punishment for crime whereof the party shall have been duly convicted, shall exist within the United States, or any place subject to their jurisdiction.

Section 2 Congress shall have power to enforce this article by appropriate legislation.

AMENDMENT XIV

Section 1 All persons born or naturalized in the United States and subject to the jurisdiction thereof, are citizens of the United States and of the State wherein they reside. No State shall make or enforce any law which shall abridge the privileges or immunities of citizens of the United States; nor shall any State deprive any person of life, liberty, or property, without due process of law; nor deny to any person within its jurisdiction the equal protection of the laws.

Section 2 Representatives shall be apportioned among the several States according to their respective numbers, counting the whole number of persons in each State, excluding Indians not taxed. But when the right to vote at any election for the choice of electors for President and Vice President of the United States, Representatives in Congress, the Executive and Judicial officers of a State, or the members of the Legislature thereof, is denied to any of the male inhabitants of such State, being twenty-one years of age, and citizens of the United States, or in any way abridged except for participation in rebellion, or other crime, the basis of representation therein shall be reduced in the proportion which the number of such male citizens shall bear to the whole number of male citizens twenty-one years in such State.

Section 3 No person shall be a Senator or Representative in Congress, or elector of President and Vice President, or hold any office, civil or military, under the United States, or under any State, who, having previously taken an oath as a member of Congress, or as an officer of the United States, or as a member of any State legislature, or as an executive or judicial officer of any State, to support the Constitution of the United States, shall have engaged in insurrection or rebellion against the same, or given aid or comfort to the enemies thereof. But Congress may by a vote of two-thirds of each House, remove such disability.

Section 4 The validity of the public debt of the United States, authorized by law, including debts incurred for payment of pensions and bounties for services in suppressing insurrection or rebellion, shall not be questioned. But neither the United States nor any State shall assume or pay any debt or obligation incurred in aid of insurrection or rebellion against the United States, or any claim for the loss or emancipation of any slave; but all such debts, obligations and claims shall be held illegal and void.

Section 5 The Congress shall have power to enforce, by appropriate legislation, the provisions of this article.

AMENDMENT XV

Section 1 The right of citizens of the United States to vote shall not be denied or abridged by the United States or by any State on account of race, color, or previous condition of servitude.

Section 2 The Congress shall have power to enforce this article by appropriate legislation.

AMENDMENT XVI

The Congress shall have power to lay and collect taxes on incomes, from whatever source derived, without apportionment among the several States, and without regard to any census or enumeration.

AMENDMENT XVII

The Senate of the United States shall be composed of two Senators from each State, elected by the people thereof, for six years; and each Senator shall have one vote. The electors in each State shall have the qualifications requisite for electors of the most numerous branch of the State legislatures.

When vacancies happen in the representation of any State in the Senate, the executive authority of such State shall issue writs of election to fill such vacancies; *Provided*, That the legislature of any State may empower the executive thereof to make temporary appointments until the people fill the vacancies by election as the legislature may direct.

This amendment shall not be so construed as to affect the election or term of any Senator chosen before it becomes valid as part of the Constitution.

AMENDMENT XVIII

Section 1 After one year from the ratification of this article the manufacture, sale, or transportation of intoxicating liquors within, the importation thereof into, or the exportation thereof from the United States and all territory subject to the jurisdiction thereof for beverage purposes is hereby prohibited.

Section 2 The Congress and the several States shall have concurrent power to enforce this article by appropriate legislation.

Section 3 This article shall be inoperative unless it shall have been ratified as an amendment to the Constitution by the legislatures of the several States, as provided in the Constitution, within seven years from the date of the submission hereof to the States by the Congress.

AMENDMENT XIX

The right of citizens of the United States to vote shall not be denied or abridged by the United States or by any State on account of sex.

Congress shall have power to enforce this article by appropriate legislation.

AMENDMENT XX

Section 1 The terms of the President and Vice President shall end at noon on the 20th day of January, and the terms of Senators and Representatives at noon on the 3d day of January, of the years in which such terms would have ended if this article had not been ratified; and the terms of their successors shall then begin.

Section 2 The Congress shall assemble at least once in every year, and such meeting shall begin at noon on the 3d day of January, unless they shall by law appoint a different day.

Section 3 If, at the time fixed for the beginning of the term of the President, the President elect shall have died, the Vice President elect shall become President. If a President shall not have been chosen before the time fixed for the beginning of his term, or if the President elect shall have failed to qualify, then the Vice President elect shall act as President until a President shall have qualified; and the Congress may by law provide for the case wherein neither a President elect nor a Vice President elect shall have qualified, declaring who shall then act as President, or the manner in which one who is to act shall be selected, and such person shall act accordingly until a President or Vice President shall have qualified.

Section 4 The Congress may by law provide for the case of the death of any of the persons from whom the House of Representatives may choose a President whenever the right of choice shall have devolved upon them, and for the case of the death of any of the persons from whom the Senate may choose a Vice President whenever the right of choice shall have devolved upon them.

Section 5 Sections 1 and 2 shall take effect on the 15th day of October following the ratification of this article.

Section 6 This article shall be inoperative unless it shall have been ratified as an amendment to the Constitution by the legislatures of three-fourths of the several States within seven years from the date of its submission.

AMENDMENT XXI

Section 1 The eighteenth article of amendment to the Constitution of the United States is hereby repealed.

Section 2 The transportation or importation into any State, Territory, or possession of the United States for delivery or use therein of intoxicating liquors, in violation of the laws thereof, is hereby prohibited.

Section 3 This article shall be inoperative unless it shall have been ratified as an amendment to the Constitution by conventions in the several States, as provided in the Constitution, within seven years from the date of the submission hereof to the States by the Congress.

AMENDMENT XXII

Section 1 No person shall be elected to the office of the President more than twice, and no person who has held the office of President, or acted as President, for more than two years of a term to which some other person was elected President shall be elected to the office of the President more than once. But this Article shall not apply to any person holding the office of President when this Article was proposed by the Congress, and shall not prevent any person who may be holding the office of President, or acting as President, during the term within which this Article becomes operative from holding the office of President or acting as President during the remainder of such term.

Section 2 This Article shall be inoperative unless it shall have been ratified as an amendment to the Constitution by the legislatures of three-fourths of the several States within seven years from the date of its submission to the States by the Congress.

AMENDMENT XXIII

Section 1 The District constituting the seat of Government of the United States shall appoint in such manner as the Congress may direct:

A number of electors of President and Vice President equal to the whole number of Senators and Representatives in Congress to which the District would be entitled if it were a State, but in no event more than the least populous State; they shall be in addition to those appointed by the States, but they shall be considered, for the purposes of the election of President and Vice President, to be electors appointed by a State; and they shall meet in the District and perform such duties as provided by the twelfth article of amendment.

Section 2 The Congress shall have power to enforce this article by appropriate legislation.

AMENDMENT XXIV

Section 1 The right of citizens of the United States to vote in any primary or other election for President or Vice President, for electors for President or Vice President, or for Senator or Representative in Congress, shall not be denied or abridged by the United States or any State by reason of failure to pay any poll tax or other tax.

Section 2 The Congress shall have power to enforce this article by appropriate legislation.

AMENDMENT XXV

Section 1 In case of the removal of the President from office or of his death or resignation, the Vice President shall become President.

Section 2 Whenever there is a vacancy in the office of the Vice President, the President shall nominate a Vice President who shall take office upon confirmation by a majority vote of both Houses of Congress.

Section 3 Whenever the President transmits to the President pro tempore of the Senate and the Speaker of the House of Representatives his written declaration that he is unable to discharge the powers and duties of his office, and until he transmits to them a written declaration to the contrary, such powers and duties shall be discharged by the Vice President as Acting President.

Section 4 Whenever the Vice President and a majority of either the principal officers of the executive departments or of such other body as Congress may by law provide, transmit to the President pro tempore of the Senate and the Speaker of the House of Representatives their written declaration that the President is unable to discharge the powers and duties of his office, the Vice President shall immediately assume the powers and duties of the office as Acting President; otherwise, the President shall resume the powers and duties of his office.

AMENDMENT XXVI

Section 1 The right of citizens of the United States, who are eighteen years of age or older, to vote shall not be denied or abridged by the United States or by any State on account of age.

Section 2 The Congress shall have power to enforce this article by appropriate legislation.

AMENDMENT XXVII

No law, varying the compensation for the services of the Senators and Representatives, shall take effect, until an election of Representatives shall have intervened.

—5—

FAREWELL ADDRESS

George Washington

September 19, 1796

Few figures in American history have played as great a role as George Washington. Without his steadfast leadership as commanding general in the War of Independence, the new nation might well have perished. Unanimously elected the first president under the Constitution, Washington matched his enormous prestige with true political skill to ensure the success of the new form of government. Throughout his presidency, he sought to maintain national unity, balancing Thomas Jefferson and James Madison (who together founded the Democratic-Republican party) against Alexander Hamilton and the Federalists. In 1796, as his second term neared its end, Washington remained universally popular, and he could easily have won a third term in office.

As early as 1792, however, Washington had asked James Madison for advice on a final speech to announce his retirement at the end of his second term. As his final year in office drew to a close, he drafted his Farewell Address with the help of Alexander Hamilton, John Jay, and Madison, who suggested revisions and additions to Washington's original version. On September 19, 1796, Washington delivered the address to widespread acclaim. Famous now for its appeal that the nation avoid foreign alliances and internal divisions, the Farewell Address captured Washington's noble vision for the young republic, and it immediately joined the Declaration of Independence and the Constitution as one of our central statements of national purpose.

FAREWELL ADDRESS

Friends, and Fellow-Citizens: The period for a new election of a Citizen, to Administer the Executive government of the United States, being not far distant, and the time actually arrived, when your thoughts must be employed in designating the person, who is to be cloathed with that important trust, it appears to me proper, especially as it may conduce to a more distinct expression of the public voice, that I should now apprise you of the resolution I have formed, to decline being considered among the number of those, out of whom a choice is to be made.

I beg you, at the same time, to do me the justice to be assured, that this resolution has not been taken, without a strict regard to all the considerations appertaining to the relation, which binds a dutiful citizen to his country, and that, in with drawing the tender of service which silence in my situation might imply, I am influenced by no diminution of zeal for your future interest, no deficiency of grateful respect for your past kindness; but am supported by a full conviction that the step is compatible with both.

The acceptance of, and continuance hitherto in, the office to which your Suffrages have twice called me, have been a uniform sacrifice of inclination to the opinion of duty, and to a deference for what appeared to be your desire. I constantly hoped, that it would have been much earlier in my power, consistently with motives, which I was not at liberty to disregard, to return to that retirement, from which I had been reluctantly drawn. The strength of my inclination to do this, previous to the last Election, had even led to the preparation of an address to declare it to you; but mature reflection on the then perplexed and critical posture of our Affairs with foreign Nations, and the unanimous advice of persons entitled to my confidence, impelled me to abandon the idea.

I rejoice, that the state of your concerns, external as well as internal, no longer renders the pursuit of inclination incompatible with the sentiment of duty, or propriety; and am persuaded whatever partiality may be retained for my services, that in the present circumstances of our country, you will not disapprove my determination to retire.

The impressions, with which I first undertook the arduous trust, were explained on the proper occasion. In the discharge of this trust, I will only say, that I have, with good intentions, contributed towards the Organization and Administration of the government, the best exertions of which a very fallible judgment was capable. Not unconscious, in the outset, of the inferiority of my qualifications, experience in my own eyes, perhaps still more in the eyes of others, has strengthened the motives to diffidence of myself; and every day the encreasing weight of years admonishes me more and more, that the shade of retirement is as necessary to me as it will be welcome. Satisfied that if any circumstances have given peculiar value to my services, they were temporary, I have the consolation to believe, that while choice and prudence invite me to quit the political scene, patriotism does not forbid it.

In looking forward to the moment, which is intended to terminate the career of my public life, my feelings do not permit me to suspend the deep acknowledgment of that debt of gratitude which I owe to my beloved country, for the many honors it has conferred upon me; still more for the stedfast confidence with which it has supported me; and for the opportunities I have thence enjoyed of manifesting my inviolable attachment, by services faithful and persevering, though in usefulness unequal to my zeal. If benefits have resulted to our country from these services, let it always be remembered to your praise, and as an instructive example in our annals, that, under circumstances in which the Passions agitated in every direction were liable to mislead, amidst appearances sometimes dubious, viscissitudes of fortune often discouraging, in situations in which not unfrequently want of Success has countenanced the spirit of criticism, the constancy of your support was the essential prop of the efforts, and a guarantee of the plans by which they were effected. Profoundly penetrated with this idea, I shall carry it with me to my grave, as a strong incitement to unceasing vows that Heaven may continue to you the choicest tokens of its beneficence; that your Union and brotherly affection may be perpetual; that the free constitution, which is the work of your hands, may be sacredly maintained; that its Administration in every department may be stamped with wisdom and Virtue; that, in fine, the happiness of the people of these States, under the auspices of liberty, may be made complete, by so careful a preservation and so prudent a use of this blessing as will acquire to them the glory of recommending it to the applause, the affection, and adoption of every nation which is yet a stranger to it.

Here, perhaps, I ought to stop. But a solicitude for your welfare, which cannot end but with my life, and the apprehension of danger, natural to that solicitude, urge me on an occasion like the present, to offer to your solemn contemplation, and to recommend to your frequent review, some sentiments; which are the result of much reflection, of no inconsiderable observation, and which appear to me all important to the permanency of your felicity as a People. These will be offered to you with the more freedom, as you can only see in them the disinterested warnings of a parting friend, who can possibly have no personal motive to biass his counsel. Nor can I forget, as an encouragement to it, your endulgent reception of my sentiments on a former and not dissimilar occasion.

Interwoven as is the love of liberty with every ligament of your hearts, no recommendation of mine is necessary to fortify or confirm the attachment.

The Unity of Government which constitutes you one people is also now dear to you. It is justly so; for it is a main Pillar in the Edifice of your real independence, the support of your tranquility at home; your peace abroad; of your safety; of your prosperity; of that very Liberty which you so highly prize. But as it is easy to foresee, that from different causes and from different quarters, much pains will be taken, many artifices employed, to weaken in your minds the conviction of this truth; as this is the point in your political fortress against which the batteries of internal and external enemies will be most constantly and actively (though often covertly and insidiously) directed, it is of infinite moment, that you should properly estimate the immense value of your national Union to your collective and individual happiness; that you should cherish a cordial, habitual and immoveable attachment to it; accustoming yourselves to think and speak of it as of the Palladium of your political safety and prosperity; watching for its preservation with jealous anxiety; discountenancing whatever may suggest even a suspicion that it can in any event be abandoned, and indignantly frowning upon the first dawning of every attempt to alienate any portion of our Country from the rest, or to enfeeble the sacred ties which now link together the various parts.

For this you have every inducement of sympathy and interest. Citizens by birth or choice, of a common country, that country has a right to concentrate your affections. The name of AMERICAN, which belongs to you, in your national capacity, must always exalt the just pride of Patriotism, more than any appellation derived from local discriminations. With slight shades of difference, you have the same Religion, Manners, Habits and political Principles. You have in a common cause fought and triumphed together. The independence and liberty you possess are the work of joint councils, and joint efforts; of common dangers, sufferings and successes.

But these considerations, however powerfully they address themselves to your sensibility are greatly outweighed by those which apply more immediately to your Interest. Here every portion of our country finds the most commanding motives for carefully guarding and preserving the Union of the whole.

The *North*, in an unrestrained intercourse with the *South*, protected by the equal Laws of a common government, finds in the productions of the latter, great additional resources of Maratime and commercial enterprise and precious materials of manufacturing industry. The *South* in the same Intercourse, benefitting by the Agency of the *North*, sees its agriculture grow and its commerce expand. Turning partly into its own channels the seamen of the *North*, it finds its particular navigation envigorated; and while it contributes, in different ways, to nourish and increase the general mass of the National navigation, it looks forward to the protection of a Maratime strength, to which itself is unequally adapted. The *East*, in a like intercourse with the *West*, already finds, and in the progressive improvement of interior communications, by land and water, will more and more find a valuable vent for the commodities which it brings from abroad, or manufactures at home. The *West* derives from the *East* supplies requisite to its growth and comfort, and what is perhaps of still greater consequence, it must of necessity owe the secure enjoyment of indispensable outlets for its own productions to the weight, influence, and the future Maritime strength of the Atlantic side of the Union, directed by an indissoluble community of Interest as one Nation. Any other tenure by which the *West* can hold this essential advantage, whether derived from its own separate strength, or from an apostate and unnatural connection with any foreign Power, must be intrinsically precarious.

While then every part of our country thus feels an immediate and particular Interest in Union, all the parts combined cannot fail to find in the united mass of means and efforts greater strength, greater resource, proportionably greater security from external danger, a less frequent interruption of their Peace by foreign Nations; and, what is of inestimable value! they must derive from Union an exemption from those broils and Wars between themselves, which so frequently afflict neighbouring countries, not tied together by the same government; which their own rivalships alone would be sufficient to produce, but which opposite foreign alliances, attachments and intriegues would stimulate and imbitter. Hence likewise they will avoid the necessity of those overgrown Military establishments, which under any form of Government are inauspicious to liberty, and which are to be regarded as particularly hostile to Republican Liberty: In this sense it is, that your Union ought to be considered as a main prop of your liberty, and that the love of the one ought to endear to you the preservation of the other.

These considerations speak a persuasive language to every reflecting and virtuous mind, and exhibit the continuance of the UNION as a primary object of Patriotic desire. Is there a doubt, whether a common government can embrace so large a sphere? Let experience solve it. To listen to mere speculation in such a case were criminal. We are authorized to hope that a proper organization of the whole, with the auxiliary agency of governments for the respective Sub divisions, will afford a happy issue to the experiment. 'Tis well worth a fair and full experiment With such powerful and obvious motives to Union, affecting all parts of our country, while experience shall not have demonstrated its impracticability, there will always be reason, to distrust the patriotism of those, who in any quarter may endeavor to weaken its bands.

In contemplating the causes wch. may disturb our Union, it occurs as matter of serious concern, that any ground should have been furnished for characterizing parties by Geographical discriminations: *Northern* and *Southern; Atlantic* and *Western*; whence designing men may endeavour to excite a belief that there is a real difference of local interests and views. One of the expedients of Party to acquire influence, within particular districts, is to misrepresent the opinions and aims of other Districts. You cannot shield yourselves too much against the jealousies and heart burnings which spring from these misrepresentations. They tend to render Alien to each other those who ought to be bound together by fraternal affection. The Inhabitants of our Western country have lately had a useful lesson on this head. They have seen, in the Negociation by the Executive, and in the unanimous ratification by the Senate, of the Treaty with Spain, and in the universal satisfaction at that event, throughout the United States, a decisive proof how unfounded were the suspicions propagated among them of a policy in the General Government and in the Atlantic States unfriendly to their Interests in regard to the MISSISSIPPI. They have been witnesses to the formation of two Treaties, that with G: Britain and that with Spain, which secure to them every thing they could desire, in respect to our Foreign relations, towards confirming their prosperity. Will it not be their wisdom to rely for the preservation of these advantages on the UNION by wch. they were procured? Will they not henceforth be deaf to those advisers, if such there are, who would sever them from their Brethren and connect them with Aliens?

To the efficacy and permanency of Your Union, a Government for the whole is indispensable. No Alliances however strict between the parts can be an adequate substitute. They must inevitably experience the infractions and interruptions which all Alliances in all times have experienced. Sensible of this momentous truth, you have improved upon your first essay, by the adoption of a Constitution of Government, better calculated than your former for an intimate Union, and for the efficacious management of your common concerns. This government, the offspring of our own choice uninfluenced and unawed, adopted upon full investigation and mature deliberation, completely free in its principles, in the distribution of its powers, uniting security with energy, and containing within itself a provision for its own amendment, has a just claim to your confidence and your support. Respect for its authority, compliance with its Laws, acquiescence in its measures, are duties enjoined by the fundamental maxims of true Liberty. The basis of our political systems is the right of the people to make and to alter their Constitutions of Government. But the Constitution which at any time exists, 'till changed by an explicit and authentic act of the whole People, is sacredly obligatory upon all. The very idea of the power and the right of the People to establish

Government presupposes the duty of every Individual to obey the established Government.

All obstructions to the execution of the Laws, all combinations and Associations, under whatever plausible character, with the real design to direct, controul counteract, or awe the regular deliberation and action of the Constituted authorities are distructive of this fundamental principle and of fatal tendency. They serve to organize faction, to give it an artificial and extraordinary force; to put in the place of the delegated will of the Nation, the will of a party; often a small but artful and enterprizing minority of the Community; and, according to the alternate triumphs of different parties, to make the public administration the Mirror of the ill concerted and incongruous projects of faction, rather than the organ of consistent and wholesome plans digested by common councils and modefied by mutual interests. However combinations or Associations of the above description may now and then answer popular ends, they are likely, in the course of time and things, to become potent engines, by which cunning, ambitious and unprincipled men will be enabled to subvert the Power of the People, and to usurp for themselves the reins of Government; destroying afterwards the very engines which have lifted them to unjust dominion.

Towards the preservation of your Government and the permanency of your present happy state, it is requisite, not only that you steadily discountenance irregular oppositions to its acknowledged authority, but also that you resist with care the spirit of innovation upon its principles however specious the pretexts. one method of assault may be to effect, in the forms of the Constitution, alterations which will impair the energy of the system, and thus to undermine what cannot be directly overthrown. In all the changes to which you may be invited, remember that time and habit are at least as necessary to fix the true character of Governments, as of other human institutions; that experience is the surest standard, by which to test the real tendency of the existing Constitution of a country; that facility in changes upon the credit of mere hypotheses and opinion exposes to perpetual change, from the endless variety of hypotheses and opinion: and remember, especially, that for the efficient management of your common interests, in a country so extensive as ours, a Government of as much vigour as is consistent with the perfect security of Liberty is indispensable. Liberty itself will find in such a Government, with powers properly distributed and adjusted, its surest Guardian.

It is indeed little else than a name, where the Government is too feeble to withstand the enterprises of faction, to confine each member of the Society within the limits prescribed by the laws and to maintain all in the secure and tranquil enjoyment of the rights of person and property.

I have already intimated to you the danger of Parties in the State, with particular reference to the founding of them on Geographical discriminations. Let me now take a more comprehensive view, and warn you in the most solemn manner against the baneful effects of the Spirit of Party, generally.

This spirit, unfortunately, is inseperable from our nature, having its root in the strongest passions of the human Mind. It exists under different shapes in all Governments, more or less stifled, controuled, or repressed; but, in those of the popular form it is seen in its greatest rankness and is truly their worst enemy.

The alternate domination of one faction over another, sharpened by the spirit of revenge natural to party dissention, which in different ages and countries has perpetrated the most horrid enormities, is itself a frightful despotism. But this leads at length to a more formal and permanent despotism. The disorders and miseries, which result, gradually incline the minds of men to seek security and repose in the absolute power of an Individual: and sooner or later the chief of some prevailing faction more able or more fortunate than his competitors, turns this disposition to the purposes of his own elevation, on the ruins of Public Liberty.

Without looking forward to an extremity of this kind (which nevertheless ought not to be entirely out of sight) the common and continual mischiefs of the spirit of Party are sufficient to make it the interest and the duty of a wise People to discourage and restrain it.

It serves always to distract the Public Councils and enfeeble the Public administration. It agitates the Community with ill founded jealousies and false alarms, kindles the animosity of one part against another, foments occasionally riot and insurrection. It opens the door to foreign influence and corruption, which find a facilitated access to the government itself through the channels of party passions. Thus the policy and the will of one country, are subjected to the policy and will of another.

There is an opinion that parties in free countries are useful checks upon the Administration of the Government and serve to keep alive the spirit of Liberty. This within certain limits is probably true, and in Governments of a Monarchical cast Patriotism may look with endulgence, if not with favour, upon the spirit of party. But in those of the popular character, in Governments purely elective, it is a spirit not to be encouraged. From their natural tendency, it is certain there will always be enough of that spirit for every salutary purpose. And there being constant danger of excess, the effort ought to be, by force of public opinion, to mitigate and assuage it. A fire not to be quenched; it demands a uniform vigilance to prevent its bursting into a flame, lest instead of warming it should consume.

It is important, likewise, that the habits of thinking in a free Country should inspire caution in those entrusted with its administration, to confine themselves within their respective Constitutional spheres; avoiding in the exercise of the Powers of one department to encroach upon another. The spirit of encroachment tends to consolidate the powers of all the departments in one, and thus to create whatever the form of government, a real despotism. A just estimate of that love of power, and proneness to abuse it, which predominates in the human heart is sufficient to satisfy us of the truth of this position. The necessity of reciprocal checks in the exercise of political power; by dividing and distributing it into different depositories, and constituting each the Guardian of the Public Weal against invasions by the others, has been evinced by experiments ancient and modern; some of them in our country and under our own eyes. To preserve them must be as necessary as to institute them. If in the opinion of the People, the distribution or modification of the Constitutional powers be in any particular wrong, let it be corrected by an amendment in the way which the Constitution designates. But let there be no change by usurpation; for though this, in one instance, may be the instrument of good, it is the customary weapon by which free governments are destroyed. The precedent must always greatly overbalance in permanent evil any partial or transient benefit which the use can at any time yield.

Of all the dispositions and habits which lead to political prosperity, Religion and morality are indispensable supports. In vain would that man claim the tribute of Patriotism, who should labour to subvert these great Pillars of human happiness, these firmest props of the duties of Men and citizens. The mere Politician, equally with the pious man ought to respect and to cherish them. A volume could not trace all their connections with private and public felicity. Let it simply be asked where is the security for property, for reputation, for life, if the sense of religious obligation desert the oaths, which are the instruments of investigation in Courts of Justice? And let us with caution indulge the supposition, that morality can be maintained without religion. Whatever may be conceded to the influence of refined education on minds of peculiar structure, reason and experience both forbid us to expect that National morality can prevail in exclusion of religious principle.

'Tis substantially true, that virtue or morality is a necessary spring of popular government. The rule indeed extends with more or less force to every species of free Government. Who that is a sincere friend to it, can look with indifference upon attempts to shake the foundation of the fabric.

Promote then as an object of primary importance, Institutions for the general diffusion of knowledge. In proportion as the structure of a government gives force to public opinion, it is essential that public opinion should be enlightened.

As a very important source of strength and security, cherish public credit. One method of preserving it is to use it as sparingly as possible: avoiding occasions of expence by cultivating peace, but remembering also that timely disbursements to prepare for danger frequently prevent much greater disbursements to repel it; avoiding likewise the accumulation of debt, not only by shunning occasions of expence, but by vigorous exertions in time of Peace to discharge the Debts which unavoidable wars may have occasioned, not ungenerously throwing upon posterity the burthen which we ourselves ought to bear. The execution of these maxims belongs to your Representatives, but it is necessary that public opinion should cooperate. To facilitate to them the performance of their duty, it is essential that you should practically bear in mind, that towards the payment of debts there must be Revenue; that to have Revenue there must be taxes; that no taxes can be devised which are not more or less inconvenient and unpleasant; that the intrinsic embarrassment inseperable from the selection of the proper objects (which is always a choice of difficulties) ought to be a decisive motive for a candid construction of the Conduct of the Government in making it, and for a spirit of acquiescence in the measures for obtaining Revenue which the public exigencies may at any time dictate.

Observe good faith and justice towds. all Nations. Cultivate peace and harmony with all. Religion and morality enjoin this conduct; and can it be that good policy does not equally enjoin it? It will be worthy of a free, enlightened, and, at no distant period, a great Nation, to give to mankind the magnanimous and too novel example of a People always guided by an exalted justice and benevolence. Who can doubt that in the course of time and things the fruits of such a plan would richly repay any temporary advantages wch. might be lost by a steady adherence to it? Can it be, that Providence has not connected the permanent felicity of a Nation with its virtue? The experiment, at least, is recommended by every sentiment which ennobles human Nature. Alas! is it rendered impossible by its vices?

In the execution of such a plan nothing is more essential than that permanent, inveterate antipathies against particular Nations and passionate attachments for others should be excluded; and that in place of them just and amicable feelings towards all should be cultivated. The Nation, which indulges towards another an habitual hatred, or an habitual fondness, is in some degree a slave. It is a slave to its animosity or to its affection, either of which is sufficient to lead it astray from its duty and its interest. Antipathy in one Nation against another, disposes each more readily to offer insult and injury, to lay hold of slight causes of umbrage, and to be haughty and intractable, when accidental or trifling occasions of dispute occur. Hence frequent collisions, obstinate envenomed and bloody contests. The Nation, prompted by illwill and resentment sometimes impels to War the Government, contrary to the best calculations of policy. The Government sometimes participates in the national propensity, and adopts through passion what reason would reject; at other times, it makes the animosity of the Nation subservient to projects of hostility instigated by pride, ambition and other sinister and pernicious motives. The peace often, sometimes perhaps the Liberty, of Nations has been the victim.

So likewise, a passionate attachment of one Nation for another produces a variety of evils. Sympathy for the favourite nation, facilitating the illusion of an imaginary common interest, in cases where no real common interest exists, and infusing into one the enmities of the other, betrays the former into a participation in the quarrels and Wars of the latter, without adequate inducement or justification: It leads also to concessions to the favourite Nation of priviledges denied to others, which is apt doubly to injure the Nation making the concessions; by unnecessarily parting with what ought to have been retained; and by exciting jealousy, ill will, and a disposition to retaliate, in the parties from whom eql. priviledges are withheld: And it gives to ambitious, corrupted, or deluded citizens (who devote themselves to the favourite Nation) facility to betray, or sacrifice the interests of their own country, without odium, sometimes even with popularity; gilding with the appearances of a virtuous sense of obligation a commendable deference for public opinion, or a laudable zeal for public good, the base or foolish compliances of ambition corruption or infatuation.

As avenues to foreign influence in innumerable ways, such attachments are particularly alarming to the truly enlightened and independent Patriot. How many opportunities do they afford to tamper with domestic factions, to practice the arts of seduction, to mislead public opinion, to influence or awe the public Councils! Such an attachment of a small or weak, towards a great and powerful Nation, dooms the former to be the satellite of the latter.

Against the insidious wiles of foreign influence, (I conjure you to believe me fellow citizens) the jealousy of a free people ought to be constantly awake; since history and experience prove that foreign influence is one of the most baneful foes of Republican Government. But that jealousy to be useful must be impartial; else it becomes the instrument of the very influence to be avoided, instead of a defence against it. Excessive partiality for one foreign nation and excessive dislike of another, cause those whom they actuate to see danger only on one side, and serve to veil and even second the arts of influence on the other. Real Patriots, who may resist the intriegues of the favourite, are liable to become suspected and odious; while its tools and dupes usurp the applause and confidence of the people, to surrender their interests.

The Great rule of conduct for us, in regard to foreign Nations is in extending our commercial relations to have with them as little political connection as possible. So far as we have already formed engagements let them be fulfilled, with perfect good faith. Here let us stop.

Europe has a set of primary interests, which to us have none, or a very remote relation. Hence she must be engaged in frequent controversies, the causes of which are essentially foreign to our concerns. Hence therefore it must be unwise in us to implicate ourselves, by artificial ties, in the ordinary vicissitudes of her politics, or the ordinary combinations and collisions of her friendships, or enmities:

Our detached and distant situation invites and enables us to pursue a different course. If we remain one People, under an efficient government, the period is not far off, when we may defy material injury from external annoyance; when we may take such an attitude as will cause the neutrality we may at any time resolve upon to be scrupulously respected; when belligerent nations, under the impossibility of making acquisitions upon us, will not lightly hazard the giving us provocation; when we may choose peace or war, as our interest guided by our justice shall Counsel.

Why forego the advantages of so peculiar a situation? Why quit our own to stand upon foreign ground? Why, by interweaving our destiny with that of any part of Europe, entangle our peace and prosperity in the toils of European Ambition, Rivalship, Interest, Humour or Caprice?

'Tis our true policy to steer clear of permanent Alliances, with any portion of the foreign world. So far, I mean, as we are now at liberty to do it, for let me not be understood as capable of patronising infidelity to existing engagements (I hold the maxim no less applicable to public than to private affairs, that honesty is always the best policy). I repeat it therefore, let those engagements be observed in their genuine sense. But in my opinion, it is unnecessary and would be unwise to extend them.

Taking care always to keep ourselves, by suitable establishments, on a respectably defensive posture, we may safely trust to temporary alliances for extraordinary emergencies.

Harmony, liberal intercourse with all Nations, are recommended by policy, humanity and interest. But even our Commercial policy should hold an equal and impartial hand: neither seeking nor granting exclusive favours or preferences; consulting the natural course of things; diffusing and deversifying by gentle means the streams of Commerce, but forcing nothing; establishing with Powers so disposed; in order to give to trade a stable course, to define the rights of our Merchants, and to enable the Government to support them; conventional rules of intercourse, the best that present circumstances and mutual opinion will permit, but temporary, and liable to be from time to time abandoned or varied, as experience and circumstances shall dictate; constantly keeping in view, that 'tis folly in one Nation to look for disinterested favors from another; that it must pay with a portion of its Independence for whatever it may accept under that character; that by such acceptance, it may place itself in the condition of having given equivalents for nominal favours and yet of being reproached with ingratitude for not giving more. There can be no greater error than to expect, or calculate upon real favours from Nation to Nation. 'Tis an illusion which experience must cure, which a just pride ought to discard.

In offering to you, my Countrymen these counsels of an old and affectionate friend, I dare not hope they will make the strong and lasting impression, I could wish; that they will controul the usual current of the passions, or prevent our Nation from running the course which has hitherto marked the Destiny of Nations: But if I may even flatter myself, that they may be productive of some partial benefit, some occasional good; that they may now and then recur to moderate the fury of party spirit, to warn against the mischiefs of foreign Intriegue, to guard against the Impostures of pretended patriotism; this hope will be a full recompence for the solicitude for your welfare, by which they have been dictated.

How far in the discharge of my Official duties, I have been guided by the principles which have been delineated, the public Records and other evidences of my conduct must Witness to You and to the world. To myself, the assurance of my own conscience is, that I have at least believed myself to be guided by them.

In relation to the still subsisting War in Europe, my Proclamation of the 22d. of April 1793 is the index to my Plan. Sanctioned by your approving voice and by that of Your Representatives in both Houses of Congress, the spirit of that measure has continually governed me; uninfluenced by any attempts to deter or divert me from it.

After deliberate examination with the aid of the best lights I could obtain I was well satisfied that our Country, under all the circumstances of the case, had a right to take, and was bound in duty and interest, to take a Neutral position. Having taken it, I determined, as far as should depend upon me, to maintain it, with moderation, perseverence and firmness.

The considerations, which respect the right to hold this conduct, it is not necessary on this occasion to detail. I will only observe, that according to my understanding of the matter, that right, so far from being denied by any of the Belligerent Powers has been virtually admitted by all.

The duty of holding a Neutral conduct may be inferred, without any thing more, from the obligation which justice and humanity impose on every Nation, in cases in which it is free to act, to maintain inviolate the relations of Peace and amity towards other Nations.

The inducements of interest for observing that conduct will best be referred to your own reflections and experience. With me, a predominant motive has been to endeavour to gain time to our country to settle and mature its yet recent institutions, and to progress without interruption, to that degree of strength and consistency, which is necessary to give it, humanly speaking, the command of its own fortunes.

Though in reviewing the incidents of my Administration, I am unconscious of intentional error, I am nevertheless too sensible of my defects not to think it probable that I may have committed many errors. Whatever they may be I fervently beseech the Almighty to avert or mitigate the evils to which they may tend. I shall also carry with me the hope that my Country will never cease to view them with indulgence; and that after forty five years of my life dedicated to its Service, with an upright zeal, the faults of incompetent abilities will be consigned to oblivion, as myself must soon be to the Mansions of rest.

Relying on its kindness in this as in other things, and actuated by that fervent love towards it, which is so natural to a Man, who views in it the native soil of himself and his progenitors for several Generations; I anticipate with pleasing expectation that retreat, in which I promise myself to realize, without alloy, the sweet enjoyment of partaking, in the midst of my fellow Citizens, the benign influence of good Laws under a free Government, the ever favourite object of my heart, and the happy reward, as I trust, of our mutual cares, labours and dangers.

—6—

ADDRESS TO THE BRITISH PEOPLE

Frederick Douglass

May 12, 1846

In 1838, a self-educated slave escaped from his master in Maryland and made his way North. A passionate and eloquent speaker, Frederick Douglass soon emerged as the most important black leader in the country as he lectured for the Massachusetts Anti-Slavery Society after 1841. His powerful attacks on slavery provided a boost to the abolitionist movement, and undermined the racism that prevailed in the North as well as the South. During the Civil War he made major contributions toward recruiting African-American troops for the Union army, and he later served in high office, including consul general to Haiti. Rising to the forefront of public life at a time when the obstacles faced by Black Americans were truly immense, Frederick Douglass showed himself to be one of the greatest figures—of any race—in American history.

In the early 1840s, however, Douglass's newly won fame attracted the attention of his former slaveowner, who could legally capture him and bring him back to slavery in the South. In order to earn the money to buy his own freedom, Douglass traveled to Great Britain, where he conducted a public speaking tour. The tour was a tremendous success; his fiery lectures on the horrors of slavery made him an international figure. The speech that follows was delivered shortly after his arrival in Britain, offering one of his classic statements on American slavery.

ADDRESS TO THE BRITISH PEOPLE

I feel exceedingly glad of the opportunity now afforded me of presenting the claims of my brethren in bonds in the United States, to so many in London and from various parts of Britain, who have assembled here on the present occasion. I have nothing to commend me to your consideration in the way of learning, nothing in the way of education, to entitle me to your attention; and you are aware that slavery is a very bad school for rearing teachers of morality and religion. Twenty-one years of my life have been spent in slavery—personal slavery—surrounded by degrading influences, such as can exist nowhere beyond the pale of slavery; and it will not be strange, if under such circumstances, I should betray, in what I have to say to you, a deficiency of that refinement which is seldom or ever found, except among persons that have experienced superior advantages to those which I have enjoyed. But I will take it for granted that you know something about the degrading influences of slavery, and that you will not expect great things from me this evening, but simply such facts as I may be able to advance immediately in connection with my own experience of slavery.

Now, what is this system of slavery? This is the subject of my lecture this evening—what is the character of this institution? I am about to answer the inquiry, what is American slavery? I do this the more readily, since I have found persons in this country who have identified the term slavery with that which I think it is not, and in some instances, I have feared, in so doing, have rather (unwittingly, I know,) detracted much from the horror with which the term slavery is contemplated. It is common in this country to distinguish every bad thing by the name of slavery. Intemperance is slavery; to be deprived of the right to vote is slavery, says one; to have to work hard is slavery, says another; and I do not know but that if we should let them go on, they would say that to eat when we are hungry, to walk when we desire to have exercise, or to minister to our necessities, or have necessities at all, is slavery. I do not wish for a moment to detract from the horror with which the evil of intemperance is contemplated—not at all; nor do I wish to throw the slightest obstruction in the way of any political freedom that any class of persons in this country may desire to obtain. But I am here to say that I think the term slavery is sometimes abused by identifying it with that which it is not. Slavery in the United States is the granting of that power by which one man exercises and enforces a right of property in the body and soul of another. The condition of a slave is simply that of the brute beast. He is a piece of property—a marketable commodity, in the language of the law, to be bought or sold at the will and caprice of the master who claims him to be his property; he is spoken of, thought of, and treated as property. His own good, his conscience, his intellect, his affections, are all set aside by the master. The will and the wishes of the master are the law of the slave. He is as much a piece of property as a horse. If he is fed, he is fed because he is property. If he is clothed, it is with a view to the increase of his value as property. Whatever of comfort is necessary to him for his body or soul that is inconsistent with his being property, is carefully wrested from him, not only by public opinion, but by the law of the country. He is carefully deprived of everything that tends in the slightest degree to detract from his value as property. He is deprived of education. God has given him an intellect; the slaveholder declares it shall not be cultivated. If his moral perception leads him in a course contrary to his value as property, the slaveholder declares he shall not exercise it. The marriage institution cannot exist among slaves, and one-sixth of the population of democratic America is denied its privileges by the law of the land. What is to be thought of a nation boasting of its liberty, boasting of its humanity, boasting of its christianity, boasting of its love of justice and purity, and yet having within its own borders three millions of persons denied by law the right of marriage?—what must be the condition of that people? I need not lift up the veil by giving you any experience of my own. Every one that can put two ideas together, must see the most fearful results from such a state of things as I have just mentioned. If any of these three millions find for themselves companions, and prove themselves honest, upright, virtuous persons to each other, yet in these cases—few as I am bound to confess they are—the virtuous live in constant apprehension of being torn asunder by the merciless men-stealers that claim them as their property. This is American slavery; no marriage—no education—the light of the gospel shut out from the dark mind of the bondman—and he forbidden by law to learn to read. If a mother shall teach her children to read, the law in Louisiana proclaims that she may be hanged by the neck. If the father attempt to give his son a knowledge of letters, he may be punished by the whip in one instance, and in another be killed, at the discretion of the court. Three millions of people shut out from the light of knowledge! It is easy for you to conceive the evil that must result from such a state of things.

I now come to the physical evils of slavery. I do not wish to dwell at length upon these, but it seems right to speak of them, not so much to influence your minds on this question, as to let the slaveholders of America know that the curtain which conceals their crimes is being lifted abroad; that we are opening the dark cell, and leading the people into the horrible recesses of what they are pleased to call their domestic institution. We want them to know that a knowledge of their whippings, their scourgings, their brandings, their chainings, is not confined to their plantations, but that some negro of theirs has broken loose from his chains—has burst through the dark incrustation of slavery, and is now exposing their deeds of deep damnation to the gaze of the christian people of England.

The slaveholders resort to all kinds of cruelty. If I were disposed, I have matter enough to interest you on this question for five or six evenings, but I will not dwell at length upon these cruelties. Suffice it to say, that all the peculiar modes of torture that were resorted to in the West India islands, are resorted to, I believe, even more frequently, in the United States of America. Starvation, the bloody whip, the chain, the gag, the thumb-screw, cat-hauling, the cat-o'-nine-tails, the dungeon, the blood-hound, are all in requisition to keep the slave in his condition as a slave in the United States. If any one has a doubt upon this point, I would ask him to read the chapter on slavery in Dickens's *Notes on America*. If any man has a doubt upon it, I have here the "testimony of a thousand witnesses," which I can give at any length, all going to prove the truth of my statement. The blood-hound is regularly trained in the United States, and advertisements are to be found in the southern papers of the Union, from persons advertising themselves as blood-hound trainers, and offering to hunt down slaves at fifteen dollars a piece, recommending their hounds as the fleetest in the neighborhood, never known to fail. Advertisements are from time to time inserted, stating that slaves have escaped with iron collars about their necks, with bands of iron about their feet, marked with the lash, branded with red-hot irons, the initials of their master's name burned into their flesh; and the masters advertise the fact of their being thus branded with their own signature, thereby proving to the world, that, however damning it may appear to non-slaveholders, such practices are not regarded discreditable among the slaveholders themselves. Why, I believe if a man should brand his horse in this country—burn the initials of his name into any of his cattle, and publish the ferocious deed here—that the united execrations of christians in Britain would descend upon him. Yet in the United States, human beings are thus branded. As Whittier says—

"...Our countrymen in chains,
The whip on woman's shrinking flesh,
Our soil yet reddening with the stains
Caught from her scourgings warm and fresh."

The slave-dealer boldly publishes his infamous acts to the world. Of all things that have been said of slavery to which exception has been taken by slaveholders, this, the charge of cruelty, stands foremost, and yet there is no charge capable of clearer demonstration, than that of the most barbarous inhumanity on the part of the slaveholders toward their slaves. And all this is necessary; it is necessary to resort to these cruelties, in order to *make the slave a slave*, and to *keep him a slave*. Why, my experience all goes to prove the truth of what you will call a marvelous proposition, that the better you treat a slave, the more you destroy his value *as a slave*, and enhance the probability of his eluding the grasp of the slaveholder; the more kindly you treat him, the more wretched you make him, while you keep him in the condition of a slave. My experience, I say, confirms the truth of this proposition. When I was treated exceedingly ill; when my back was being scourged daily; when I was whipped within an inch of my life—*life* was all I cared for. "Spare my life," was my continual prayer. When I was looking for the blow about to be inflicted upon my head, I was not thinking of my liberty; it was my life. But, as soon as the blow was not to be feared, then came the longing for liberty. If a slave has a bad master, his ambition is to get a better; when he gets a better, he aspires to have the best; and when he gets the best, he aspires to be his own master. But the slave must be brutalized to keep him as a slave. The slaveholder feels this necessity. I admit this necessity. If it be right to hold slaves at all, it is right to hold them in the only way in which they can be held; and this can be done only by shutting out the light of education from their minds, and brutalizing their persons. The whip, the chain, the gag, the thumb-screw, the blood-hound, the stocks, and all the other bloody paraphernalia of the slave system, are indispensably necessary to the relation of master and slave. The slave must be subjected to these, or he ceases to be a slave. Let him know that the whip is burned; that the fetters have been turned to some useful and profitable employment; that the chain is no longer for his limbs; that the blood-hound is no longer to be put upon his track; that his master's authority over him is no longer to be enforced by taking his life—and immediately he walks out from the house of bondage and asserts his freedom as a man. The slaveholder finds it necessary to have these implements to keep the slave in bondage; finds it necessary to be able to say, "Unless you do so and so; unless you do as I bid you—I will take away your life!"

Some of the most awful scenes of cruelty are constantly taking place in the middle states of the Union. We have in those states what are called the slave-breeding states. Allow me to speak plainly. Although it is harrowing to your feelings, it is necessary that the facts of the case should be stated. We have in the United States slave-breeding states. The very state from which the minister from our court to yours comes, is one of these states—Maryland, where men, women, and children are reared for the market, just as horses, sheep, and swine are raised for the market. Slave-rearing is there looked upon as a legitimate trade; the law sanctions it, public opinion upholds it, the church does not condemn it. It goes on in all its bloody horrors, sustained by the auctioneer's block. If you would see the cruelties of this system, hear the following narrative. Not long since the following scene occurred. A slave-woman and a slave-man had united themselves as man and wife in the absence of any law to protect them as man and wife. They had lived together by the permission, not by right, of their master, and they had reared a family. The master found it expedient, and for his interest, to sell them. He did not ask them their wishes in regard to the matter at all; they were not consulted. The man and woman were brought to the auctioneer's block, under the sound of the hammer. The cry was raised, "Here goes; who bids cash?" Think of it—a man and wife to be sold! The woman was placed on the auctioneer's block; her limbs, as is customary, were brutally exposed to the purchasers, who examined her with all the freedom with which they would examine a horse. There stood the husband, powerless; no right to his wife; the master's right preëminent. She was sold. He was next brought to the auctioneer's block. His eyes followed his wife in the distance; and he looked beseechingly, imploringly, to the man that had bought his wife, to buy him also. But he was at length bid off to another person. He was about to be separated forever from her he loved. No word of his, no work of his, could save him from this separation. He asked permission of his new master to go and take the hand of his wife at parting. It was denied him. In the agony of his soul he rushed from the man who had just bought him, that he might take a farewell of his wife; but his way was obstructed, he was struck over the head with a loaded whip, and was held for a moment; but his agony was too great. When he was let go, he fell a corpse at the feet of his master. His heart was broken. Such scenes are the every-day fruits of American slavery. Some two years since, the Hon. Seth M. Gates, an anti-slavery gentleman of the state of New York, a representative in the congress of the United States, told me he saw with his own eyes the following circumstance. In the national District of Columbia, over which the star-spangled emblem is constantly waving, where orators are ever holding forth on the subject of American liberty, American democracy, American republicanism, there are two slave prisons. When going across a bridge, leading to one of these prisons, he saw a young woman run out, barefooted and bare-headed, and with very little clothing on. She was running with all speed to the bridge he was approaching. His eye was fixed upon her, and he stopped to see what was the matter. He had not paused long before he saw three men run out after her. He now knew what the nature of the case was; a slave escaping from her chains—a young woman, a sister—escaping from the bondage in which she had been held. She made her way to the bridge, but had not reached it, ere from the Virginia side there came two slaveholders. As soon as they saw them, her pursuers called out, "Stop her!" True to their Virginian instincts, they came to the rescue of their brother kidnappers, across the bridge. The poor girl now saw that there was no chance for her. It was a trying time. She knew if she went back, she must be a slave forever—she must be dragged down to the scenes of pollution which the slaveholders continually provide for most of the poor, sinking, wretched young women, whom they call their property. She formed her resolution; and just as those who were about to take her, were going to put hands upon her, to drag her back, she leaped over the balustrades of the bridge, and down she went to rise no more. She chose death, rather than to go back into the hands of those christian slaveholders from whom she had escaped.

Can it be possible that such things as these exist in the United States? Are not these the exceptions? Are any such scenes as this general? Are not such deeds condemned by the law and denounced by public opinion? Let me read to you a few of the laws of the slaveholding states of America. I think no better exposure of slavery can be made than is made by the laws of the states in which slavery exists. I prefer reading the laws to making any statement in confirmation of what I have said myself; for the slaveholders cannot object to this testimony, since it is the calm, the cool, the deliberate enactment of their wisest heads, of their most clearsighted, their own constituted representatives. "If more than seven slaves together are found in any road without a white person, twenty lashes a piece; for visiting a plantation without a written pass, ten lashes; for letting loose a boat from where it is made fast, thirty-nine lashes for the first offense; and for the second, shall have cut off from his head one ear; for keeping or carrying a club, thirty-nine lashes; for having any article for sale, without a ticket from his master, ten lashes; for traveling in any other than the most usual and accustomed road, when going alone to any place, forty lashes; for traveling in the night without a pass, forty lashes." I am afraid you do not understand the awful character of these lashes. You must bring it before your mind. A human being in a perfect state of nudity, tied hand and foot to a stake, and a strong man standing behind with a heavy whip, knotted at the end, each blow cutting into the flesh, and leaving the warm blood dripping to the feet; and for these trifles. "For being found in another person's negro-quarters, forty lashes; for hunting with dogs in the woods, thirty lashes; for being on horseback without the written permission of his master, twenty-five lashes; for riding or going abroad in the night, or riding horses in the day time, without leave, a slave may be whipped, cropped, or branded in the cheek with the letter R, or otherwise punished, such punishment not extending to life, or so as to render him unfit for labor.'' The laws referred to, may be found by consulting Brevard's Digest; Haywood's Manual; Virginia Revised Code; Prince's Digest; Missouri Laws; Mississippi Revised Code. A man, for going to visit his brethren, without the permission of his master—and in many instances he may not have that permission; his master, from caprice or other reasons, may not be willing to allow it—may be caught on his way, dragged to a post, the branding-iron heated, and the name of his master or the letter R branded into his cheek or on his forehead. They treat slaves thus, on the principle that they must punish for light offenses, in order to prevent the commission of larger ones. I wish you to mark that in the single state of Virginia there are seventy-one crimes for which a colored man may be executed; while there are only three of these crimes, which, when committed by a white man, will subject him to that punishment. There are many of these crimes which if the white man did not commit, he would be regarded as a scoundrel and a coward. In the state of Maryland, there is a law to this effect: that if a slave shall strike his master, he may be hanged, his head severed from his body, his body quartered, and his head and quarters set up in the most prominent places in the neighborhood. If a colored woman, in the defense of her own virtue, in defense of her own person, should shield herself from the brutal attacks of her tyrannical master, or make the slightest resistance, she may be killed on the spot. No law whatever will bring the guilty man to justice for the crime.

But you will ask me, can these things be possible in a land professing christianity? Yes, they are so; and this is not the worst. No; a darker feature is yet to be presented than the mere existence of these facts. I have to inform you that the religion of the southern states, at this time, is the great supporter, the great sanctioner of the bloody atrocities to which I have referred. While America is printing tracts and bibles; sending missionaries abroad to convert the heathen; expending her money in various ways for the promotion of the gospel in foreign lands—the slave not only lies forgotten, uncared for, but it trampled under foot by the very churches of the land. What have we in America? Why, we have slavery made part of the religion of the land. Yes, the pulpit there stands up as the great defender of this cursed *institution*, as it is called. Ministers of religion come forward and torture the hallowed pages of inspired wisdom to sanction the bloody deed.

They stand forth as the foremost, the strongest defenders of this "institution." As a proof of this, I need not do more than state the general fact, that slavery has existed under the droppings of the sanctuary of the south for the last two hundred years, and there has not been any war between the *religion* and the *slavery* of the south. Whips, chains, gags, and thumb-screws have all lain under the droppings of the sanctuary, and instead of rusting from off the limbs of the bondman, those droppings have served to preserve them in all their strength. Instead of preaching the gospel against this tyranny, rebuke, and wrong, ministers of religion have sought, by all and every means, to throw in the back-ground whatever in the bible could be construed into opposition to slavery, and to bring forward that which they could torture into its support. This I conceive to be the darkest feature of slavery, and the most difficult to attack, because it is identified with religion, and exposes those who denounce it to the charge of infidelity. Yes, those with whom I have been laboring, namely, the old organization anti-slavery society of America, have been again and again stigmatized as infidels, and for what reason? Why, solely in consequence of the faithfulness of their attacks upon the slaveholding religion of the southern states, and the northern religion that sympathizes with it. I have found it difficult to speak on this matter without persons coming forward and saying, "Douglass, are you not afraid of injuring the cause of Christ? You do not desire to do so, we know; but are you not undermining religion?" This has been said to me again and again, even since I came to this country, but I cannot be induced to leave off these exposures. I love the religion of our blessed Savior. I love that religion that comes from above, in the "wisdom of God," which is first pure, then peaceable, gentle, and easy to be entreated, full of mercy and good fruits, without partiality and without hypocrisy. I love that religion that sends its votaries to bind up the wounds of him that has fallen among thieves. I love that religion that makes it the duty of its disciples to visit the fatherless and the widow in their affliction. I love that religion that is based upon the glorious principle, of love to God and love to man; which makes its followers do unto others as they themselves would be done by. If you demand liberty to yourself, it says, grant it to your neighbors. If you claim a right to think for yourself, it says, allow your neighbors the same right. If you claim to act for yourself, it says, allow your neighbors the same right. It is because I love this religion that I hate the slaveholding, the woman-whipping, the mind-darkening, the soul-destroying religion that exists in the southern states of America. It is because I regard the one as good, and pure, and holy, that I cannot but regard the other as bad, corrupt, and wicked. Loving the one I must hate the other; holding to the one I must reject the other.

I may be asked, why I am so anxious to bring this subject before the British public—why I do not confine my efforts to the United States? My answer is, first, that slavery is the common enemy of mankind, and all mankind should be made acquainted with its abominable character. My next answer is, that the slave is a man, and, as such, is entitled to your sympathy as a brother. All the feelings, all the susceptibilities, all the capacities, which you have, he has. He is a part of the human family. He has been the prey—the common prey—of christendom for the last three hundred years, and it is but right, it is but just, it is but proper, that his wrongs should be known throughout the world. I have another reason for bringing this matter before the British public, and it is this: slavery is a system of wrong, so blinding to all around, so hardening to the heart, so corrupting to the morals, so deleterious to religion, so sapping to all the principles of justice in its immediate vicinity, that the community surrounding it lack the moral stamina necessary to its removal. It is a system of such gigantic evil, so strong, so overwhelming in its power, that no one nation is equal to its removal. It requires the humanity of christianity, the morality of the world to remove it. Hence, I call upon the people of Britain to look at this matter, and to exert the influence I am about to show they possess, for the removal of slavery from America. I can appeal to them, as strongly by their regard for the slaveholder as for the slave, to labor in this cause. I am here, because you have an influence on America that no other nation can have. You have been drawn together by the power of steam to a marvelous extent; the distance between London and Boston is now reduced to some twelve or fourteen days, so that the denunciations against slavery, uttered in London this week, may be heard in a fortnight in the streets of Boston, and reverberating amidst the hills of Massachusetts. There is nothing said here against slavery that will not be recorded in the United States. I am here, also, because the slaveholders do not want me to be here; they would rather that I were not here. I have adopted a maxim laid down by Napoleon, never to occupy ground which the enemy would like me to occupy. The slaveholders would much rather have me, if I will denounce slavery, denounce it in the northern states, where their friends and supporters are, who will stand by and mob me for denouncing it. They feel something as the man felt, when he uttered his prayer, in which he made out a most horrible case for himself, and one of his neighbors touched him and said, "My friend, I always had the opinion of you that you have now expressed for yourself—that you are a very great sinner." Coming from himself, it was all very well, but coming from a stranger it was rather cutting. The slaveholders felt that when slavery was denounced among themselves, it was not so bad; but let one of the slaves get loose, let him summon the people of Britain, and make known to them the conduct of the slaveholders toward their slaves, and it cuts them to the quick, and produces a sensation such as would be produced by nothing else. The power I exert now is something like the power that is exerted by the man at the end of the lever; my influence now is just in proportion to the distance that I am from the United States. My exposure of slavery abroad will tell more upon the hearts and consciences of slaveholders, than if I was attacking them in America; for almost every paper that I now receive from the United States, comes teeming with statements about this fugitive negro, calling him a "glib-tongued scoundrel," and saying that he is running out against the institutions and people of America. I deny the charge that I am saying a word against the institutions of America, or the people, as such. What I have to say is against slavery and slaveholders. I feel at liberty to speak on this subject. I have on my back the marks of the lash; I have four sisters and one brother now under the galling chain. I feel it my duty to cry aloud and spare not. I am not averse to having the good opinion of my fellow-creatures. I am not averse to being kindly regarded by all men; but I am bound, even at the hazard of making a large class of religionists in this country hate me, oppose me, and malign me as they have done—I am bound by the prayers, and tears, and entreaties of three millions of kneeling bondsmen, to have no compromise with men who are in any shape or form connected with the slaveholders of America. I expose slavery in this country, because to expose it is to kill it. Slavery is one of those monsters of darkness to whom the light of truth is death. Expose slavery, and it dies. Light is to slavery what the heat of the sun is to the root of a tree; it must die under it. All the slaveholder asks of me is silence. He does not ask me to go abroad and preach *in favor* of slavery; he does not ask any one to do that. He would not say that slavery is a good thing, but the best under the circumstances.

The slaveholders want total darkness on the subject. They want the hatchway shut down, that the monster may crawl in his den of darkness, crushing human hopes and happiness, destroying the bondman at will, and having no one to reprove or rebuke him. Slavery shrinks from the light; it hateth the light, neither cometh to the light, lest its deeds should be reproved. To tear off the mask from this abominable system, to expose it to the light of heaven, aye, to the heat of the sun, that it may burn and wither it out of existence, is my object in coming to this country. I want the slaveholder surrounded, as by a wall of anti-slavery fire, so that he may see the condemnation of himself and his system glaring down in letters of light. I want him to feel that he has no sympathy in England, Scotland, or Ireland; that he has none in Canada, none in Mexico, none among the poor wild Indians; that the voice of the civilized, aye, and savage world is against him. I would have condemnation blaze down upon him in every direction, till, stunned and overwhelmed with shame and confusion, he is compelled to let go the grasp he holds upon the persons of his victims, and restore them to their long-lost rights.

—7—

FIRST INAUGURAL ADDRESS

Abraham Lincoln

March 4, 1861

Slavery divided the North and South from the very beginnings of the United States, but tensions reached new heights in the 1850s. The Mexican War of 1846–48 and the Kansas-Nebraska Act of 1854 were seen by many in the North (including Abraham Lincoln) as attempts by aggressive Southern slaveowners to expand the system of human bondage into new territories, to create new slave states. Fighting between pro- and antislavery settlers in Kansas in the late 1850s and John Brown's raid on Harpers Ferry in 1859 sparked new fury between North and South. In the North, antislavery forces formed the Republican Party, while some leaders in the Southern states called for secession from the Union.

In this explosive atmosphere, no less than four major candidates ran for president in 1860, as the Democratic Party split into three parts over the issue of slavery. Lincoln and the Republican Party, facing such a divided opposition, won a narrow victory. Southern extremists painted Lincoln as a man determined to abolish slavery as soon as possible, and after his election several Southern states broke away to form the Confederate States of America on February 8, 1861. Lincoln, however, did not believe in immediate abolition; though he opposed slavery, he believed in slow, careful measures to bring it to an end. In his inaugural address on March 4, 1861, he sought to ease Southern fears, speaking with moderation in the face of open rebellion. But this address also reveals the firmness of his commitment to national unity, obvious in his warning that "the Union of these States is perpetual," that secession would not be tolerated. With this speech, Lincoln began what was probably the single most important presidential administration in American history—and he began his own role as the unifier of a long divided nation.

FIRST INAUGURAL ADDRESS

Fellow Citizens of the United States: In compliance with a custom as old as the government itself, I appear before you to address you briefly, and to take in your presence the oath prescribed by the Constitution of the United States to be taken by the President "before he enters on the execution of his office."

I do not consider it necessary at present for me to discuss those matters of administration about which there is no special anxiety or excitement.

Apprehension seems to exist among the people of the Southern states that by the accession of a Republican administration their property and their peace and personal security are to be endangered. There has never been any reasonable cause for such apprehension. Indeed, the most ample evidence to the contrary has all the while existed and been open to their inspection. It is found in nearly all the published speeches of him who now addresses you. I do but quote from one of those speeches when I declare that "I have no purpose, directly or indirectly, to interfere with the institution of slavery in the states where it exists. I believe I have no lawful right to do so, and I have no inclination to do so." Those who nominated and elected me did so with full knowledge that I had made this and many similar declarations, and had never recanted them. And, more than this, they placed in the platform for my acceptance, and as a law to themselves and to me, the clear and emphatic resolution which I now read:

"*Resolved,* That the maintenance inviolate of the rights of the states, and especially the right of each state to order and control its own domestic institutions according to its own judgment exclusively, is essential to that balance of power on which the perfection and endurance of our political fabric depend, and we denounce the lawless invasion by armed force of the soil of any state or territory, no matter under what pretext, as among the gravest of crimes.''

I now reiterate these sentiments; and, in doing so, I only press upon the public attention the most conclusive evidence of which the case is susceptible, that the property, peace, and security of no section are to be in any wise endangered by the now incoming administration. I add, too, that all the protection which, consistently with the Constitution and the laws, can be given, will be cheerfully given to all the states when lawfully demanded, for whatever cause—as cheerfully to one section as to another.

There is much controversy about the delivering up of fugitives from service or labor. The clause I now read is as plainly written in the Constitution as any other of its provisions:

``No person held to service or labor in one state, under the laws thereof, escaping into another, shall in consequence of any law or regulation therein be discharged from such service or labor, but shall be delivered up on claim of the party to whom such service or labor may be due.''

It is scarcely questioned that this provision was intended by those who made it for the reclaiming of what we call fugitive slaves; and the intention of the lawgiver is the law. All members of Congress swear their support to the whole Constitution—to this provision as much as to any other. To the proposition, then, that slaves whose cases come within the terms of this clause ``shall be delivered up,'' their oaths are unanimous. Now, if they would make the effort in good temper, could they not with nearly equal unanimity frame and pass a law by means of which to keep good that unamimous oath?

There is some difference of opinion whether this clause should be enforced by national or by state authority; but surely that difference is not a very material one. If the slave is to be surrendered, it can be of but little consequence to him or to others by which authority it is done. And should anyone in any case be content that his oath shall go unkept on a merely unsubstantial controversy as to how it shall be kept?

Again, in any law upon this subject, ought not all the safeguards of liberty known in civilized and humane jurisprudence to be introduced, so that a free man be not, in any case, surrendered as a slave? And might it not be well at the same time to provide by law for the enforcement of that clause in the Constitution which guarantees that "the citizen of each state shall be entitled to all privileges and immunities of citizens in the several states"?

I take the official oath today with no mental reservations, and with no purpose to construe the Constitution or laws by any hypercritical rules. And while I do not choose now to specify particular acts of Congress as proper to be enforced, I do suggest that it will be much safer for all, both in official and private stations, to conform to and abide by all those acts which stand unrepealed, than to violate any of them, trusting to find impunity in having them held to be unconstitutional.

It is seventy-two years since the first inauguration of a president under our national Constitution. During that period fifteen different and greatly distinguished citizens have, in succession, administered the executive branch of the government. They have conducted it through many perils, and generally with great success. Yet, with all this scope of precedent, I now enter upon the same task for the brief constitutional term of four years under great and peculiar difficulty. A disruption of the federal Union, heretofore only menaced, is now formidably attempted.

I hold that, in contemplation of universal law and of the Constitution, the union of these states is perpetual. Perpetuity is implied, if not expressed, in the fundamental law of all national governments. It is safe to assert that no government proper ever had a provision in its organic law for its own termination. Continue to execute all the express provisions of our national Constitution, and the Union will endure forever—it being impossible to destroy it except by some action not provided for in the instrument itself.

Again, if the United States be not a government proper, but an association of states in the nature of contract merely, can it, as a contract, be peaceably unmade by less than all the parties who made it? One party to a contract may violate it—break it, so to speak; but does it not require all to lawfully rescind it?

Descending from these general principles, we find the proposition that, in legal contemplation the Union is perpetual confirmed by the history of the Union itself. The Union is much older than the Constitution. It was formed, in fact, by the Articles of Association in 1774. It was matured and continued by the Declaration of Independence in 1776. It was further matured, and the faith of all the then thirteen states expressly plighted and engaged that it should be perpetual, by the Articles of Confederation in

1778. And, finally, in 1787 one of the declared objects for ordaining and establishing the Constitution was "to form a more perfect Union."

But if the destruction of the Union by one or by a part only of the states be lawfully possible, the Union is less perfect than before the Constitution, having lost the vital element of perpetuity.

It follows from these views that no state upon its own mere motion can lawfully get out of the Union; that resolves and ordinances to that effect are legally void; and that acts of violence, within any state or states, against the authority of the United States, are insurrectionary or revolutionary, according to circumstances.

I therefore consider that, in view of the Constitution and the laws, the Union is unbroken and to the extent of my ability I shall take care, as the Constitution itself expressly enjoins upon me, that the laws of the Union be faithfully executed in all the states. Doing this I deem to be only a simple duty on my part; and I shall perform it so far as practicable, unless my rightful masters, the American people, shall withhold the requisite means, or in some authoritative manner direct the contrary. I trust this will not be regarded as a menace, but only as the declared purpose of the Union that it will constitutionally defend and maintain itself.

In doing this there needs to be no bloodshed or violence; and there shall be none, unless it be forced upon the national authority. The power confided to me will be used to hold, occupy, and possess the property and places belonging to the government, and to collect the duties and imposts; but beyond what may be necessary for these objects, there will be no invasion, no using of force against or among the people anywhere. Where hostility to the United States, in any interior locality, shall be so great and universal as to prevent competent resident citizens from holding the federal offices, there will be no attempt to force obnoxious strangers among the people for that object. While the strict legal right may exist in the government to enforce the exercise of these offices, the attempt to do so would be so irritating, and so nearly impracticable withal, that I deem it better to forego for the time the uses of such offices.

The mails, unless repelled, will continue to be furnished in all parts of the Union. So far as possible, the people everywhere shall have that sense of perfect security which is most favorable to calm thought and reflection. The course here indicated will be followed unless current events and experience shall show a modification or change to be proper, and in every case and exigency my best discretion will be exercised according to circumstances actually existing, and with a view and a hope of a peaceful solution of the national troubles and the restoration of fraternal sympathies and affections.

That there are persons in one section or another who seek to destroy the Union at all events, and are glad of any pretext to do it, I will neither affirm nor deny; but if there be such, I need address no word to them. To those, however, who really love the Union may I not speak?

Before entering upon so grave a matter as the destruction of our national fabric, with all its benefits, its memories, and its hopes, would it not be wise to ascertain precisely why we do it? Will you hazard so desperate a step while there is any possibility that any portion of the ills you fly from have no real existence? Will you, while the certain ills you fly to are greater than all the real ones you fly from—will you risk the commission of so fearful a mistake?

All profess to be content in the Union if all constitutional rights can be maintained. Is it true, then, that any right, plainly written in the Constitution, has been denied? I think not. Happily the human mind is so constituted that no party can reach to the audacity of doing this. Think, if you can, of a single instance in which a plainly written provision of the Constitution has ever been denied. If by the mere force of numbers a majority should deprive a minority of any clearly written constitutional right, it might, in a moral point of view, justify revolution—certainly would if such a right were a vital one. But such is not our case. All the vital rights of minorities and of individuals are so plainly assured to them by affirmations and negations, guarantees and prohibitions, in the Constitution, that controversies never arise concerning them. But no organic law can ever be framed with a provision specifically applicable to every question which may occur in practical administration. No foresight can anticipate, nor any document of reasonable length contain, express provisions for all possible questions. Shall fugitives from labor be surrendered by national or by state authority? The Constitution does not expressly say. *May* Congress prohibit slavery in the territories? The Constitution does not expressly say. *Must* Congress protect slavery in the territories? The Constitution does not expressly say.

From questions of this class spring all our constitutional controversies, and we divide upon them into majorities and minorities. If the minority will not acquiesce, the majority must, or the government must cease. There is no other alternative; for continuing the government is acquiescence on one side or the other.

If a minority in such case will secede rather than acquiesce, they make a precedent which in turn will divide and ruin them; for a minority of their own will secede from them whenever a majority refuses to be controlled by such minority. For instance, why may not any portion of a new confederacy a year or two hence arbitrarily secede again, precisely as portions of the present Union now claim to secede from it? All who cherish disunion sentiments are now being educated to the exact temper of doing this.

Is there such perfect identity of interests among the states to compose a new Union, as to produce harmony only, and prevent renewed secession?

Plainly, the central idea of secession is the essence of anarchy. A majority held in restraint by constitutional checks and limitations, and always changing easily with deliberate changes of popular opinions and sentiments, is the only true sovereign of a free people. Whoever rejects it does, of necessity, fly to anarchy or to despotism. Unanimity is impossible; the rule of a minority, as a permanent arrangement, is wholly inadmissible, so that, rejecting the majority principle, anarchy or despotism in some form is all that is left.

I do not forget the position, assumed by some, that constitutional questions are to be decided by the Supreme Court; nor do I deny that such decisions must be binding, in any case, upon the parties to a suit, as to the object of that suit, while they are also entitled to very high respect and consideration in all parallel cases by all other departments of the government. And while it is obviously possible that such decisions may be erroneous in any given case, still the evil effect following it, being limited to that particular case, with the chance that it may be overruled and never become a precedent for other cases, can better be borne than could the evils of a different practice. At the same time, the candid citizen must confess that if the policy of the government, upon vital questions affecting the whole people, is to be irrevocably fixed by decisions of the Supreme Court, the instant they are made, in ordinary litigation between parties in personal actions, the people will have ceased to be their own rulers, having to that extent practically resigned their government into the hands of that eminent tribunal. Nor is there in this view any assault upon the court or the judges. It is a duty from which they may not shrink to decide cases properly brought before them, and it is no fault of theirs if others seek to turn their decisions to political purposes.

One section of our country believes slavery is right, and ought to be extended, while the other believes it is wrong, and ought not be extended. This is the only substantial dispute. The fugitive-slave clause of the Constitution, and the law for the suppression of the foreign slave-trade, are each as well enforced, perhaps, as any law can ever be in a community where the moral sense of the people imperfectly supports the law itself. The great body of the people abide by the dry legal obligation in both cases, and a few break over in each. This, I think, cannot be perfectly cured; and it would be worse in both cases after the separation of the sections than before. The foreign slave-trade, now imperfectly suppressed, would be ultimately revived, without restriction, in one section, while fugitive slaves, now only partially surrendered, would not be surrendered at all by the other.

Physically speaking, we cannot separate. We cannot remove our respective sections from each other, nor build an impassable wall between them. A husband and wife may be divorced, and go out of the presence and beyond the reach of each other; but the different parts of our country cannot do this. They cannot but remain face to face, and intercourse, either amicable or hostile, must continue between them. Is it possible, then, to make that intercourse more advantageous or more satisfactory after separation than before? Can aliens make treaties easier than friends can make laws? Can treaties be more faithfully enforced between aliens than laws can among friends? Suppose you go to war, you cannot fight always; and when, after much loss on both sides, and no gain on either, you cease fighting, the identical old questions as to terms of intercourse are again upon you.

This country, with its institutions, belongs to the people who inhabit it. Whenever they shall grow weary of the existing government, they can exercise their constitutional right of amending it, or their revolutionary right to dismember or overthrow it. I cannot be ignorant of the fact that many worthy and patriotic citizens are desirous of having the national Constitution amended. While I make no recommendation of amendments, I fully recognize the rightful authority of the people over the whole subject, to be exercised in either of the modes prescribed in the instrument itself; and I should, under existing circumstances, favor rather than oppose a fair opportunity being afforded the people to act upon it. I will venture to add that to me the convention mode seems preferable, in that it allows amendments to originate with the people themselves, instead of only permitting them to take or reject propositions originated by others not especially chosen for the purpose, and which might not be precisely such as they would wish to either accept or refuse. I understand a proposed amendment to the Constitution—which amendment, however, I have not seen—has passed Congress, to the effect that the federal government shall never interfere with the domestic institutions of the states, including that of persons held to service. To avoid misconstruction of what I have said, I depart from my purpose not to speak of particular amendments so far as to say that, holding such a provision to now be implied constitutional law, I have no objections to its being made express and irrevocable.

The chief magistrate derives all his authority from the people, and they have conferred none upon him to fix terms for the separation of the states. The people themselves can do this also if they choose; but the executive, as such, has nothing to do with it. His duty is to administer the present government, as it came to his hands, and to transmit it, unimpaired by him, to his successor.

Why should there not be a patient confidence in the ultimate justice of the people? Is there any better or equal hope in the world? In our present differences is either party without faith of being in the right? If the Almighty Ruler of Nations, with His eternal truth and justice, be on your side of the North, or on yours of the South, that truth and that justice will surely prevail by the judgment of this great tribunal of the American people.

By the frame of the government under which we live, this same people have wisely given their public servants but little power for mischief; and have, with equal wisdom, provided for the return of that little to their own hands at very short intervals. While the people retain their virtue and vigilance, no administration, by any extreme of wickedness or folly, can very seriously injure the government in the short space of four years.

My countrymen, one and all, think calmly and well upon this whole subject. Nothing valuable can be lost by taking time. If there be an object to hurry any of you in hot haste to a step which you would never take deliberately, that object will be frustrated by taking time; but no good object can be frustrated by it. Such of you as are now dissatisfied, still have the old Constitution unimpaired, and, on the sensitive point, the laws of your own framing under it; while the new administration will have no immediate power, if it would, to change either. If it were admitted that you who are dissatisfied hold the right side in the dispute, there still is no single good reason for precipitate action. Intelligence, patriotism, Christianity, and a firm reliance on Him who has never yet forsaken this favored land, are still competent to adjust in the best way all our present difficulty.

In your hands, my dissatisfied fellow-countrymen, and not in mine, is the momentous issue of civil war. The government will not assail you. You can have no conflict without being yourselves the aggressors. You have no oath registered in heaven to destroy the government, while I shall have the most solemn one to ''preserve, protect, and defend it.''

I am loathe to close. We are not enemies, but friends. We must not be enemies. Though passion may have strained, it must not break our bonds of affection. The mystic chords of memory, stretching from every battlefield and patriot grave to every living heart and hearthstone all over this broad land, will yet swell the chorus of the Union when again touched, as surely they will be, by the better angels of our nature.

—8—

THE EMANCIPATION PROCLAMATION

Abraham Lincoln

September 22, 1862

For the first year of the Civil War, the official goal of the Union was to put an end to the rebellion of the Southern states. President Lincoln made no mention of slavery as one of the causes of the war, or abolition as one of its ends. But as the war dragged on, it became clear that the conflict would drag on for months, even years. The war turned into a brutal, life-and-death struggle as a series of defeats in the East brought Northern morale to desperately low levels. Meanwhile, thousands of slaves crossed Union lines to freedom with each passing month, disrupting slavery as the Union army advanced in the West and captured beachheads along the seacoast.

In July, 1862, as gloom over Union defeats settled over the North, Lincoln announced to his cabinet his intention to declare the emancipation of slaves in Confederate-held territory. His decision combined both political and moral reasoning: By declaring slaves in the rebel states to be free, he hoped to encourage more of them to flee to Northern lines, and weaken the Confederacy's war effort by reducing its slave labor reserves. To avoid angering the border states, which had stayed with the Union but maintained slavery, he limited the declaration to *only* Confederate territory.

Lincoln did, of course, oppose slavery, and the proclamation gave a new, moral purpose to the war effort.

Before delivering the proclamation, the President waited until the federal forces in the East could claim a victory. Then, on September 17, 1862, the Union army under General George McClellan turned back an attempted invasion of the North by Confederate General Robert E. Lee at the Battle of Antietam. On September 22, 1862, Lincoln issued the Emancipation Proclamation.

Many scholars believe that Lincoln went far beyond the limits of the Constitution with the Emancipation Proclamation, by relying on his own authority as President to declare the slaves free. The Proclamation, in fact, was only one instance of how he took on unprecedented new powers in his effort to save the Union. At the same time, Lincoln recognized the new, more radical turn the war had taken as the fighting had spread. In the end, the Emancipation Proclamation gave the Constitution even greater vitality by giving new meaning to the principles of freedom and liberty enshrined there.

THE EMANCIPATION PROCLAMATION

BY THE PRESIDENT OF THE UNITED STATES OF AMERICA:
A Proclamation.

Whereas on the 22d day of September, A.D. 1862, a proclamation was issued by the President of the United States, containing, among other things, the following, to wit:

"That on the 1st day of January, A.D. 1863, all persons held as slaves within any State or designated part of a State the people whereof shall then be in rebellion against the United States shall be then, thenceforward, and forever free; and the executive government of the United States, including the military and naval authority thereof, will recognize and maintain the freedom of such persons and will do no act or acts to repress such persons, or any of them, in any efforts they may make for their actual freedom.

"That the executive will on the 1st day of January aforesaid, by proclamation, designate the States and parts of States, if any, in which the people thereof, respectively, shall then be in rebellion against the United States; and the fact that any State or the people thereof shall on that day be in good faith represented in the Congress of the United States by members chosen thereto at elections wherein a majority of the qualified voters of such States shall have participated shall, in the absence of strong countervailing testimony, be deemed conclusive evidence that such State and the people thereof are not then in rebellion against the United States.''

Now, therefore, I, Abraham Lincoln, President of the United States, by virtue of the power in me vested as Commander-in-Chief of the Army and Navy of the United States in time of actual armed rebellion against the authority and government of the United States, and as a fit and necessary war measure for suppressing said rebellion, do, on this 1st day of January, A.D. 1863, and in accordance with my purpose so to do, publicly proclaimed for the full period of one hundred days from the first day above mentioned, order and designate as the States and parts of States wherein the people thereof, respectively, are this day in rebellion against the United States the following, to wit:

Arkansas, Texas, Louisiana (except the parishes of St. Bernard, Plaquemines, Jefferson, St. John, St. Charles, St. James, Ascension, Assumption, Terrebonne, Lafourche, St. Mary, St. Martín, and Orleans, including the city of New Orleans), Mississippi, Alabama, Florida, Georgia, South Carolina, North Carolina, and Virginia (except the forty-eight counties designated as West Virginia, and also the counties of Berkeley, Accomac, Northhampton, Elizabeth City, York, Princess Anne, and Norfolk, including the cities of Norfolk and Portsmouth), and which excepted parts are for the present left precisely as if this proclamation were not issued.

And by virtue of the power and for the purpose aforesaid, I do order and declare that all persons held as slaves within said designated States and parts of States are, and henceforward shall be, free; and that the Executive Government of the United States, including the military and naval authorities thereof, will recognize and maintain the freedom of said persons.

And I hereby enjoin upon the people so declared to be free to abstain from all violence, unless in necessary self-defense; and I recommend to them that, in all cases when allowed, they labor faithfully for reasonable wages.

And I further declare and make known that such persons of suitable condition will be received into the armed service of the United States to garrison forts, positions, stations, and other places, and to man vessels of all sorts in said service.

And upon this act, sincerely believed to be an act of justice, warranted by the Constitution upon military necessity, I invoke the considerate judgment of mankind and the gracious favor of Almighty God.

9

THE GETTYSBURG ADDRESS

Abraham Lincoln

November 19, 1863

On November 18, 1863, President Abraham Lincoln traveled to the town of Gettysburg, Pennsylvania, to make some remarks at the dedication of a national cemetery. It was at Gettysburg, in July, 1863, that the Union army had defeated Lee's second and last attempt to invade the North, in the biggest battle of the Civil War; together with the capture of Vicksburg on the Mississippi at about the same time, it proved to be the war's turning point. On November 19, he attended the ceremony on the great battlefield. The President was not the main speaker, and was not expected to make a long address. The principal speech of the day, by Edward Everett, ran on for two hours (common for public speeches in the nineteenth century), but it has long since disappeared in the shadow of Lincoln's three short paragraphs.

Few documents as brief as the Gettysburg Address have played so great a role in the American consciousness. Speaking in the midst of the most terrible war our nation has ever endured, Lincoln transformed our sense of national purpose. Before the Civil War, the United States was considered plural—a Union of separate states. Loyalty to one's state often took priority over loyalty to the nation (Robert E. Lee, for example, did not like either slavery or secession, but he joined the Confederate army when his home state of Virginia left the Union). In the Gettysburg Address, Lincoln referred to the *nation*—a single country, not a collection of states. In this sense, the Address represents a key moment in the unification of the nation, and in Lincoln's role in speeding that transformation through his foresight and eloquence.

The Gettysburg Address was also the culmination of the emerging moral crusade that first appeared a year before in the Emancipation Proclamation. Harking back to the Declaration of Independence, Lincoln declared that they were fighting the war not simply to suppress a rebellion, but to fulfill the promise held out at America's founding, to secure equal rights for everyone, regardless of race. With the Gettysburg Address, Lincoln filled the North with a new sense of purpose in the midst of our most bitter war. He also set out a vision for the nation that Americans struggle to meet to this day.

THE GETTYSBURG ADDRESS

Four score and seven years ago our fathers brought forth on this continent, a new nation, conceived in Liberty, and dedicated to the proposition that all men are created equal.

Now we are engaged in a great civil war, testing whether that nation or any nation so conceived and so dedicated, can long endure. We are met on a great battle-field of that war. We have come to dedicate a portion of that field, as a final resting place for those who here gave their lives that that nation might live. It is altogether fitting and proper that we should do this.

But, in a larger sense, we can not dedicate—we can not consecrate—we can not hallow—this ground. The brave men, living and dead, who struggled here, have consecrated it, far above our poor power to add or detract. The world will little note, nor long remember what we say here, but it can never forget what they did here. It is for us the living, rather, to be dedicated here to the unfinished work which they who fought here have thus far so nobly advanced. It is rather for us to be here dedicated to the great task remaining before us—that from these honored dead we take increased devotion to that cause for which they gave the last full measure of devotion—that we here highly resolve that these dead shall not have died in vain—that this nation, under God, shall have a new birth of freedom—and that government of the people, by the people, for the people, shall not perish from the earth.

—10—

SECOND INAUGURAL ADDRESS

Abraham Lincoln

March 4, 1865

As a congressman, Abraham Lincoln opposed war with Mexico; as he took the oath of office in 1861, he sought to soothe Southern fears with his moderation; but as President he was relentless in his determination to crush the Confederate cause. He constantly prodded his generals to fight harder, and he promoted those, like Ulysses S. Grant, who aggressively attacked the Southern armies. But as the Confederacy crumbled in late 1864 and early 1865, he turned his attention to reuniting the nation and spoke of the dangers of vindictiveness against the South. ''Enemies!'' he once snapped. ''Never again must we repeat that word.''

On March 4, 1865, Lincoln took the oath of office for the second time. The address that followed demonstrated the depth of his statesmanship and the sincerity of his vision of a newly united people and nation. While radical members of his own party called for the South to be treated like a conquered province, Lincoln declared his desire to restore the rebellious states to an equal place in the country, despite the savagery of the Civil War. ''With malice toward none, with charity for all, let us strive on to finish the work we are in,'' he declared. A little over a month later, he died from an assassin's bullet, and his generous vision of Reconstruction disappeared in a bitter dispute between the Radical Republican Congress and President Andrew Johnson. Nevertheless, this Second Inaugural Address remains one of our most profound statements on the essential unity of the American people—even at the close of a vicious conflict that nearly destroyed the nation.

SECOND INAUGURAL ADDRESS

Fellow countrymen, at this second appearing to take the oath of the presidential office, there is less occasion for an extended address than there was at the first. Then a statement, somewhat in detail, of a course to be pursued, seemed fitting and proper. Now, at the expiration of four years, during which public declarations have been constantly called forth on every point and phase of the great contest which still absorbs the attention, and engrosses the energies of the nation, little that is new could be presented. The progress of our arms, upon which all else chiefly depends, is as well known to the public as to myself; and it is, I trust, reasonably satisfactory and encouraging to all. With high hope for the future, no prediction in regard to it is ventured.

On the occasion corresponding to this four years ago, all thoughts were anxiously directed to an impending civil-war. All dreaded it—all sought to avert it. While the inaugural address was being delivered from this place, devoted altogether to *saving* the Union without war, insurgent agents were in the city seeking to *destroy* it without war—seeking to dissolve the Union, and divide effects, by negotiation. Both parties deprecated war; but one of them would *make* war rather than let the nation survive; and the other would *accept* war rather than let it perish. And the war came.

One eighth of the whole population were colored slaves, not distributed generally over the Union, but localized in the Southern part of it. These slaves constituted a peculiar and powerful interest. All knew that this interest was, somehow, the cause of the war. To strengthen, perpetuate, and extend this interest was the object for which the insurgents would rend the Union, even by war; while the government claimed no right to do more than to restrict the territorial enlargement of it. Neither party expected for the war, the magnitude, or the duration, which it has already attained. Neither anticipated that the *cause* of the conflict might cease with, or even before, the conflict itself should cease. Each looked for an easier triumph, and a result less fundamental and astounding. Both read the same Bible, and pray to the same God; and each invokes His aid against the other. It may seem strange that any men should dare to ask a just God's assistance in wringing their bread from the sweat of other men's faces; but let us judge not that we be not judged. The prayers of both could not be answered; that of neither has been answered fully. The Almighty has His own purposes. "Woe unto the world because of offences! for it must needs be that offences come; but woe to that man by whom the offence cometh!" If we shall suppose that American Slavery is one of those offences which, in the providence of God, must needs come, but which, having continued through His appointed time, He now wills to remove, and that He gives to both North and South, this terrible war, as the woe due to those by whom the offence came, shall we discern therein any departure from those divine attributes which the believers in a Living God always ascribe to Him? Fondly do we hope—fervently do we pray—that this mighty scourge of war may speedily pass away. Yet, if God wills that it continue, until all the wealth piled by the bond-man's two hundred and fifty years of unrequited toil shall be sunk, and until every drop of blood drawn with the lash, shall be paid by another drawn with the sword, as was said three thousand years ago, so still it must be said "the judgments of the Lord, are true and righteous altogether."

With malice toward none; with charity for all; with firmness in the right, as God gives us to see the right, let us strive on to finish the work we are in; to bind up the nation's wounds; to care for him who shall have borne the battle, and for his widow, and his orphan—to do all which may achieve and cherish a just, and a lasting peace, among ourselves, and with all nations.

—11—

ON INDIAN AFFAIRS, FROM HIS SECOND ANNUAL MESSAGE TO CONGRESS

Andrew Jackson

1830

From the very beginning of white settlement in North America, westward expansion has been at the center of the American imagination. Through the end of the nineteenth century, whites saw the freedom to settle in the West almost as a right, even though it came at the expense of native peoples who had lived there for thousands of years. As early as 1763, King George III's decision to reserve the lands west of the Appalachians for the Indians sparked bitter resentment among white Americans. After the Revolution, whites filled up the lands between both oceans—always driving the Indians out before them. One of the leaders most closely associated with the drive west, and with the wars against the Indian nations, was Andrew Jackson, a frontiersman, general, and President of the United States from 1829 to 1837.

Like most presidents in the nineteenth century, Jackson spent a great deal of time dealing with Indian affairs. The following passage formed a substantial portion of his second annual message to Congress. One of the earliest crises of his presidency occurred when the Supreme Court ruled that the state of Georgia had no jurisdiction in the lands of the Cherokee nation. Jackson ignored the ruling, reportedly declaring, "[Chief Justice] John

Marshall has made his decision; now let him enforce it.'' Indians living within the boundaries of a state, he stated, were subject to its laws. The solution to tensions between white and Native Americans, he suggested, would be to pay the Indians to move to the unsettled lands west of the Mississippi. But the passage that follows reveals his ruthless view of the destruction of Native American life. The Indians, he wrote, were savages who foolishly resisted the benefits of white civilization. He added that the destruction of the Indians was inevitable; simply a case of the triumph of the strong over the weak. This process, he believed, was beyond the government's control; if anything, the government should encourage rather than delay it. Unfortunately, Jackson spoke for most Americans, and the Native Americans barely survived the nineteenth century's wholesale destruction of their people and culture.

ON INDIAN AFFAIRS

It gives me pleasure to announce to Congress that the benevolent policy of the Government, steadily pursued for nearly thirty years, in relation to the removal of the Indians beyond the white settlements is approaching to a happy consummation. Two important tribes have accepted the provision made for their removal at the last session of Congress, and it is believed that their example will induce the remaining tribes also to seek the same obvious advantages.

The consequence of a speedy removal will be important to the United States, to individual States, and to the Indians themselves. . . .

It will separate the Indians from immediate contact with settlements of whites; free them from the power of the States; enable them to pursue happiness in their own way and under their own rude institutions; will retard the progress of decay, which is lessening their numbers, and perhaps cause them gradually, under the protection of the Government and through the influence of good counsels, to cast off their savage habits and become an interesting, civilized, and Christian community. These consequences, some of them so certain and the rest so probable, make the complete execution of the plan sanctioned by Congress at their last session an object of much solicitude.

Toward the aborigines of the country no one can indulge a more friendly feeling than myself, or would go further in attempting to reclaim them from their wandering habits and make them a happy, prosperous people. . . .

Humanity has often wept over the fate of the aborigines of this country, and Philanthropy has been long busily employed in devising means to avert it, but its progress has never for a moment been arrested, and one by one have many powerful tribes disappeared from the earth. To follow to the tomb the last of his race and to tread on the graves of extinct nations excite melancholy reflections. But true philanthropy reconciles the mind to these vicissitudes as it does to the extinction of one generation to make room for another. In the monuments and fortresses of an unknown people, spread over the extensive regions of the West, we behold the memorials of a once powerful race, which was exterminated or has disappeared to make room for the existing savage tribes. Nor is there anything in this which, upon a comprehensive view of the general interests of the human race, is to be regretted. Philanthropy could not wish to see this continent restored to the condition in which it was found by our forefathers. What good man would prefer a country covered with forests and ranged by a few thousand savages to our extensive Republic, studded with cities, towns, and prosperous farms, embellished with all the improvements which art can devise or industry execute, occupied by more than 12,000,000 happy people, and filled with all the blessings of liberty, civilization, and religion?

The present policy of the Government is but a continuation of the same progressive change by a milder process. The tribes which occupied the countries now constituting the Eastern States were annihilated or have melted away to make room for the whites. The waves of population and civilization are rolling to the westward, and we now propose to acquire the countries occupied by the red men of the South and West by a fair exchange, and, at the expense of the United States, to send them to a land where their existence may be prolonged and perhaps made perpetual. Doubtless it will be painful to leave the graves of their fathers; but what do they more than our ancestors did or than our children are now doing? To better their condition in an unknown land our forefathers left all that was dear in earthly objects. Our children by thousands yearly leave the land of their birth to seek new homes in distant regions. Does Humanity weep at these painful separations from everything, animate and inanimate, with which the young heart has become entwined? Far from it. It is rather a source of joy that our country affords scope where our young population may range unconstrained in body or in mind, developing the power and faculties of man in their highest perfection. These remove hundreds and almost thousands of miles at their own expense, purchase the lands they occupy, and support themselves at their new homes from the moment of their arrival. Can it be cruel in this Government when, by events which it can not control, the Indian is made discontented in his ancient home to purchase his lands, to give him a new and extensive territory, to pay the expense of his removal, and support him a year in his new abode? How many thousands of our own people would gladly embrace the opportunity of removing to the West on such conditions! If the offers made to the Indians were extended to them, they would be hailed with gratitude and joy.

And is it supposed that the wandering savage has a stronger attachment to his home than the settled, civilized Christian? Is it more afflicting to him to leave the graves of his fathers than it is to our brothers and children? Rightly considered, the policy of the General Government toward the red man is not only liberal, but generous. He is unwilling to submit to the laws of the States and mingle with their population. To save him from this alternative, or perhaps utter annihilation, the General Government kindly offers him a new home, and proposes to pay the whole expense of his removal and settlement.

—12—

AN INDIAN'S VIEWS OF INDIAN AFFAIRS

Chief Joseph

April, 1879

When Andrew Jackson advocated sending the Indians across the Mississippi to prevent conflicts between the United States and the Indian nations, few whites lived in the far West; within a few decades, millions of settlers flooded the region, driving Native Americans into ever more restricted lands. Gradually, most Indian tribes found themselves forced onto a few small reservations—a bitter end to centuries of free travel across enormous territory as a part of their annual rhythm of life. Few white Americans saw anything wrong in this process; they believed Native Americans were uncivilized savages who were simply falling to the march of time and progress. Today, few Americans would call the Indians "savages," and many consider the destruction of Native American culture and peoples one of the great tragedies in our history.

In 1877, this era of vast land seizures was drawing to a close. In that year, one of the last wars fought between the United States Army and Native Americans took place in the northern Rocky Mountains. The Indians were a group of Nez Percés, led by In-mut-too-yah-lat-lat (Thunder Traveling Over the Mountains), also known as Chief Joseph, a name given him by a white missionary.

When Chief Joseph's band refused to move with the rest of the Nez Percés onto a reservation, he skillfully led them in a guerrilla campaign against the U.S. cavalry as they marched toward Canada. Only a short distance from the border they were surrounded and forced to surrender; there he spoke the famous line, "From where the sun now stands I will fight no more." In April, 1879, Chief Joseph published this essay in the *North American Review*, recounting the suffering of his tribe at the hands of the United States government. In straightforward, eloquent language, Chief Joseph destroyed the white image of the Indian as a savage; his plea for decency and respect for human rights remains as powerful as anything written by the founding fathers.

AN INDIAN'S VIEWS OF INDIAN AFFAIRS

My friends, I have been asked to show you my heart. I am glad to have a chance to do so. I want the white people to understand my people. Some of you think an Indian is like a wild animal. This is a great mistake. I will tell you all about our people, and then you can judge whether an Indian is a man or not. I believe much trouble and blood would be saved if we opened our hearts more. I will tell you in my way how the Indian sees things. The white man has more words to tell you how they look to him, but it does not require many words to speak the truth. What I have to say will come from my heart, and I will speak with a straight tongue. Ah-cum-kin-i-ma-me-hut (the Great Spirit) is looking at me, and will hear me.

My name is In-mut-too-yah-lat-lat (Thunder Traveling Over the Mountains). I am chief of the Wal-lam-wat-kin band of Chute-pa-lu, or Nez Percés (nose-pierced Indians). I was born in eastern Oregon, thirty-eight winters ago. My father was chief before me. When a young man, he was called Joseph by Mr. Spaulding, a missionary. He died a few years ago. There was no stain on his hands of the blood of a white man. He left a good name on the earth. He advised me well for my people.

Our fathers gave us many laws, which they had learned from their fathers. These laws were good. They told us to treat all men as they treated us; that we should never be the first to break a bargain; that it was a disgrace to tell a lie; that we should speak only the truth; that it was a shame for one man to take from another his wife, or his property without paying for it. We were taught to believe that the Great Spirit sees and hears everything, and that he never forgets; that hereafter he will give every man a spirit-home according to his deserts: if he has been a good man, he will have a good home; if he has been a bad man, he will have a bad home. This I believe, and all my people believe the same.

We did not know there were other people besides the Indian until about one hundred winters ago, when some men with white faces came to our country. They brought many things with them to trade for furs and skins. They brought tobacco, which was new to us. They brought guns with flint stones on them, which frightened our women and children. Our people could not talk with these white-faced men, but they used signs which all people understand. These men were Frenchmen, and they called our people "Nez Percés," because they wore rings in their noses for ornaments. Although very few of our people wear them now, we are still called by the same name. These French trappers said a great many things to our fathers, which have been planted in our hearts. Some were good for us, but some were bad. Our people were divided in opinion about these men. Some thought they taught more bad than good. An Indian respects a brave man, but he despises a coward. He loves a straight tongue, but he hates a forked tongue. The French trappers told us some truths and some lies.

The first white men of your people who came to our country were named Lewis and Clarke. They also brought many things that our people had never seen. They talked straight, and our people gave them a great feast, as a proof that their hearts were friendly. These men were very kind. They made presents to our chiefs and our people made presents to them. We had a great many horses, of which we gave them what they needed, and they gave us guns and tobacco in return. All the Nez Percés made friends with Lewis and Clarke, and agreed to let them pass through their country, and never to make war on white men. This promise the Nez Percés have never broken. No white man can accuse them of bad faith, and speak with a straight tongue. It has always been the pride of the Nez Percés that they were the friends of the white men. When my father was a young man there came to our country a white man (Rev. Mr. Spaulding) who talked spirit law. He won the affections of our people because he spoke good things to them. At first he did not say anything about white men wanting to settle on our lands. Nothing was said about that until about twenty winters ago, when a number of white people came into our country and built houses and made farms. At first our people made no complaint. They thought there was room enough for all to live in peace, and they were learning many things from the white men that seemed to be good. But we soon found that the white men were growing rich very fast, and were greedy to possess everything the Indian had. My father was the first to see through the schemes of the white men, and he warned his tribe to be careful about trading with them. He had suspicion of men who seemed so anxious to make money. I was a boy then, but I remember well my father's caution. He had sharper eyes than the rest of our people.

Next there came a white officer (Governor Stevens), who invited all the Nez Percés to a treaty council. After the council was opened he made known his heart. He said there were a great many white people in the country, and many more would come; that he wanted the land marked out so that the Indians and white men could be separated. If they were to live in peace it was necessary, he said, that the Indians should have a country set apart for them, and in that country they must stay. My father, who represented his band, refused to have anything to do with the council, because he wished to be a free man. He claimed that no man owned any part of the earth, and a man could not sell what he did not own.

Mr. Spaulding took hold of my father's arm and said, "Come and sign the treaty." My father pushed him away, and said: "Why do you ask me to sign away my country? It is your business to talk to us about spirit matters, and not to talk to us about parting with our land." Governor Stevens urged my father to sign his treaty, but he refused. "I will not sign your paper," he said; "you go where you please, so do I; you are not a child, I am no child; I can think for myself. No man can think for me. I have no other home than this. I will not give it up to any man. My people would have no home. Take away your paper. I will not touch it with my hand."

My father left the council. Some of the chiefs of the other bands of the Nez Percés signed the treaty, and then Governor Stevens gave them presents of blankets. My father cautioned his people to take no presents, for "after a while," he said, "they will claim that you have accepted pay for your country." Since that time four bands of the Nez Percés have received annuities from the United States. My father was invited to many councils, and they tried hard to make him sign the treaty, but he was firm as the rock, and would not sign away his home. His refusal caused a difference among the Nez Percés.

Eight years later (1863) was the next treaty council. A chief called Lawyer, because he was a great talker, took the lead in this council, and sold nearly all the Nez Percés country. My father was not there. He said to me: "When you go into council with the white man, always remember your country. Do not give it away. The white man will cheat you out of your home. I have taken no pay from the United States. I have never sold our land." In this treaty Lawyer acted without authority from our band. He had no right to sell the Wallowa (*winding water*) country. That had always belonged to my father's own people, and the other bands had never disputed our right to it. No other Indians ever claimed Wallowa.

In order to have all people understand how much land we owned, my father planted poles around it and said:

"Inside is the home of my people—the white man may take the land outside. Inside this boundary all our people were born. It circles around the graves of our fathers, and we will never give up these graves to any man."

The United States claimed they had bought all the Nez Percés country outside of Lapwai Reservation, from Lawyer and other chiefs, but we continued to live on this land in peace until eight years ago, when white men began to come inside the bounds my father had set. We warned them against this great wrong, but they would not leave our land, and some bad blood was raised. The white men represented that we were going upon the war-path. They reported many things that were false.

The United States Government again asked for a treaty council. My father had become blind and feeble. He could no longer speak for his people. It was then that I took my father's place as chief. In this council I made my first speech to white men. I said to the agent who held the council:

"I did not want to come to this council, but I came hoping that we could save blood. The white man has no right to come here and take our country. We have never accepted any presents from the Government. Neither Lawyer nor any other chief had authority to sell this land. It has always belonged to my people. It came unclouded to them from our fathers, and we will defend this land as long as a drop of Indian blood warms the hearts of our men."

The agent said he had orders, from the Great White Chief at Washington, for us to go upon the Lapwai Reservation, and that if we obeyed he would help us in many ways. "You *must* move to the agency,'' he said. I answered him: ''I will not. I do not need your help; we have plenty, and we are contented and happy if the white man will let us alone. The reservation is too small for so many people with all their stock. You can keep your presents; we can go to your towns and pay for all we need; we have plenty of horses and cattle to sell, and we won't have any help from you; we are free now; we can go where we please. Our fathers were born here. Here they lived, here they died, here are their graves. We will never leave them.'' The agent went away, and we had peace for a little while.

Soon after this my father sent for me. I saw he was dying. I took his hand in mine. He said: ''My son, my body is returning to my mother earth, and my spirit is going very soon to see the Great Spirit Chief. When I am gone, think of your country. You are the chief of these people. They look to you to guide them. Always remember that your father never sold his country. You must stop your ears whenever you are asked to sign a treaty selling your home. A few years more, and white men will be all around you. They have their eyes on this land. My son, never forget my dying words. This country holds your father's body. Never sell the bones of your father and your mother.'' I pressed my father's hand and told him I would protect his grave with my life. My father smiled and passed away to the spirit-land.

I buried him in that beautiful valley of winding waters. I love that land more than all the rest of the world. A man who would not love his father's grave is worse than a wild animal.

For a short time we lived quietly. But this could not last. White men had found gold in the mountains around the land of winding water. They stole a great many horses from us, and we could not get them back because we were Indians. The white men told lies for each other. They drove off a great many of our cattle. Some white men branded our young cattle so they could claim them. We had no friend who would plead our cause before the law councils. It seemed to me that some of the white men in Wallowa were doing these things on purpose to get up a war. They knew that we were not strong enough to fight them. I labored hard to avoid trouble and bloodshed. We gave up some of our country to the white men, thinking that then we could have peace. We were mistaken. The white man would not let us alone. We could have avenged our wrongs many times, but we did not. Whenever the Government has asked us to help them against other Indians, we have never refused. When the white men were few and we were strong we could have killed them all off, but the Nez Percés wished to live at peace.

If we have not done so, we have not been to blame. I believe that the old treaty has never been correctly reported. If we ever owned the land, we own it still, for we never sold it. In the treaty councils the commissioners have claimed that our country had been sold to the Government. Suppose a white man should come to me and say, "Joseph, I like your horses, and I want to buy them." I say to him, "No, my horses suit me, I will not sell them." Then he goes to my neighbor, and says to him: "Joseph has some good horses. I want to buy them, but he refuses to sell." My neighbor answers, "Pay me the money, and I will sell you Joseph's horses." The white man returns to me, and says, "Joseph, I have bought your horses, and you must let me have them." If we sold our lands to the Government, this is the way they were bought.

On account of the treaty made by the other bands of the Nez Percés, the white men claimed my lands. We were troubled greatly by white men crowding over the line. Some of these were good men, and we lived on peaceful terms with them, but they were not all good.

Nearly every year the agent came over from Lapwai and ordered us on to the reservation. We always replied that we were satisfied to live in Wallowa. We were careful to refuse the presents or annuities which he offered.

Through all the years since the white men came to Wallowa we have been threatened and taunted by them and the treaty Nez Percés. They have given us no rest. We have had a few good friends among white men, and they have always advised my people to bear these taunts without fighting. Our young men were quick-tempered, and I have had great trouble in keeping them from doing rash things. I have carried a heavy load on my back ever since I was a boy. I learned then that we were but few, while the white men were many, and that we could not hold our own with them. We were like deer. They were like grizzly bears. We had a small country. Their country was large. We were contented to let things remain as the Great Spirit Chief made them. They were not; and would change the rivers and mountains if they did not suit them.

Year after year we have been threatened, but no war was made upon my people until General Howard came to our country two years ago and told us that he was the white war-chief of all that country. He said: "I have a great many soldiers at my back. I am going to bring them up here, and then I will talk to you again. I will not let white men laugh at me the next time I come. The country belongs to the Government, and I intend to make you go upon the reservation."

I remonstrated with him against bringing more soldiers to the Nez Percés country. He had one house full of troops all the time at Fort Lapwai.

The next spring the agent at Umatilla agency sent an Indian runner to tell me to meet General Howard at Walla Walla. I could not go myself, but I sent my brother and five other head men to meet him, and they had a long talk.

General Howard said: "You have talked straight, and it is all right. You can stay in Wallowa." He insisted that my brother and his company should go with him to Fort Lapwai. When the party arrived there General Howard sent out runners and called all the Indians in to a grand council. I was in that council. I said to General Howard, "We are ready to listen." He answered that he would not talk then, but would hold a council next day, when he would talk plainly. I said to General Howard: "I am ready to talk to-day. I have been in a great many councils, but I am no wiser. We are all sprung from a woman, although we are unlike in many things. We can not be made over again. You are as you were made, and as you were made you can remain. We are just as we were made by the Great Spirit, and you can not change us; then why should children of one mother and one father quarrel—why should one try to cheat the other? I do not believe that the Great Spirit Chief gave one kind of men the right to tell another kind of men what they must do."

General Howard replied: "You deny my authority, do you? You want to dictate to me, do you?"

Then one of my chiefs—Too-hool-hool-suit—rose in the council and said to General Howard: "The Great Spirit Chief made the world as it is, and as he wanted it, and he made a part of it for us to live upon. I do not see where you get authority to say that we shall not live where he placed us."

General Howard lost his temper and said: "Shut up! I don't want to hear any more of such talk. The law says you shall go upon the reservation to live, and I want you to do so, but you persist in disobeying the law" (meaning the treaty). "If you do not move, I will take the matter into my own hand, and make you suffer for your disobedience.''

Too-hool-hool-suit answered: ''Who are you, that you ask us to talk, and then tell me I sha'n't talk? Are you the Great Spirit? Did you make the world? Did you make the sun? Did you make the rivers to run for us to drink? Did you make the grass to grow? Did you make all these things, that you talk to us as though we were boys? If you did, then you have the right to talk as you do.''

General Howard replied, ''You are an impudent fellow, and I will put you in the guard-house,'' and then ordered a soldier to arrest him.

Too-hool-hool-suit made no resistance. He asked General Howard: ''Is that your order? I don't care. I have expressed my heart to you. I have nothing to take back. I have spoken for my country. You can arrest me, but you can not change me or make me take back what I have said.''

The soldiers came forward and seized my friend and took him to the guard-house. My men whispered among themselves whether they should let this thing be done. I counseled them to submit. I knew if we resisted that all the white men present, including General Howard would be killed in a moment, and we would be blamed. If I had said nothing, General Howard would never have given another unjust order against my men. I saw the danger, and, while they dragged Too-hool-hool-suit to prison, I arose and said: ''*I am going to talk now.* I don't care whether you arrest me or not.'' I turned to my people and said: ''The arrest of Too-hool-hool-suit was wrong, but we will not resent the insult. We were invited to this council to express our hearts, and we have done so.'' Too-hool-hool-suit was prisoner for five days before he was released.

The council broke up for that day. On the next morning General Howard came to my lodge, and invited me to go with him and White-Bird and Looking-Glass, to look for land for my people. As we rode along we came to some good land that was already occupied by Indians and white people. General Howard, pointing to this land, said: ''If you will come on to the reservation, I will give you these lands and move these people off.''

I replied: ''No. It would be wrong to disturb these people. I have no right to take their homes. I have never taken what did not belong to me. I will not now.''

We rode all day upon the reservation, and found no good land unoccupied. I have been informed by men who do not lie that General Howard sent a letter that night, telling the soldiers at Walla Walla to go to Wallowa Valley, and drive us out upon our return home.

In the council, next day, General Howard informed me, in a haughty spirit, that he would give my people *thirty days* to go back home, collect all their stock, and move on to the reservation, saying, "If you are not here in that time, I shall consider that you want to fight, and will send my soldiers to drive you on."

I said: "War can be avoided, and it ought to be avoided. I want no war. My people have always been the friends of the white man. Why are you in such a hurry? I can not get ready to move in thirty days. Our stock is scattered, and Snake River is very high. Let us wait until fall, then the river will be low. We want time to hunt up our stock and gather supplies for winter."

General Howard replied, "If you let the time run over one day, the soldiers will be there to drive you on to the reservation, and all your cattle and horses outside of the reservation at that time will fall into the hands of the white men."

I knew I had never sold my country, and that I had no land in Lapwai; but I did not want bloodshed. I did not want my people killed. I did not want anybody killed. Some of my people had been murdered by white men, and the white murderers were never punished for it. I told General Howard about this, and again said I wanted no war. I wanted the people who lived upon the lands I was to occupy at Lapwai to have time to gather their harvest.

I said in my heart that, rather than have war, I would give up my country. I would give up my father's grave. I would give up everything rather than have the blood of white men upon the hands of my people.

General Howard refused to allow me more than thirty days to move my people and their stock. I am sure that he began to prepare for war at once.

When I returned to Wallowa I found my people very much excited upon discovering that the soldiers were already in the Wallowa Valley. We held a council, and decided to move immediately, to avoid bloodshed.

Too-hool-hool-suit, who felt outraged by his imprisonment, talked for war, and made many of my young men willing to fight rather than be driven like dogs from the land where they were born. He declared that blood alone would wash out the disgrace General Howard had put upon him. It required a strong heart to stand up against such talk, but I urged my people to be quiet, and not to begin a war.

We gathered all the stock we could find, and made an attempt to move. We left many of our horses and cattle in Wallowa, and we lost several hundred in crossing the river. All of my people succeeded in getting across in safety. Many of the Nez Percés came together in Rocky Cañon to hold a grand council. I went with all my people. This council lasted ten days. There was a great deal of war-talk, and a great deal of excitement. There was one young brave present whose father had been killed by a white man five years before. This man's blood was bad against white men, and he left the council calling for revenge.

Again I counseled peace, and I thought the danger was past. We had not complied with General Howard's order because we could not, but we intended to do so as soon as possible. I was leaving the council to kill beef for my family, when news came that the young man whose father had been killed had gone out with several other hot-blooded young braves and killed four white men. He rode up to the council and shouted: "Why do you sit here like women? The war has begun already." I was deeply grieved. All the lodges were moved except my brother's and my own. I saw clearly that the war was upon us when I learned that my young men had been secretly buying ammunition. I heard then that Too-hool-hool-suit, who had been imprisoned by General Howard, had succeeded in organizing a war-party. I knew that their acts would involve all my people. I saw that the war could not then be prevented. The time had passed. I counseled peace from the beginning. I knew that we were too weak to fight the United States. We had many grievances, but I knew that war would bring more. We had good white friends, who advised us against taking the war-path. My friend and brother, Mr. Chapman, who has been with us since the surrender, told us just how the war would end. Mr. Chapman took sides against us, and helped General Howard. I do not blame him for doing so. He tried hard to prevent bloodshed. We hoped the white settlers would not join the soldiers. Before the war commenced we had discussed this matter all over, and many of my people were in favor of warning them that if they took no part against us they should not be molested in the event of war being begun by General Howard. This plan was voted down in the war-council.

There were bad men among my people who had quarreled with white men, and they talked of their wrongs until they roused all the bad hearts in the council. Still I could not believe that they would begin the war. I know that my young men did a great wrong, but I ask, Who was first to blame? They had been insulted a thousand times; their fathers and brothers had been killed; their mothers and wives had been disgraced; they had been driven to madness by whisky sold to them by white men; they had been told by General Howard that all their horses and cattle which they had been unable to drive out of Wallowa were to fall into the hands of white men; and, added to all this, they were homeless and desperate.

I would have given my own life if I could have undone the killing of white men by my people. I blame my young men and I blame the white men. I blame General Howard for not giving my people time to get their stock away from Wallowa. I do not acknowledge that he had the right to order me to leave Wallowa at any time. I deny that either my father or myself ever sold that land. It is still our land. It may never again be our home, but my father sleeps there, and I love it as I love my mother. I left there, hoping to avoid bloodshed.

If General Howard had given me plenty of time to gather up my stock, and treated Too-hool-hool-suit as a man should be treated, there *would have been no war*.

My friends among white men have blamed me for the war. I am not to blame. When my young men began the killing, my heart was hurt. Although I did not justify them, I remembered all the insults I had endured, and my blood was on fire. Still I would have taken my people to the buffalo country without fighting, if possible.

I could see no other way to avoid a war. We moved over to White Bird Creek, sixteen miles away, and there encamped, intending to collect our stock before leaving; but the soldiers attacked us, and the first battle was fought. We numbered in that battle sixty men, and the soldiers a hundred. The fight lasted but a few minutes, when the soldiers retreated before us for twelve miles. They lost thirty-three killed, and had seven wounded. When an Indian fights, he only shoots to kill; but soldiers shoot at random. None of the soldiers were scalped. We do not believe in scalping, nor in killing wounded men. Soldiers do not kill many Indians unless they are wounded and left upon the battle-field. Then they kill Indians.

Seven days after the first battle, General Howard arrived in the Nez Percés country, bringing seven hundred more soldiers. It was now war in earnest. We crossed over Salmon River, hoping General Howard would follow. We were not disappointed. He did follow us, and we got back between him and his supplies, and cut him off for three days. He sent out two companies to open the way. We attacked them, killing one officer, two guides, and ten men.

We withdrew, hoping the soldiers would follow, but they had got fighting enough for that day. They intrenched themselves, and next day we attacked them again. The battle lasted all day, and was renewed next morning. We killed four and wounded seven or eight.

About this time General Howard found out that we were in his rear. Five days later he attacked us with three hundred and fifty soldiers and settlers. We had two hundred and fifty warriors. The fight lasted twenty-seven hours. We lost four killed and several wounded. General Howard's loss was twenty-nine men killed and sixty wounded.

The following day the soldiers charged upon us, and we retreated with our families and stock a few miles, leaving eighty lodges to fall into General Howard's hands.

Finding that we were outnumbered, we retreated to Bitter Root Valley. Here another body of soldiers came upon us and demanded our surrender. We refused. They said, "You can not get by us." We answered, "We are going by you without fighting if you will let us, but we are going by you anyhow." We then made a treaty with these soldiers. We agreed not to molest any one, and they agreed that we might pass through the Bitter Root country in peace. We bought provisions and traded stock with white men there.

We understood that there was to be no more war. We intended to go peaceably to the buffalo country, and leave the question of returning to our country to be settled afterward.

With this understanding we traveled on for four days, and, thinking that the trouble was all over, we stopped and prepared tent-poles to take with us. We started again, and at the end of two days we saw three white men passing our camp. Thinking that peace had been made, we did not molest them. We could have killed or taken them prisoners, but we did not suspect them of being spies, which they were.

That night the soldiers surrounded our camp. About daybreak one of my men went out to look after his horses. The soldiers saw him and shot him down like a coyote. I have since learned that these soldiers were not those we had left behind. They had come upon us from another direction. The new white war-chief's name was Gibbon. He charged upon us while some of my people were still asleep. We had a hard fight. Some of my men crept around and attacked the soldiers from the rear. In this battle we lost nearly all our lodges, but we finally drove General Gibbon back.

Finding that he was not able to capture us, he sent to his camp a few miles away for his big guns (cannons), but my men had captured them and all the ammunition. We damaged the big guns all we could, and carried away the powder and lead. In the fight with General Gibbon we lost fifty women and children and thirty fighting men. We remained long enough to bury our dead. The Nez Percés never make war on women and children; we could have killed a great many women and children while the war lasted, but we would feel ashamed to do so cowardly an act.

We never scalp our enemies, but when General Howard came up and joined General Gibbon, their Indian scouts dug up our dead and scalped them. I have been told that General Howard did not order this great shame to be done.

We retreated as rapidly as we could toward the buffalo country. After six days General Howard came close to us, and we went out and attacked him, and captured nearly all his horses and mules (about two hundred and fifty head). We then marched on to the Yellowstone Basin.

On the way we captured one white man and two white women. We released them at the end of three days. They were treated kindly. The women were not insulted. Can the white soldiers tell me of one time when Indian women were taken prisoners, and held three days and then released without being insulted? Were the Nez Percés women who fell into the hands of General Howard's soldiers treated with as much respect? I deny that a Nez Percé was ever guilty of such a crime.

A few days later we captured two more white men. One of them stole a horse and escaped. We gave the other a poor horse and told him he was free.

Nine days' march brought us to the mouth of Clarke's Fork of the Yellowstone. We did not know what had become of General

Howard, but we supposed that he had sent for more horses and mules. He did not come up, but another new war-chief (General Sturgis) attacked us. We held him in check while we moved all our women and children and stock out of danger, leaving a few men to cover our retreat.

Several days passed, and we heard nothing of General Howard, or Gibbon, or Sturgis. We had repulsed each in turn, and began to feel secure, when another army, under General Miles, struck us. This was the fourth army, each of which outnumbered our fighting force, that we had encountered within sixty days.

We had no knowledge of General Miles's army until a short time before he made a charge upon us, cutting our camp in two, and capturing nearly all of our horses. About seventy men, myself among them, were cut off. My little daughter, twelve years of age, was with me. I gave her a rope, and told her to catch a horse and join the others who were cut off from the camp. I have not seen her since, but I have learned that she is alive and well.

I thought of my wife and children, who were now surrounded by soldiers, and I resolved to go to them or die. With a prayer in my mouth to the Great Spirit Chief who rules above, I dashed unarmed through the line of soldiers. It seemed to me that there were guns on every side, before and behind me. My clothes were cut to pieces and my horse was wounded, but I was not hurt. As I reached the door of my lodge, my wife handed me my ride, saying: ''Here's your gun. Fight!''

The soldiers kept up a continuous fire. Six of my men were killed in one spot near me. Ten or twelve soldiers charged into our camp and got possession of two lodges, killing three Nez Percés and losing three of their men, who fell inside our lines. I called my men to drive them back. We fought at close range, not more than twenty steps apart, and drove the soldiers back upon their main line, leaving their dead in our hands. We secured their arms and ammunition. We lost, the first day and night, eighteen men and three women. General Miles lost twenty-six killed and forty wounded. The following day General Miles sent a messenger into my camp under protection of a white flag. I sent my friend Yellow Bull to meet him.

Yellow Bull understood the messenger to say that General Miles wished me to consider the situation; that he did not want to kill my people unnecessarily. Yellow Bull understood this to be a demand for me to surrender and save blood. Upon reporting this message to me, Yellow Bull said he wondered whether General Miles was in earnest. I sent him back with my answer, that I had not made up my mind, but would think about it and send word soon. A little later he sent some Cheyenne scouts with another message. I went out to meet them. They said they believed that General Miles was sincere and really wanted peace. I walked on to General Miles's tent. He met me and we shook hands. He said, "Come, let us sit down by the fire and talk this matter over." I remained with him all night; next morning Yellow Bull came over to see if I was alive, and why I did not return.

General Miles would not let me leave the tent to see my friend alone.

Yellow Bull said to me: "They have got you in their power, and I am afraid they will never let you go again. I have an officer in our camp, and I will hold him until they let you go free."

I said: "I do not know what they mean to do with me, but if they kill me you must not kill the officer. It will do no good to avenge my death by killing him."

Yellow Bull returned to my camp. I did not make any agreement that day with General Miles. The battle was renewed while I was with him. I was very anxious about my people. I knew that we were near Sitting Bull's camp in King George's land, and I thought maybe the Nez Percés who had escaped would return with assistance. No great damage was done to either party during the night.

On the following morning I returned to my camp by agreement, meeting the officer who had been held a prisoner in my camp at the flag of truce. My people were divided about surrendering. We could have escaped from Bear Paw Mountain if we had left our wounded, old women, and children behind. We were unwilling to do this. We had never heard of a wounded Indian recovering while in the hands of white men.

On the evening of the fourth day General Howard came in with a small escort, together with my friend Chapman. We could now talk understandingly. General Miles said to me in plain words, "If you will come out and give up your arms, I will spare your lives and send you to your reservation." I do not know what passed between General Miles and General Howard.

I could not bear to see my wounded men and women suffer any longer; we had lost enough already. General Miles had promised that we might return to our own country with what stock we had left. I thought we could start again. I believed General Miles, or *I never would have surrendered.* I have heard that he has been censured for making the promise to return us to Lapwai. He could not have made any other terms with me at that time. I would have held him in check until my friends came to my assistance, and then neither of the generals nor their soldiers would have ever left Bear Paw Mountain alive.

On the fifth day I went to General Miles and gave up my gun, and said, "From where the sun now stands I will fight no more." My people needed rest—we wanted peace.

I was told we could go with General Miles to Tongue River and stay there until spring, when we would be sent back to our country. Finally it was decided that we were to be taken to Tongue River. We had nothing to say about it. After our arrival at Tongue River, General Miles received orders to take us to Bismarck. The reason given was, that subsistence would be cheaper there.

General Miles was opposed to this order. He said: "You must not blame me. I have endeavored to keep my word, but the chief who is over me has given the order, and I must obey it or resign. That would do you no good. Some other officer would carry out the order."

I believe General Miles would have kept his word if he could have done so. I do not blame him for what we have suffered since the surrender. I do not know who is to blame. We gave up all our horses—over eleven hundred—and all our saddles—over one hundred—and we have not heard from them since. Somebody has got our horses.

General Miles turned my people over to another soldier, and we were taken to Bismarck. Captain Johnson, who now had charge of us, received an order to take us to Fort Leavenworth. At Leavenworth we were placed on a low river bottom, with no water except river-water to drink and cook with. We had always lived in a healthy country, where the mountains were high and the water was cold and clear. Many of my people sickened and died, and we buried them in this strange land. I can not tell how much my heart suffered for my people while at Leavenworth. The Great Spirit Chief who rules above seemed to be looking some other way, and did not see what was being done to my people.

During the hot days (July, 1878) we received notice that we were to be moved farther away from our own country. We were not asked if we were willing to go. We were ordered to get into the railroad-cars. Three of my people died on the way to Baxter

Springs. It was worse to die there than to die fighting in the mountains.

We were moved from Baxter Springs (Kansas) to the Indian Territory, and set down without our lodges. We had but little medicine, and we were nearly all sick. Seventy of my people have died since we moved there.

We have had a great many visitors who have talked many ways. Some of the chiefs (General Fish and Colonel Stickney) from Washington came to see us, and selected land for us to live upon. We have not moved to that land, for it is not a good place to live.

The Commissioner Chief (E. A. Hayt) came to see us. I told him, as I told every one, that I expected General Miles's word would be carried out. He said it "could not be done; that white men now lived in my country and all the land was taken up; that, if I returned to Wallowa, I could not live in peace; that law-papers were out against my young men who began the war, and that the Government could not protect my people." This talk fell like a heavy stone upon my heart. I saw that I could not gain anything by talking to him. Other law chiefs (Congressional Committee) came to see me and said they would help me to get a healthy country. I did not know who to believe. The white people have too many chiefs. They do not understand each other. They do not all talk alike.

The Commissioner Chief (Mr. Hayt) invited me to go with him and hunt for a better home than we have now. I like the land we found (west of the Osage reservation) better than any place I have seen in that country; but it is not a healthy land. There are no mountains and rivers. The water is warm. It is not a good country for stock. I do not believe my people can live there. I am afraid they will all die. The Indians who occupy that country are dying off. I promised Chief Hayt to go there, and do the best I could until the Government got ready to make good General Miles's word. I was not satisfied, but I could not help myself.

Then the Inspector Chief (General McNiel) came to my camp and we had a long talk. He said I ought to have a home in the mountain country north, and that he would write a letter to the Great Chief at Washington. Again the hope of seeing the mountains of Idaho and Oregon grew up in my heart.

At last I was granted permission to come to Washington and bring my friend Yellow Bull and our interpreter with me. I am glad we came. I have shaken hands with a great many friends, but there are some things I want to know which no one seems able to explain. I can not understand how the Government sends a man out to fight us, as it did General Miles, and then breaks his word. Such a Government has something wrong about it. I can not understand why so many chiefs are allowed to talk so many different ways, and promise so many different things. I have seen the Great Father Chief (the President), the next Great Chief (Secretary of the Interior), the Commissioner Chief (Hayt), the Law Chief (General Butler), and many other law chiefs (Congressmen), and they all say they are my friends, and that I shall have justice, but while their mouths all talk right I do not understand why nothing is done for my people. I have heard talk and talk, but nothing is done. Good words do not last long unless they amount to something. Words do not pay for my dead people. They do not pay for my country, now overrun by white men. They do not protect my father's grave. They do not pay for all my horses and cattle. Good words will not give me back my children. Good words will not make good the promise of your War Chief General Miles. Good words will not give my people good health and stop them from dying. Good words will not get my people a home where they can live in peace and take care of themselves. I am tired of talk that comes to nothing. It makes my heart sick when I remember all the good words and all the broken promises. There has been too much talking by men who had no right to talk. Too many misrepresentations have been made, too many misunderstandings have come up between the white men about the Indians. If the white man wants to live in peace with the Indian he can live in peace. There need be no trouble. Treat all men alike. Give them all the same law. Give them all an even chance to live and grow. All men were made by the same Great Spirit Chief. They are all brothers. The earth is the mother of all people, and all people should have equal rights upon it. You might as well expect the rivers to run backward as that any man who was born a free man should be contented when penned up and denied liberty to go where he pleases. If you tie a horse to a stake, do you expect he will grow fat? If you pen an Indian up on a small spot of earth, and compel him to stay there, he will not be contented, nor will he grow and prosper. I have asked some of the great white chiefs where they get their authority to say to the Indian that he shall stay in one place, while he sees white men going where they please. They can not tell me.

I only ask of the Government to be treated as all other men are treated. If I can not go to my own home, let me have a home in some country where my people will not die so fast. I would like to go to Bitter Root Valley. There my people would be healthy; where they are now they are dying. Three have died since I left my camp to come to Washington.

When I think of our condition my heart is heavy. I see men of my race treated as outlaws and driven from country to country, or shot down like animals.

I know that my race must change. We can not hold our own with the white men as we are. We only ask an even chance to live as other men live. We ask to be recognized as men. We ask that the same law shall work alike on all men. If the Indian breaks the law, punish him by the law. If the white man breaks the law, punish him also.

Let me be a free man—free to travel, free to stop, free to work, free to trade where I choose, free to choose my own teachers, free to follow the religion of my fathers, free to think and talk and act for myself—and I will obey every law, or submit to the penalty.

Whenever the white man treats the Indian as they treat each other, then we will have no more wars. We shall all be alike—brothers of one father and one mother, with one sky above us and one country around us, and one government for all. Then the Great Spirit Chief who rules above will smile upon this land, and send rain to wash out the bloody spots made by brothers' hands from the face of the earth. For this time the Indian race are waiting and praying. I hope that no more groans of wounded men and women will ever go to the ear of the Great Spirit Chief above, and that all people may be one people.

In-mut-too-yah-lat-lat has spoken for his people.

YOUNG JOSEPH.

—13—

THE CONSTITUTIONAL ARGUMENT FOR THE WOMAN'S RIGHT TO VOTE

Susan B. Anthony

June, 1873

The movement for the woman's right to vote had its origins in a convention held in Seneca Falls, New York, in 1848. Two organizations led the fight through the middle of the century: the American Woman Suffrage Association (led by Lucy Stone and Julia Ward Howe) and the National Woman Suffrage Association (led by Elizabeth Cady Stanton and Susan B. Anthony). These groups (known as the suffragettes) eventually united in the 1890s. One of the fiercest champions of woman suffrage, from before the Civil War to the turn of the century, was Susan B. Anthony.

The daughter of Massachusetts Quaker parents, Anthony devoted her life to the cause. In 1872, following in the footsteps of Henry David Thoreau, she deliberately challenged the law by voting in the general election in Rochester, New York. Her arrest and subsequent trial attracted attention nationwide, greatly advancing the cause of the woman's right to vote. As seen in the following speech, delivered shortly before her trial in June, 1873, Anthony argued that women were entitled to vote both by natural right and the amendments to the Constitution ratified during Reconstruction (particularly the Fourteenth Amendment). Though her argument was not accepted at the time, she brought the issue to the forefront of American politics. During the 1890s and early 1900s, several states extended the right to vote to women; in 1920, the states ratified the Nineteenth Amendment to the Constitution, guaranteeing all women the vote.

CONSTITUTIONAL ARGUMENT

Friends and Fellow Citizens:—I stand before you under indictment for the alleged crime of having voted at the last presidential election, without having a lawful right to vote. It shall be my work this evening to prove to you that in thus doing, I not only committed no crime, but instead simply exercised my citizen's right, guaranteed to me and all United States citizens by the National Constitution beyond the power of any State to deny.

Our democratic-republican government is based on the idea of the natural right of every individual member thereof to a voice and a vote in making and executing the laws. We assert the province of government to be to secure the people in the enjoyment of their inalienable rights. We throw to the winds the old dogma that government can give rights. No one denies that before governments were organized each individual possessed the right to protect his own life, liberty and property. When 100 to 1,000,000 people enter into a free government, they do not barter away their natural rights; they simply pledge themselves to protect each other in the enjoyment of them through prescribed judicial and legislative tribunals. They agree to abandon the methods of brute force in the adjustment of their differences and adopt those of civilization. . . . The Declaration of Independence, the United States Constitution, the constitutions of the several States and the organic laws of the Territories, all alike propose to *protect* the people in the exercise of their God-given rights. Not one of them pretends to bestow rights.

> All men are created equal, and endowed by their Creator with certain inalienable rights. Among these are life, liberty

> and the pursuit of happiness. To secure these, governments are instituted among men, deriving their just powers from the consent of the governed.

Here is no shadow of government authority over rights, or exclusion of any class from their full and equal enjoyment. Here is pronounced the right of all men, and "consequently," as the Quaker preacher said, "of all women," to a voice in the government. And here, in this first paragraph of the Declaration, is the assertion of the natural right of all to the ballot; for how can "the consent of the governed" be given, if the right to vote be denied? . . . The women, dissatisfied as they are with this form of government, that enforces taxation without representation—that compels them to obey laws to which they never have given their consent—that imprisons and hangs them without a trial by a jury of their peers—that robs them, in marriage, of the custody of their own persons, wages and children—are this half of the people who are left wholly at the mercy of the other half, in direct violation of the spirit and letter of the declarations of the framers of this government, every one of which was based on the immutable principle of equal rights to all. By these declarations, kings, popes, priests, aristocrats, all were alike dethroned and placed on a common level, politically, with the lowliest born subject or serf. By them, too, men, as such, were deprived of their divine right to rule and placed on a political level with women. By the practice of these declarations all class and caste distinctions would be abolished, and slave, serf, plebeian, wife, woman, all alike rise from their subject position to the broader platform of equality.

The preamble of the Federal Constitution says:

> We, the people of the United States, in order to form a more perfect union, establish justice, insure domestic tranquillity, provide for the common defence, promote the general welfare and secure the blessings of liberty to ourselves and our posterity, do ordain and establish this Constitution for the United States of America.

It was we, the people, not we, the white male citizens, nor we, the male citizens; but we, the whole people, who formed this Union. We formed it not to give the blessings of liberty but to secure them; not to the half of ourselves and the half of our posterity, but to the whole people—women as well as men. It is downright mockery to talk to women of their enjoyment of the blessings of liberty while they are denied the only means of securing them provided by this democratic-republican government—the ballot.

The early journals of Congress show that, when the committee reported to that body the original articles of confederation, the very first one which became the subject of discussion was that respecting equality of suffrage. . . .

James Madison said:

> Under every view of the subject, it seems indispensable that the mass of the citizens should not be without a voice in making the laws which they are to obey, and in choosing the magistrates who are to administer them. . . . Let it be remembered, finally, that it has ever been the pride and the boast of America that the rights for which she contended were the rights of human nature.

These assertions by the framers of the United States Constitution of the equal and natural right of all the people to a voice in the government, have been affirmed and reaffirmed by the leading statesmen of the nation throughout the entire history of our government. Thaddeus Stevens, of Pennsylvania, said in 1866: "I have made up my mind that the elective franchise is one of the inalienable rights meant to be secured by the Declaration of Independence." . . .

Charles Sumner, in his brave protests against the Fourteenth and Fifteenth Amendments, insisted that so soon as by the Thirteenth Amendment the slaves became free men, the original powers of the United States Constitution guaranteed to them equal rights—the right to vote and to be voted for. . . .

The preamble of the constitution of the State of New York declares the same purpose. It says: "We, the people of the State of New York, grateful to Almighty God for our freedom, in order to secure its blessings, do establish this constitution." Here is not the slightest intimation either of receiving freedom from the United States Constitution, or of the State's conferring the blessings of liberty upon the people; and the same is true of every other State constitution. Each and all declare rights God-given, and that to secure the people in the enjoyment of their inalienable rights is their one and only object in ordaining and establishing government. All of the State constitutions are equally emphatic in their recognition of the ballot as the means of securing the people in the enjoyment of these rights. . . .

I submit that in view of the explicit assertions of the equal right of the whole people, both in the preamble and previous article of the constitution, this omission of the adjective "female" should not be construed into a denial; but instead should be considered as of no effect. . . . No barriers whatever stand today between women and the exercise of their right to vote save those of precedent and prejudice, which refuse to expunge the word "male" from the constitution.

. . . When, in 1871, I asked that senator to declare the power of the United States Constitution to protect women in their right to vote—as he had done for black men—he handed me a copy of all his speeches during that reconstruction period, and said:

> Put "sex" where I have "race" or "color," and you have here the best and strongest argument I can make for woman. There is not a doubt but women have the constitutional right to vote, and I will never vote for a Sixteenth Amendment to guarantee it to them. I voted for both the Fourteenth and Fifteenth under protest; would never have done it but for the pressing emergency of that hour; would have insisted that the power of the original Constitution to protect all citizens in the equal enjoyment of their rights should have been vindicated through the courts. But the newly-made freedmen had neither the intelligence, wealth nor time to await that slow process. Women do possess all these in an eminent degree, and I insist that they shall appeal to the courts, and through them establish the powers of our American magna charta to protect every citizen of the republic.

But, friends, when in accordance with Senator Sumner's counsel I went to the ballot-box, last November, and exercised my citizen's right to vote, the courts did not wait for me to appeal to them—they appealed to me, and indicted me on the charge of having voted illegally. Putting sex where he did color, Senator Sumner would have said:

> Qualifications can be in their nature permanent or insurmountable. Sex can not be a qualification any more than size, race, color or previous condition of servitude. A permanent or insurmountable qualification is equivalent to a deprivation

of the suffrage. In other words, it is the tyranny of taxation without representation, against which our Revolutionary mothers, as well as fathers, rebelled.

For any State to make sex a qualification, which must ever result in the disfranchisement of one entire half of the people, is to pass a bill of attainder, an ex post facto law, and is therefore a violation of the supreme law of the land. By it the blessings of liberty are forever withheld from women and their female posterity. For them, this government has no just powers derived from the consent of the governed. For them this government is not a democracy; it is not a republic. It is the most odious aristocracy ever established on the face of the globe. An oligarchy of wealth, where the rich govern the poor; an oligarchy of learning, where the educated govern the ignorant; or even an oligarchy of race, where the Saxon rules the African, might be endured; but this oligarchy of sex which makes father, brothers, husband, sons, the oligarchs over the mother and sisters, the wife and daughters of every household; which ordains all men sovereigns, all women subjects—carries discord and rebellion into every home of the nation. This most odious aristocracy exists, too, in the face of Section 4, Article IV, which says: ''The United States shall guarantee to every State in the Union a republican form of government.'' . . .

It is urged that the use of the masculine pronouns *he, his* and *him* in all the constitutions and laws, is proof that only men were meant to be included in their provisions. If you insist on this version of the letter of the law, we shall insist that you be consistent and accept the other horn of the dilemma, which would compel you to exempt women from taxation for the support of the government and from penalties for the violation of laws. There is no *she* or *her* or *hers* in the tax laws, and this is equally true of all the criminal laws.

Take for example the civil rights law which I am charged with having violated; not only are all the pronouns in it masculine, but everybody knows that it was intended expressly to hinder the rebel men from voting. It reads, ''If any person shall knowingly vote without *his* having a lawful right.'' . . . I insist if government officials may thus manipulate the pronouns to tax, fine, imprison and hang women, it is their duty to thus change them in order to protect us in our right to vote. . . .

Though the words persons, people, inhabitants, electors, citizens, are all used indiscriminately in the national and State constitutions, there was always a conflict of opinion, prior to the war, as to whether they were synonymous terms, but whatever room there was for doubt, under the old regime, the adoption of the Fourteenth Amendment settled that question forever in its first sentence:

> All persons born or naturalized in the United States, and subject to the jurisdiction thereof, are citizens of the United States, and of the State wherein they reside.

The second settles the equal status of all citizens:

> No State shall make or enforce any law which shall abridge the privileges or immunities of citizens of the United States; nor shall any State deprive any person of life, liberty or property without due process of law, or deny to any person within its jurisdiction the equal protection of the laws.

The only question left to be settled now is: Are women persons? I scarcely believe any of our opponents will have the hardihood to say they are not. Being persons, then, women are citizens, and no State has a right to make any new law, or to enforce any old law, which shall abridge their privileges or immunities. Hence, every discrimination against women in the constitutions and laws of the several States is today null and void, precisely as is every one against negroes.

Is the right to vote one of the privileges or immunities of citizens? I think the disfranchised ex-rebels and ex-State prisoners all will agree that it is not only one of them, but the one without which all the others are nothing. Seek first the kingdom of the ballot and all things else shall be added, is the political injunction. . . .

I am proud to mention the names of the two United States judges who have given opinions honorable to our republican idea, and honorable to themselves—Judge Howe, of Wyoming Territory, and Judge Underwood, of Virginia. The former gave it as his opinion a year ago, when the legislature seemed likely to revoke the law enfranchising the women of that Territory that, in case they succeeded, the women would still possess the right to vote under the Fourteenth Amendment. The latter, in noticing the recent decision of Judge Cartter, of the Supreme Court of the District of Columbia, denying to women the right to vote under the Fourteenth and Fifteenth Amendments, says:

> If the people of the United States, by amendment of their Constitution, could expunge, without any explanatory or assisting legislation, an adjective of five letters from all State and local constitutions, and thereby raise millions of our most ignorant fellow-citizens to all of the rights and privileges of electors, why should not the same people, by the same amendment, expunge an adjective of four letters from the same State and local constitutions, and thereby raise other millions of more educated and better informed citizens to equal rights and privileges, without explanatory or assisting legislation?

If the Fourteenth Amendment does not secure to all citizens the right to vote, for what purpose was that grand old charter of the fathers lumbered with its unwieldy proportions? The Republican party, and Judges Howard and Bingham, who drafted the document, pretended it was to do something for black men; and if that something were not to secure them in their right to vote and hold office, what could it have been? For by the Thirteenth Amendment black men had become people, and hence were entitled to all the privileges and immunities of the government, precisely as were the women of the country and foreign men not naturalized. According to Associate-Justice Washington, they already had:

> Protection of the government, the enjoyment of life and liberty, with the right to acquire and possess property of every kind, and to pursue and obtain happiness and safety, subject to such restraints as the government may justly prescribe for the general welfare of the whole; the right of a citizen of one State to pass through or to reside in any other State for the purpose of trade, agriculture, professional pursuit, or otherwise; to claim the benefit of the writ of habeas corpus, to institute and maintain actions of any kind in the courts of the State; to take, hold, and dispose of property, either real or personal, and an exemption from higher taxes or impositions than are paid by the other citizens of the State.

Thus, you see, those newly-freed men were in possession of every possible right, privilege and immunity of the government, except that of suffrage, and hence needed no constitutional amendment for any other purpose. What right in this country has the Irishman the day after he receives his naturalization papers that he did not possess the day before, save the right to vote and hold office? The Chinamen now crowding our Pacific coast are in precisely the same position. What privilege or immunity has California or Oregon the right to deny them, save that of the ballot? Clearly, then, if the Fourteenth Amendment was not to secure to black men their right to vote it did nothing for them, since they possessed everything else before. But if it was intended to prohibit the States from denying or abridging their right to vote, then it did the same for all persons, white women included, born or naturalized in the United States; for the amendment does not say that all male persons of African descent, but that all persons are citizens.

The second section is simply a threat to punish the States by reducing their representation on the floor of Congress, should they disfranchise any of their male citizens, and can not be construed into a sanction to disfranchise female citizens, nor does it in any wise weaken or invalidate the universal guarantee of the first section.

However much the doctors of the law may disagree as to whether people and citizens, in the original Constitution, were one and the same, or whether the privileges and immunities in the Fourteenth Amendment include the right of suffrage, the question of the citizen's right to vote is forever settled by the Fifteenth Amendment. "The right of citizens of the United States to vote shall not be denied or abridged by the United States, or by any State, on account of race, color or previous condition of servitude." How can the State deny or abridge the right of the citizen, if the citizen does not possess it? There is no escape from the conclusion that to vote is the citizen's right, and the specifications of race, color or previous condition of servitude can in no way impair the force of that emphatic assertion that the citizen's right to vote shall not be denied or abridged. . . .

If once we establish the false principle that United States citizenship does not carry with it the right to vote in every State in this Union, there is no end to the petty tricks and cunning devices which will be attempted to exclude one and another class of citizens from the right of suffrage. It will not always be the men combining to disfranchise all women; native born men combining to abridge the rights of all naturalized citizens, as in Rhode Island. It will not always be the rich and educated who may combine to cut off the poor and ignorant; but we may live to see the hard-working, uncultivated day laborers, foreign and native born, learning the power of the ballot and their vast majority of numbers, combine and amend State constitutions so as to disfranchise the Vanderbilts, the Stewarts, the Conklings and the Fentons. It is a poor rule that won't work more ways than one. Establish this precedent, admit the State's right to deny suffrage, and there is no limit to the confusion, discord and disruption that may await us. There is and can be but one safe principle of government—equal rights to all. Discrimination against any class on account of color, race, nativity, sex, property, culture, can but embitter and disaffect that class, and thereby endanger the safety of the whole people. Clearly, then, the national government not only must define the rights of citizens, but must stretch out its powerful hand and protect them in every State in this Union.

If, however, you will insist that the Fifteenth Amendment's emphatic interdiction against robbing United States citizens of their suffrage "on account of race, color or previous condition of servitude," is a recognition of the right of either the United States or any State to deprive them of the ballot for any or all other reasons, I will prove to you that the class of citizens for whom I now plead are, by all the principles of our government and many of the laws of the States, included under the term "previous conditions of servitude."

Consider first married women and their legal status. What is servitude? "The condition of a slave." What is a slave? "A person who is robbed of the proceeds of his labor; a person who is subject to the will of another." By the laws of Georgia, South Carolina and all the States of the South, the negro had no right to the custody and control of his person. He belonged to his master. If he were disobedient, the master had the right to use correction. If the negro did not like the correction and ran away, the master had the right to use coercion to bring him back. By the laws of almost every State in this Union today, North as well as South, the married woman has no right to the custody and control of her person. The wife belongs to the husband; and if she refuse obedience he may use moderate correction, and if she do not like his moderate correction and leave his "bed and board," the husband may use moderate coercion to bring her back. The little word "moderate," you see, is the saving clause for the wife, and would doubtless be overstepped should her offended husband administer his correction with the "cat-o'-nine-tails," or accomplish his coercion with blood-hounds.

Again the slave had no right to the earnings of his hands, they belonged to his master; no right to the custody of his children, they belonged to his master; no right to sue or be sued, or to testify in the courts. If he committed a crime, it was the master who must sue or be sued. In many of the States there has been special legislation, giving married women the right to property inherited or received by bequest, or earned by the pursuit of any avocation outside the home; also giving them the right to sue and be sued in matters pertaining to such separate property; but not a single State of this Union has ever secured the wife in the enjoyment of her right to equal ownership of the joint earnings of the marriage copartnership. And since, in the nature of things, the vast majority of married women never earn a dollar by work outside their families, or inherit a dollar from their fathers, it follows that from the day of their marriage to the day of the death of their husbands not one of them ever has a dollar, except it shall please her husband to let her have it. . . .

A good farmer's wife in Illinois, who had all the rights she wanted, had made for herself a full set of false teeth. The dentist pronounced them an admirable fit, and the wife declared it gave her fits to wear them. The dentist sued the husband for his bill; his counsel brought the wife as witness; the judge ruled her off the stand, saying, "A married woman can not be a witness in matters of joint interest between herself and her husband." Think of it, ye good wives, the false teeth in your mouths are a joint interest with your husbands, about which you are legally incompetent to speak! If a married woman is injured by accident, in nearly all of the States it is her husband who must sue, and it is to him that the damages will be awarded. . . . Isn't such a position humiliating enough to be called "servitude?" That husband sued and obtained damages for the loss of the services of his wife, precisely as he would have done had it been his ox, cow or horse; and exactly as the master, under the old regime, would have recovered for the services of his slave.

I submit the question, if the deprivation by law of the ownership of one's own person, wages, property, children, the denial of the right as an individual to sue and be sued and testify in the courts, is not a condition of servitude most bitter and absolute, even though under the sacred name of marriage? . . . The facts also prove that, by all the great fundamental principles of our free government, not only married women but the entire womanhood of the nation are in a "condition of servitude" as surely as were our Revolutionary fathers when they rebelled against King George. Women are taxed without representation, governed without their consent, tried, convicted and punished without a jury of their peers. Is all this tyranny any less humiliating and degrading to women under our democratic-republican government today than it was to men under their aristocratic, monarchial government one hundred years ago? . . .

Is anything further needed to prove woman's condition of servitude sufficient to entitle her to the guarantees of the Fifteenth Amendment? Is there a man who will not agree with me that to talk of freedom without the ballot is mockery to the women of this republic, precisely as New England's orator, Wendell Phillips, at the close of the late war declared it to be to the newly emancipated black man? I admit that, prior to the rebellion, by common consent, the right to enslave, as well as to disfranchise both native and foreign born persons, was conceded to the States. But the one grand principle settled by the war and the reconstruction legislation, is the supremacy of the national government to protect the citizens of the United States in their right to freedom and the elective franchise, against any and every interference on the part of the several States; and again and again have the American people asserted the triumph of this principle by their overwhelming majorities for Lincoln and Grant.

The one issue of the last two presidential elections was whether the Fourteenth and Fifteenth Amendments should be considered the irrevocable will of the people; and the decision was that they should be, and that it is not only the right, but the duty of the national government to protect all United States citizens in the full enjoyment and free exercise of their privileges and immunities against the attempt of any State to deny or abridge. In this conclusion Republicans and Democrats alike agree. Senator Frelinghuysen said: "The heresy of State rights has been completely buried in these amendments, and as amended, the Constitution confers not only National but State citizenship upon all persons born or naturalized within our limits." . . .

Benjamin F. Butler, in a recent letter to me, said: "I do not believe anybody in Congress doubts that the Constitution authorizes the right of women to vote, precisely as it authorizes trial by jury and many other like rights guaranteed to citizens."

It is upon this just interpretation of the United States Constitution that our National Woman Suffrage Association, which celebrates the twenty-fifth anniversary of the woman's rights movement next May in New York City, has based all its arguments and action since the passage of these amendments. We no longer petition legislature or Congress to give us the right to vote, but appeal to women everywhere to exercise their too long neglected "citizen's right." We appeal to the inspectors of election to receive the votes of all United States citizens, as it is their duty to do. We appeal to United States commissioners and marshals to arrest, as is their duty, the inspectors who reject the votes of United States citizens, and leave alone those who perform their duties and accept these votes. We ask the juries to return verdicts of "not guilty" in the cases of law-abiding United States citizens who cast their votes, and inspectors of election who receive and count them.

We ask the judges to render unprejudiced opinions of the law, and wherever there is room for doubt to give the benefit to the side of liberty and equal rights for women, remembering that, as Sumner says, "The true rule of interpretation under our National Constitution, especially since its amendments, is that anything *for* human rights is constitutional, everything *against* human rights unconstitutional." It is on this line that we propose to fight our battle for the ballot—peaceably but nevertheless persistently—until we achieve complete triumph and all United States citizens, men and women alike, are recognized as equals in the government.

—14—

FIRST INAUGURAL ADDRESS

Franklin Delano Roosevelt

March 4, 1933

As Franklin Delano Roosevelt took the oath of office in 1933, the nation struggled in the midst of the Great Depression, a time of tremendous suffering and despair. Twelve million Americans found themselves out of work as record numbers of businesses went bankrupt. The outgoing President, Herbert Hoover, seemed completely ineffectual. In this atmosphere, the voters gave Roosevelt a landslide victory in the hope that he could lift the country out of the crisis.

The new President electrified the nation with his inaugural address. In apparent contrast with the Hoover administration, Roosevelt described a bold new vision of major programs to put the country to work again. For decades, Americans had believed that the government that governs least, governs best; Roosevelt dramatically broke with the past, forever changing the nature of American politics. ''The only thing we have to fear,'' FDR announced, ''is fear itself.'' The Congress responded to his call, and within one hundred days it enacted the primary legislation of the New Deal—a legacy that has largely shaped the pattern of the federal action for the rest of the century.

FIRST INAUGURAL ADDRESS

President Hoover, Mr. Chief Justice, my friends:

This is a day of national consecration, and I am certain that my fellow-Americans expect that on my induction into the Presidency I will address them with a candor and a decision which the present situation of our nation impels.

This is pre-eminently the time to speak the truth, the whole truth, frankly and boldly. Nor need we shrink from honestly facing conditions in our country today. This great nation will endure as it has endured, will revive and will prosper.

So first of all let me assert my firm belief that the only thing we have to fear is fear itself—nameless, unreasoning, unjustified terror which paralyzes needed efforts to convert retreat into advance.

In every dark hour of our national life a leadership of frankness and vigor has met with that understanding and support of the people themselves which is essential to victory. I am convinced that you will again give that support to leadership in these critical days.

In such a spirit on my part and on yours we face our common difficulties. They concern, thank God, only material things. Values have shrunken to fantastic levels; taxes have risen; our ability to pay has fallen, government of all kinds is faced by serious curtailment of income; the means of exchange are frozen in the currents of trade; the withered leaves of industrial enterprise lie on every side; farmers find no markets for their produce; the savings of many years in thousands of families are gone.

More important, a host of unemployed citizens face the grim problem of existence, and an equally great number toil with little return. Only a foolish optimist can deny the dark realities of the moment.

Yet our distress comes from no failure of substance. We are stricken by no plague of locusts. Compared with the perils which our forefathers conquered because they believed and were not afraid, we have still much to be thankful for. Nature still offers her bounty and human efforts have multiplied it. Plenty is at our doorstep, but a generous use of it languishes in the very sight of the supply.

Primarily, this is because the rulers of the exchange of mankind's goods have failed through their own stubbornness and their own incompetence, have admitted their failure and abdicated. Practices of the unscrupulous money changers stand indicted in the court of public opinion, rejected by the hearts and minds of men.

True, they have tried, but their efforts have been cast in the pattern of an outworn tradition. Faced by failure of credit, they have proposed only the lending of more money.

Stripped of the lure of profit by which to induce our people to follow their false leadership, they have resorted to exhortations, pleading tearfully for restored confidence. They know only the rules of a generation of self-seekers.

They have no vision, and when there is no vision the people perish.

The money changers have fled from their high seats in the temple of our civilization. We may now restore that temple to the ancient truths.

The measure of the restoration lies in the extent to which we apply social values more noble than mere monetary profit.

Happiness lies not in the mere possession of money; it lies in the joy of achievement, in the thrill of creative effort.

The joy and moral stimulation of work no longer must be forgotten in the mad chase of evanescent profits. These dark days will be worth all they cost us if they teach us that our true destiny is not to be ministered unto but to minister to ourselves and to our fellow-men.

Recognition of the falsity of material wealth as the standard of success goes hand in hand with the abandonment of the false belief that public office and high political position are to be valued only by the standards of pride of place and personal profit; and there must be an end to a conduct in banking and in business which too often has given to a sacred trust the likeness of callous and selfish wrongdoing.

Small wonder that confidence languishes, for it thrives only on honesty, on honor, on the sacredness of obligations, on faithful protection, on unselfish performance. Without them it cannot live.

Restoration calls, however, not for changes in ethics alone. This nation asks for action, and action now.

Our greatest primary task is to put people to work. This is no unsolvable problem if we face it wisely and courageously.

It can be accomplished in part by direct recruiting by the government itself, treating the task as we would treat the emergency of a war, but at the same time, through this employment, accomplishing greatly needed projects to stimulate and reorganize the use of our natural resources.

Hand in hand with this, we must frankly recognize the overbalance of population in our industrial centers and, by engaging on a national scale in the redistribution, endeavor to provide a better use of the land for those best fitted for the land.

The task can be helped by definite efforts to raise the values of agricultural products and with this the power to purchase the output of our cities.

It can be helped by preventing realistically the tragedy of the growing loss, through foreclosure, of our small homes and our farms.

It can be helped by insistence that the Federal, State and local governments act forthwith on the demand that their cost be drastically reduced.

It can be helped by the unifying of relief activities which today are often scattered, uneconomical and unequal. It can be helped by national planning for and supervision of all forms of transportation and of communications and other utilities which have a definitely public character.

There are many ways in which it can be helped, but it can never be helped merely by talking about it. We must act, and act quickly.

Finally, in our progress toward a resumption of work we require two safeguards against a return of the evils of the old order; there must be a strict supervision of all banking and credits and investments; there must be an end to speculation with other people's money, and there must be provision for an adequate but sound currency.

These are the lines of attack. I shall presently urge upon a new Congress in special session detailed measures for their fulfillment, and I shall seek the immediate assistance of the several States.

Through this program of action we address ourselves to putting our own national house in order and making income balance outgo.

Our international trade relations, though vastly important, are, in point of time and necessity, secondary to the establishment of a sound national economy.

I favor as a practical policy the putting of first things first. I shall spare no effort to restore world trade by international economic readjustment, but the emergency at home cannot wait on that accomplishment.

The basic thought that guides these specific means of national recovery is not narrowly nationalistic.

It is the insistence, as a first consideration, upon the interdependence of the various elements in, and parts of, the United States—a recognition of the old and permanently important manifestation of the American spirit of the pioneer.

It is the way to recovery. It is the immediate way. It is the strongest assurance that the recovery will endure.

In the field of world policy I would dedicate this nation to the policy of the good neighbor—the neighbor who resolutely respects himself and, because he does so, respects the rights of others—the neighbor who respects his obligations and respects the sanctity of his agreements in and with a world of neighbors.

If I read the temper of our people correctly, we now realize as we have never before, our interdependence on each other; that we cannot merely take, but we must give as well; that if we are to go forward we must move as a trained and loyal army willing to sacrifice for the good of a common discipline, because, without such discipline, no progress is made, no leadership becomes effective.

We are, I know, ready and willing to submit our lives and property to such discipline because it makes possible a leadership which aims at a larger good.

This I propose to offer, pledging that the larger purposes will bind upon us all as a sacred obligation with a unity of duty hitherto evoked only in time of armed strife.

With this pledge taken, I assume unhesitatingly the leadership of this great army of our people, dedicated to a disciplined attack upon our common problems.

Action in this image and to this end is feasible under the form of government which we have inherited from our ancestors.

Our Constitution is so simple and practical that it is possible always to meet extraordinary needs by changes in emphasis and arrangement without loss of essential form.

That is why our constitutional system has proved itself the most superbly enduring political mechanism the modern world has produced. It has met every stress of vast expansion of territory, of foreign wars, of bitter internal strife, of world relations.

It is to be hoped that the normal balance of executive and legislative authority may be wholly adequate to meet the unprecedented task before us. But it may be that an unprecedented demand and need for undelayed action may call for temporary departure from that normal balance of public procedure.

I am prepared under my constitutional duty to recommend the measures that a stricken nation in the midst of a stricken world may require.

These measures, or such other measures as the Congress may build out of its experience and wisdom, I shall seek, within my constitutional authority, to bring to speedy adoption.

But in the event that the Congress shall fail to take one of these two courses, and in the event that the national emergency is still critical, I shall not evade the clear course of duty that will then confront me.

I shall ask the Congress for the one remaining instrument to meet the crisis—broad executive power to wage a war against the emergency as great as the power that would be given me if we were in fact invaded by a foreign foe.

For the trust reposed in me I will return the courage and the devotion that befit the time. I can do no less.

We face the arduous days that lie before us in the warm courage of national unity; with the clear consciousness of seeking old and precious moral values; with the clean satisfaction that comes from the stern performance of duty by old and young alike.

We aim at the assurance of a rounded and permanent national life.

We do not distrust the future of essential democracy. The people of the United States have not failed. In their need they have registered a mandate that they want direct, vigorous action.

They have asked for discipline and direction under leadership. They have made me the present instrument of their wishes. In the spirit of the gift I take it.

In this dedication of a nation we humbly ask the blessing of God. May He protect each and every one of us! May He guide me in the days to come!

—15—

THE ANNUAL MESSAGE TO THE CONGRESS— "FOUR FREEDOMS SPEECH"

Franklin Delano Roosevelt

January 6, 1941

As President Franklin Delano Roosevelt celebrated his reelection at the end of 1940, he faced wars in Europe and Asia that threatened to draw in the United States. In the Far East, Japan had taken over Manchuria and much of China, and had just occupied bases in French Indochina, placing the American-ruled Philippines at grave risk. But Roosevelt was particularly worried about the situation in Europe, where Adolf Hitler had just seized Poland, Denmark, Norway, the Low Countries, and France; only Great Britain held out. The President was hesitant to commit United States troops to the fighting without a specific provocation, but he was determined to help Britain with as much aid as he could send. American political opinion, however, was deeply divided over how far the nation should involve itself in the fighting in Europe. In order to win Congressional approval for his plans to help Britain, Roosevelt decided to spell out the basic rights at stake in the battle.

On January 6, 1941, almost a year before the U.S. entered the war, President Roosevelt delivered his annual message to Congress, focusing on the conflict in Europe. He called for a dramatic new aid program known as Lend-Lease, in which billions of dollars worth of military goods could be shipped to any country the President deemed critical to American security. At the same time, Roosevelt listed four ''essential human freedoms'' which would be the basis of a new world order: the freedom of speech and expression, freedom of worship, freedom from want, and freedom from fear. These ''Four Freedoms'' gave concrete form to the values of the Allies as they fought Germany and Japan.

THE ANNUAL MESSAGE TO THE CONGRESS

Mr. President, Mr. Speaker, Members of the Seventy-seventh Congress: I address you, the Members of the Seventy-seventh Congress, at a moment unprecedented in the history of the Union. I use the word "unprecedented," because at no previous time has American security been as seriously threatened from without as it is today.

Since the permanent formation of our Government under the Constitution, in 1789, most of the periods of crisis in our history have related to our domestic affairs. Fortunately, only one of these—the four-year War Between the States—ever threatened our national unity. Today, thank God, one hundred and thirty million Americans, in forty-eight States, have forgotten points of the compass in our national unity.

It is true that prior to 1914 the United States often had been disturbed by events in other Continents. We had even engaged in two wars with European nations and in a number of undeclared wars in the West Indies, in the Mediterranean and in the Pacific for the maintenance of American rights and for the principles of peaceful commerce. But in no case had a serious threat been raised against our national safety or our continued independence.

What I seek to convey is the historic truth that the United States as a nation has at all times maintained clear, definite opposition, to any attempt to lock us in behind an ancient Chinese wall while the procession of civilization went past. Today, thinking of our children and of their children, we oppose enforced isolation for ourselves or for any other part of the Americas.

That determination of ours, extending over all these years, was proved, for example, during the quarter century of wars following the French Revolution.

While the Napoleonic struggles did threaten interests of the United States because of the French foothold in the West Indies and in Louisiana, and while we engaged in the War of 1812 to vindicate our right to peaceful trade, it is nevertheless clear that neither France nor Great Britain, nor any other nation, was aiming at domination of the whole world.

In like fashion from 1815 to 1914—ninety-nine years—no single war in Europe or in Asia constituted a real threat against our future or against the future of any other American nation.

Except in the Maximilian interlude in Mexico, no foreign power sought to establish itself in this Hemisphere; and the strength of the British fleet in the Atlantic has been a friendly strength. It is still a friendly strength.

Even when the World War broke out in 1914, it seemed to contain only small threat of danger to our own American future. But, as time went on, the American people began to visualize what the downfall of democratic nations might mean to our own democracy.

We need not overemphasize imperfections in the Peace of Versailles. We need not harp on failure of the democracies to deal with problems of world reconstruction. We should remember that the Peace of 1919 was far less unjust than the kind of "pacification" which began even before Munich, and which is being carried on under the new order of tyranny that seeks to spread over every continent today. The American people have unalterably set their faces against that tyranny.

Every realist knows that the democratic way of life is at this moment being directly assailed in every part of the world—assailed either by arms, or by secret spreading of poisonous propaganda by those who seek to destroy unity and promote discord in nations that are still at peace.

During sixteen long months this assault has blotted out the whole pattern of democratic life in an appalling number of independent nations, great and small. The assailants are still on the march, threatening other nations, great and small.

Therefore, as your President, performing my constitutional duty to "give to the Congress information of the state of the Union," I find it, unhappily, necessary to report that the future and the safety of our country and of our democracy are overwhelmingly involved in events far beyond our borders.

Armed defense of democratic existence is now being gallantly waged in four continents. If that defense fails, all the population and all the resources of Europe, Asia, Africa and Australasia will be dominated by the conquerors. Let us remember that the total of those populations and their resources in those four continents greatly exceeds the sum total of the population and the resources of the whole of the Western Hemisphere—many times over.

In times like these it is immature—and incidentally, untrue—for anybody to brag that an unprepared America, single-handed, and with one hand tied behind its back, can hold off the whole world.

No realistic American can expect from a dictator's peace international generosity, or return of true independence, or world disarmament, or freedom of expression, or freedom of religion—or even good business.

Such a peace would bring no security for us or for our neighbors. "Those, who would give up essential liberty to purchase a little temporary safety, deserve neither liberty nor safety."

As a nation, we may take pride in the fact that we are soft-hearted; but we cannot afford to be soft-headed.

We must always be wary of those who with sounding brass and a tinkling cymbal preach the "ism" of appeasement.

We must especially beware of that small group of selfish men who would clip the wings of the American eagle in order to feather their own nests.

I have recently pointed out how quickly the tempo of modern warfare could bring into our very midst the physical attack which we must eventually expect if the dictator nations win this war.

There is much loose talk of our immunity from immediate and direct invasion from across the seas. Obviously, as long as the British Navy retains its power, no such danger exists. Even if there were no British Navy, it is not probable that any enemy would be stupid enough to attack us by landing troops in the United States from across thousands of miles of ocean, until it had acquired strategic bases from which to operate.

But we learn much from the lessons of the past years in Europe—particularly the lesson of Norway, whose essential seaports were captured by treachery and surprise built up over a series of years.

The first phase of the invasion of this Hemisphere would not be the landing of regular troops. The necessary strategic points would be occupied by secret agents and their dupes—and great numbers of them are already here, and in Latin America.

As long as the aggressor nations maintain the offensive, they—not we—will choose the time and the place and the method of their attack.

That is why the future of all the American Republics is today in serious danger.

That is why this Annual Message to the Congress is unique in our history.

That is why every member of the Executive Branch of the Government and every member of the Congress faces great responsibility and great accountability.

The need of the moment is that our actions and our policy should be devoted primarily—almost exclusively—to meeting this foreign peril. For all our domestic problems are now a part of the great emergency.

Just as our national policy in internal affairs has been based upon a decent respect for the rights and the dignity of all our fellow men within our gates, so our national policy in foreign affairs has been based on a decent respect for the rights and dignity of all nations, large and small. And the justice of morality must and will win in the end.

Our national policy is this:

First, by an impressive expression of the public will and without regard to partisanship, we are committed to all-inclusive national defense.

Second, by an impressive expression of the public will and without regard to partisanship, we are committed to full support of all those resolute peoples, everywhere, who are resisting aggression and are thereby keeping war away from our Hemisphere. By this support, we express our determination that the democratic cause shall prevail; and we strengthen the defense and the security of our own nation.

Third, by an impressive expression of the public will and without regard to partisanship, we are committed to the proposition that principles of morality and considerations for our own security will never permit us to acquiesce in a peace dictated by aggressors and sponsored by appeasers. We know that enduring peace cannot be bought at the cost of other people's freedom.

In the recent national election there was no substantial difference between the two great parties in respect to that national policy. No issue was fought out on this line before the American electorate. Today it is abundantly evident that American citizens everywhere are demanding and supporting speedy and complete action in recognition of obvious danger.

Therefore, the immediate need is a swift and driving increase in our armament production.

Leaders of industry and labor have responded to our summons. Goals of speed have been set. In some cases these goals are being reached ahead of time; in some cases we are on schedule; in other cases there are slight but not serious delays; and in some cases—and I am sorry to say very important cases—we are all concerned by the slowness of the accomplishment of our plans.

The Army and Navy, however, have made substantial progress during the past year. Actual experience is improving and speeding up our methods of production with every passing day. And today's best is not good enough for tomorrow.

I am not satisfied with the progress thus far made. The men in charge of the program represent the best in training, in ability, and in patriotism. They are not satisfied with the progress thus far made. None of us will be satisfied until the job is done.

No matter whether the original goal was set too high or too low, our objective is quicker and better results.

To give you two illustrations:

We are behind schedule in turning out finished airplanes; we are working day and night to solve the innumerable problems and to catch up.

We are ahead of schedule in building warships but we are working to get even further ahead of that schedule.

To change a whole nation from a basis of peacetime production of implements of peace to a basis of wartime production of implements of war is no small task. And the greatest difficulty comes at the beginning of the program, when new tools, new plant facilities, new assembly lines, and new ship ways must first be constructed before the actual matériel begins to flow steadily and speedily from them.

The Congress, of course, must rightly keep itself informed at all times of the progress of the program. However, there is certain information, as the Congress itself will readily recognize, which, in the interests of our own security and those of the nations that we are supporting, must of needs be kept in confidence.

New circumstances are constantly begetting new needs for our safety. I shall ask this Congress for greatly increased new appropriations and authorizations to carry on what we have begun.

I also ask this Congress for authority and for funds sufficient to manufacture additional munitions and war supplies of many kinds, to be turned over to those nations which are now in actual war with aggressor nations.

Our most useful and immediate role is to act as an arsenal for them as well as for ourselves. They do not need man power, but they do need billions of dollars worth of the weapons of defense.

The time is near when they will not be able to pay for them all in ready cash. We cannot, and we will not, tell them that they must surrender, merely because of present inability to pay for the weapons which we know they must have.

I do not recommend that we make them a loan of dollars with which to pay for these weapons—a loan to be repaid in dollars.

I recommend that we make it possible for those nations to continue to obtain war materials in the United States, fitting their orders into our own program. Nearly all their matériel would, if the time ever came, be useful for our own defense.

Taking counsel of expert military and naval authorities, considering what is best for our own security, we are free to decide how much should be kept here and how much should be sent abroad to our friends who by their determined and heroic resistance are giving us time in which to make ready our own defense.

For what we send abroad, we shall be repaid within a reasonable time following the close of hostilities, in similar materials, or, at our option, in other goods of many kinds, which they can produce and which we need.

Let us say to the democracies: "We Americans are vitally concerned in your defense of freedom. We are putting forth our energies, our resources and our organizing powers to give you the strength to regain and maintain a free world. We shall send you, in ever-increasing numbers, ships, planes, tanks, guns. This is our purpose and our pledge."

In fulfillment of this purpose we will not be intimidated by the threats of dictators that they will regard as a breach of international law or as an act of war our aid to the democracies which dare to resist their aggression. Such aid is not an act of war, even if a dictator should unilaterally proclaim it so to be.

When the dictators, if the dictators, are ready to make war upon us, they will not wait for an act of war on our part. They did not wait for Norway or Belgium or the Netherlands to commit an act of war.

Their only interest is in a new one-way international law, which lacks mutuality in its observance, and, therefore, becomes an instrument of oppression.

The happiness of future generations of Americans may well depend upon how effective and how immediate we can make our aid felt. No one can tell the exact character of the emergency situations that we may be called upon to meet. The Nation's hands must not be tied when the Nation's life is in danger.

We must all prepare to make the sacrifices that the emergency—almost as serious as war itself—demands. Whatever stands in the way of speed and efficiency in defense preparations must give way to the national need.

A free nation has the right to expect full cooperation from all groups. A free nation has the right to look to the leaders of business, of labor, and of agriculture to take the lead in stimulating effort, not among other groups but within their own groups.

The best way of dealing with the few slackers or trouble makers in our midst is, first, to shame them by patriotic example, and, if that fails, to use the sovereignty of Government to save Government.

As men do not live by bread alone, they do not fight by armaments alone. Those who man our defenses, and those behind them who build our defenses, must have the stamina and the courage which come from unshakable belief in the manner of life which they are defending. The mighty action that we are calling for cannot be based on a disregard of all things worth fighting for.

The Nation takes great satisfaction and much strength from the things which have been done to make its people conscious of their individual stake in the preservation of democratic life in America. Those things have toughened the fibre of our people, have renewed their faith and strengthened their devotion to the institutions we make ready to protect.

Certainly this is no time for any of us to stop thinking about the social and economic problems which are the root cause of the social revolution which is today a supreme factor in the world.

For there is nothing mysterious about the foundations of a healthy and strong democracy. The basic things expected by our people of their political and economic systems are simple. They are:

Equality of opportunity for youth and for others.

Jobs for those who can work.

Security for those who need it.

The ending of special privilege for the few.

The preservation of civil liberties for all.

The enjoyment of the fruits of scientific progress in a wider and constantly rising standard of living.

These are the simple, basic things that must never be lost sight of in the turmoil and unbelievable complexity of our modern world. The inner and abiding strength of our economic and political systems is dependent upon the degree to which they fulfill these expectations.

Many subjects connected with our social economy call for immediate improvement.

As examples:

We should bring more citizens under the coverage of old-age pensions and unemployment insurance.

We should widen the opportunities for adequate medical care.

We should plan a better system by which persons deserving or needing gainful employment may obtain it.

I have called for personal sacrifice. I am assured of the willingness of almost all Americans to respond to that call.

A part of the sacrifice means the payment of more money in taxes. In my Budget Message I shall recommend that a greater portion of this great defense program be paid for from taxation than we are paying today. No person should try, or be allowed, to get rich out of this program; and the principle of tax payments in accordance with ability to pay should be constantly before our eyes to guide our legislation.

If the Congress maintains these principles, the voters, putting patriotism ahead of pocketbooks, will give you their applause.

In the future days, which we seek to make secure, we look forward to a world founded upon four essential human freedoms.

The first is freedom of speech and expression—everywhere in the world.

The second is freedom of every person to worship God in his own way—everywhere in the world.

The third is freedom from want—which, translated into world terms, means economic understandings which will secure to every nation a healthy peacetime life for its inhabitants—everywhere in the world.

The fourth is freedom from fear—which, translated into world terms, means a world-wide reduction of armaments to such a point and in such a thorough fashion that no nation will be in a position to commit an act of physical aggression against any neighbor—anywhere in the world.

That is no vision of a distant millennium. It is a definite basis for a kind of world attainable in our own time and generation. That kind of world is the very antithesis of the so-called new order of tyranny which the dictators seek to create with the crash of a bomb.

To that new order we oppose the greater conception—the moral order. A good society is able to face schemes of world domination and foreign revolutions alike without fear.

Since the beginning of our American history, we have been engaged in change—in a perpetual peaceful revolution—a revolution which goes on steadily, quietly adjusting itself to changing conditions—without the concentration camp or the quick-lime in the ditch. The world order which we seek is the cooperation of free countries, working together in a friendly, civilized society.

This nation has placed its destiny in the hands and heads and hearts of its millions of free men and women; and its faith in freedom under the guidance of God. Freedom means the supremacy of human rights everywhere. Our support goes to those who struggle to gain those rights or keep them. Our strength is our unity of purpose.

To that high concept there can be no end save victory.

—16—

MESSAGE ASKING FOR WAR AGAINST JAPAN— "DAY OF INFAMY ADDRESS"

Franklin Delano Roosevelt

December 8, 1941

As the United States edged closer to entering the war in Europe in 1941, the Roosevelt administration engaged in negotiations with the Japanese over their recent expansion in Asia. Tensions between Japan and the U.S. had risen drastically when Roosevelt imposed economic sanctions against the Japanese to punish them for their attacks in Asia. Japan had few natural resources of its own, and its diplomats tried to convince Roosevelt to lift the sanctions even as the Japanese military laid plans for a lightning campaign to conquer the Pacific. On December 7, 1941, the Japanese navy struck a surprise blow against the American fleet at anchor at Pearl Harbor. In a few minutes, the entire battleship force of the U.S. Pacific Fleet sank or suffered crippling damage under the rain of bombs and torpedoes. The outrage that swept the nation in the aftermath has scarcely been equalled in American history. The next day, President Roosevelt delivered this address to Congress, capturing the nation's anger with the famous phrase, "day of infamy." Congress immediately voted to declare war on Japan, and war with Germany and Italy followed soon after.

MESSAGE ASKING FOR WAR AGAINST JAPAN

Yesterday, December 7, 1941—a date which will live in infamy—the United States of America was suddenly and deliberately attacked by naval and air forces of the Empire of Japan.

The United States was at peace with that nation and, at the solicitation of Japan, was still in conversation with its Government and its Emperor looking toward the maintenance of peace in the Pacific. Indeed, one hour after Japanese air squadrons had commenced bombing in Oahu, the Japanese Ambassador to the United States and his colleague delivered to the Secretary of State a formal reply to a recent American message. While this reply stated that it seemed useless to continue the existing diplomatic negotiations, it contained no threat or hint of war or armed attack.

It will be recorded that the distance of Hawaii from Japan makes it obvious that the attack was deliberately planned many days or even weeks ago. During the intervening time the Japanese Government has deliberately sought to deceive the United States by false statements and expressions of hope for continued peace.

The attack yesterday on the Hawaiian Islands has caused severe damage to American naval and military forces. Very many American lives have been lost. In addition American ships have been reported torpedoed on the high seas between San Francisco and Honolulu.

Yesterday the Japanese Government also launched an attack against Malaya. Last night Japanese forces attacked Hong Kong. Last night Japanese forces attacked Guam. Last night Japanese forces attacked the Philippine Islands. Last night the Japanese attacked Wake Island. This morning the Japanese attacked Midway Island.

Japan has, therefore, undertaken a surprise offensive extending throughout the Pacific area. The facts of yesterday speak for themselves. The people of the United States have already formed their opinions and well understand the implications to the very life and safety of our nation.

As Commander-in-Chief of the Army and Navy, I have directed that all measures be taken for our defense.

Always will we remember the character of the onslaught against us.

No matter how long it may take us to overcome this premeditated invasion, the American people in their righteous might will win through to absolute victory.

I believe I interpret the will of the Congress and of the people when I assert that we will not only defend ourselves to the uttermost but will make very certain that this form of treachery shall never endanger us again.

Hostilities exist. There is no blinking at the fact that our people, our territory and our interests are in grave danger.

With confidence in our armed forces—with the unbonded determination of our people—we will gain the inevitable triumph—so help us God.

I ask that the Congress declare that since the unprovoked and dastardly attack by Japan on Sunday, December seventh, a state of war has existed between the United States and the Japanese Empire.

17

THE UNITED NATIONS CHARTER

October 24, 1945

The first attempt at forming an international body to govern relations between states was the ineffectual League of Nations, created after the First World War. The Second World War swept away the old League, but not the ideal of an organization which would regulate international affairs and secure world peace. As the Axis powers collapsed in defeat in 1945, the Allies gathered at the San Francisco Conference to found a new body, known as the United Nations. The basic framework for the organization had been established at the Dumbarton Oaks Conference in 1944, and the name itself stemmed from President Roosevelt's term for the Allies then fighting Germany and Japan. The charter for the United Nations took effect on October 24, 1945; its headquarters was in San Francisco, though it moved to New York in 1952.

With a sense of realism about international relations, the founders of the U.N. created two general governing bodies for the new organization: the General Assembly, in which each nation is represented, and the Security Council, which features both rotating members and five permanent members. The permanent members, representing the victorious powers in the Second World War (the United States, the Soviet Union, China, Great Britain, and France—the most powerful forces in the world when the U.N.

was founded), each have a veto over any resolution that comes before the Security Council. Since the collapse of the U.S.S.R., the Soviet seat has passed to Russia, and proposals have been put forward for giving permanent seats to Germany and Japan. The U.N. also has agencies designed to promote health, development, and education, including UNESCO and UNICEF. It also has a judicial branch, represented by the International Court of Justice. During much of the U.N.'s history, it was prevented from acting effectively by the rivalry between the United States and the Soviet Union. With the end of the Cold War, however, and the growing strength of powers other than the United States, the U.N. has risen to the center of international relations.

CHARTER OF THE UNITED NATIONS

PREAMBLE

WE THE PEOPLES
OF THE UNITED NATIONS
DETERMINED

to save succeeding generations from the scourge of war, which twice in our lifetime has brought untold sorrow to mankind, and

to reaffirm faith in fundamental human rights, in the dignity and worth of the human person, in the equal rights of men and women and of nations large and small, and

to establish conditions under which justice and respect for the obligations arising from treaties and other sources of international law can be maintained, and

to promote social progress and better standards of life in larger freedom,

AND FOR THESE ENDS

to practice tolerance and live together in peace with one another as good neighbors, and to unite our strength to maintain international peace and security, and

to ensure by the acceptance of principles and the institution of methods, that armed force shall not be used, save in the common interest, and

to employ international machinery for the promotion of the economic and social advancement of all peoples,

HAVE RESOLVED TO
COMBINE OUR EFFORTS TO
ACCOMPLISH THESE AIMS

Accordingly, our respective Governments, through representatives assembled in the city of San Francisco, who have exhibited their full powers found to be in good and due form, have agreed to the present Charter of the United Nations and do hereby establish an international organization to be known as the United Nations.

CHAPTER I
PURPOSES AND PRINCIPLES

Article 1

The Purposes of the United Nations are:

1. To maintain international peace and security, and to that end: to take effective collective measures for the prevention and removal of threats to the peace, and for the suppression of acts of aggression or other breaches of the peace, and to bring about by peaceful means, and in conformity with the principles of justice and international law, adjustment or settlement of international disputes or situations which might lead to a breach of the peace;

2. To develop friendly relations among nations based on respect for the principle of equal rights and self-determination of peoples, and to take other appropriate measures to strengthen universal peace;

3. To achieve international cooperation in solving international problems of an economic, social, cultural, or humanitarian character, and in promoting and encouraging respect for human rights and for fundamental freedoms for all without distinction as to race, sex, language, or religion; and

4. To be a center for harmonizing the actions of nations in the attainment of these common ends.

Article 2

The Organization and its Members, in pursuit of the Purposes stated in Article 1, shall act in accordance with the following Principles.

1. The Organization is based on the principle of the sovereign equality of all its Members.

2. All Members, in order to ensure to all of them the rights and benefits resulting from membership, shall fulfill in good faith the obligations assumed by them in accordance with the present Charter.

3. All Members shall settle their international disputes by peaceful means in such a manner that international peace and security, and justice, are not endangered.

4. All Members shall refrain in their international relations from the threat or use of force against the territorial integrity or political independence of any state, or in any other manner inconsistent with the Purposes of the United Nations.

5. All Members shall give the United Nations every assistance in any action it takes in accordance with the present Charter, and shall refrain from giving assistance to any state against which the United Nations is taking preventive or enforcement action.

6. The Organization shall ensure that states which are not Members of the United Nations act in accordance with these Principles so far as may be necessary for the maintenance of international peace and security.

7. Nothing contained in the present Charter shall authorize the United Nations to intervene in matters which are essentially within the domestic jurisdiction of any state or shall require the Members to submit such matters to settlement under the present Charter; but this principle shall not prejudice the application of enforcement measures under Chapter VII.

CHAPTER II
MEMBERSHIP

Article 3

The original Members of the United Nations shall be the states which, having participated in the United Nations Conference on International Organization at San Francisco, or having previously signed the Declaration by United Nations of January 1, 1942, sign the present Charter and ratify it in accordance with Article 110.

Article 4

1. Membership in the United Nations is open to all other peace-loving states which accept the obligations contained in the present Charter and, in the judgment of the Organization, are able and willing to carry out these obligations.

2. The admission of any such state to membership in the United Nations will be effected by a decision of the General Assembly upon the recommendation of the Security Council.

Article 5

A Member of the United Nations against which preventive or enforcement action has been taken by the Security Council may be suspended from the exercise of the rights and privileges of membership by the General Assembly upon the recommendation of the Security Council. The exercise of these rights and privileges may be restored by the Security Council.

Article 6

A Member of the United Nations which has persistently violated the Principles contained in the present Charter may be expelled from the Organization by the General Assembly upon the recommendation of the Security Council.

CHAPTER III
ORGANS

Article 7

1. There are established as the principal organs of the United Nations: a General Assembly, a Security Council, an Economic and Social Council, a Trusteeship Council, an International Court of Justice, and a Secretariat.

2. Such subsidiary organs as may be found necessary may be established in accordance with the present Charter.

Article 8

The United Nations shall place no restrictions on the eligibility of men and women to participate in any capacity and under conditions of equality in its principal and subsidiary organs.

Chapter IV
THE GENERAL ASSEMBLY

Composition

Article 9

1. The General Assembly shall consist of all the Members of the United Nations.

2. Each member shall have not more than five representatives in the General Assembly.

Functions and Powers

Article 10

The General Assembly may discuss any questions or any matters within the scope of the present Charter or relating to the powers and functions of any organs provided for in the present Charter, and, except as provided in Article 12, may make recommendations to the Members of the United Nations or to the Security Council or to both on any such questions or matters.

Article 11

1. The General Assembly may consider the general principles of cooperation in the maintenance of international peace and security, including the principles governing disarmament and the regulation of armaments, and may make recommendations with regard to such principles to the Members or to the Security Council or to both.

2. The General Assembly may discuss any questions relating

to the maintenance of international peace and security brought before it by any Member of the United Nations, or by the Security Council, or by a state which is not a Member of the United Nations in accordance with Article 35, paragraph 2, and, except as provided in Article 12, may make recommendations with regard to any such questions to the state or states concerned or to the Security Council or to both. Any such question on which action is necessary shall be referred to the Security Council by the General Assembly either before or after discussion.

3. The General Assembly may call the attention of the Security Council to situations which are likely to endanger international peace and security.

4. The powers of the General Assembly set forth in this Article shall not limit the general scope of Article 10.

Article 12

1. While the Security Council is exercising in respect of any dispute or situation the functions assigned to it in the present Charter, the General Assembly shall not make any recommendation with regard to that dispute or situation unless the Security Council so requests.

2. The Secretary-General, with the consent of the Security Council, shall notify the General Assembly at each session of any matters relative to the maintenance of international peace and security which are being dealt with by the Security Council and shall similarly notify the General Assembly, or the Members of the United Nations if the General Assembly is not in session, immediately the Security Council ceases to deal with such matters.

Article 13

1. The General Assembly shall initiate studies and make recommendations for the purpose of:

a. promoting international cooperation in the political field and encouraging the progressive development of international law and its codification;

b. promoting international cooperation in the economic, social, cultural, educational, and health fields, and assisting in the realization of human rights and fundamental freedoms for all without distinction as to race, sex, language, or religion.

2. The further responsibilities, functions and powers of the General Assembly with respect to matters mentioned in paragraph 1(b) above are set forth in Chapters IX and X.

Article 14

Subject to the provisions of Article 12, the General Assembly may recommend measures for the peaceful adjustment of any situation, regardless of origin, which it deems likely to impair the general welfare or friendly relations among nations, including situations resulting from a violation of the provisions of the present Charter setting forth the Purposes and Principles of the United Nations.

Article 15

1. The General Assembly shall receive and consider annual and special reports from the Security Council; these reports shall include an account of the measures that the Security Council has decided upon or taken to maintain international peace and security.

2. The General Assembly shall receive and consider reports from the other organs of the United Nations.

Article 16

The General Assembly shall perform such functions with respect to the international trusteeship system as are assigned to it under Chapters XII and XIII, including the approval of the trusteeship agreements for areas not designated as strategic.

Article 17

1. The General Assembly shall consider and approve the budget of the Organization.

2. The expenses of the Organization shall be borne by the Members as apportioned by the General Assembly.

3. The General Assembly shall consider and approve any financial and budgetary arrangements with specialized agencies referred to in Article 57 and shall examine the administrative budgets of such specialized agencies with a view to making recommendations to the agencies concerned.

Voting

Article 18

1. Each member of the General Assembly shall have one vote.

2. Decisions of the General Assembly on important questions shall be made by a two-thirds majority of the members present and voting. These questions shall include: recommendations with respect to the maintenance of international peace and security, the election of the non-permanent members of the Security Council, the election of the members of the Economic and Social Council, the election of members of the Trusteeship Council in accordance with paragraph 1(c) of Article 86, the admission of new Members to the United Nations, the suspension of the rights and privileges of membership, the expulsion of Members, questions relating to the operation of the trusteeship system, and budgetary questions.

3. Decisions on other questions, including the determination of additional categories of questions to be decided by a two-thirds majority, shall be made by a majority of the members present and voting.

Article 19

A Member of the United Nations which is in arrears in the payment of its financial contributions to the Organization shall have no vote in the General Assembly if the amount of its arrears equals or exceeds the amount of the contributions due from it for the preceding two full years. The General Assembly may, nevertheless, permit such a Member to vote if it is satisfied that the failure to pay is due to conditions beyond the control of the Member.

Procedure

Article 20

The General Assembly shall meet in regular annual sessions and in such special sessions as occasion may require. Special sessions shall be convoked by the Secretary-General at the request of the Security Council or of a majority of the Members of the United Nations.

Article 21

The General Assembly shall adopt its own rules of procedure. It shall elect its President for each session.

Article 22

The General Assembly may establish such subsidiary organs as it deems necessary for the performance of its functions.

CHAPTER V
THE SECURITY COUNCIL

Composition

Article 23

1. The Security Council shall consist of fifteen Members of the United Nations. The Republic of China, France, the Union of Soviet Socialist Republics, the United Kingdom of Great Britain and Northern Ireland, and the United States of America shall be permanent members of the Security Council. The General Assembly shall elect ten other Members of the United Nations to be non-permanent members of the Security Council, due regard being specially paid, in the first instance to the contribution of Members of the United Nations to the maintenance of international peace and security and to the other purposes of the Organization, and also to equitable geographical distribution.

2. The non-permanent members of the Security Council shall be elected for a term of two years. In the first election of the non-permanent members after the increase of the membership of the Security Council from eleven to fifteen, two of the four additional members shall be chosen for a term of one year. A retiring member shall not be eligible for immediate re-election.

3. Each member of the Security Council shall have one representative.

Functions and Powers

Article 24

1. In order to ensure prompt and effective action by the United Nations, its Members confer on the Security Council primary re-

sponsibility for the maintenance of international peace and security, and agree that in carrying out its duties under this responsibility the Security Council acts on their behalf.

2. In discharging these duties the Security Council shall act in accordance with the Purposes and Principles of the United Nations. The specific powers granted to the Security Council for the discharge of these duties are laid down in Chapters VI, VII, VIII, and XII.

3. The Security Council shall submit annual and, when necessary, special reports to the General Assembly for its consideration.

Article 25

The Members of the United Nations agree to accept and carry out the decisions of the Security Council in accordance with the present Charter.

Article 26

In order to promote the establishment and maintenance of international peace and security with the least diversion for armaments of the world's human and economic resources, the Security Council shall be responsible for formulating, with the assistance of the Military Staff Committee referred to in Article 47, plans to be submitted to the Members of the United Nations for the establishment of a system for the regulation of armaments.

Voting

Article 27

1. Each member of the Security Council shall have one vote.

2. Decisions of the Security Council on procedural matters shall be made by an affirmative vote of nine members.

3. Decisions of the Security Council on all other matters shall be made by an affirmative vote of nine members including the concurring votes of the permanent members; provided that, in decisions under Chapter VI, and under paragraph 3 of Article 52, a party to a dispute shall abstain from voting.

Procedure

Article 28

1. The Security Council shall be so organized as to be able to function continuously. Each member of the Security Council shall for this purpose be represented at all times at the seat of the Organization.

2. The Security Council shall hold periodic meetings at which each of its members may, if it so desires, be represented by a member of the government or by some other specially designated representative.

3. The Security Council may hold meetings at such places other than the seat of the Organization as in its judgment will best facilitate its work.

Article 29

The Security Council may establish such subsidiary organs as it deems necessary for the performance of its functions.

Article 30

The Security Council shall adopt its own rules of procedure, including the method of selecting its President.

Article 31

Any Member of the United Nations which is not a member of the Security Council may participate, without vote, in the discussion of any question brought before the Security Council whenever the latter considers that the interests of that Member are specially affected.

Article 32

Any Member of the United Nations which is not a member of the Security Council or any state which is not a Member of the United Nations, if it is a party to a dispute under consideration by the Security Council, shall be invited to participate, without vote, in the discussion relating to the dispute. The Security Council shall lay down such conditions as it deems just for the participation of a state which is not a Member of the United Nations.

CHAPTER VI
PACIFIC SETTLEMENT OF DISPUTES

Article 33

1. The parties to any dispute, the continuance of which is likely to endanger the maintenance of international peace and security, shall, first of all, seek a solution by negotiation, enquiry, mediation, conciliation, arbitration, judicial settlement, resort to regional agencies or arrangements, or other peaceful means of their own choice.

2. The Security Council shall, when it deems necessary, call upon the parties to settle their dispute by such means.

Article 34

The Security Council may investigate any dispute, or any situation which might lead to international friction or give rise to a dispute, in order to determine whether the continuance of the dispute or situation is likely to endanger the maintenance of international peace and security.

Article 35

1. Any Member of the United Nations may bring any dispute, or any situation of the nature referred to in Article 34, to the attention of the Security Council or of the General Assembly.

2. A state which is not a Member of the United Nations may bring to the attention of the Security Council or of the General Assembly any dispute to which it is a party if it accepts in advance, for the purposes of the dispute, the obligations of pacific settlement provided in the present Charter.

3. The proceedings of the General Assembly in respect of matters brought to its attention under this Article will be subject to the provisions of Articles 11 and 12.

Article 36

1. The Security Council may, at any stage of a dispute of the nature referred to in Article 33 or of a situation of like nature, recommend appropriate procedures or methods of adjustment.

2. The Security Council should take into consideration any procedures for the settlement of the dispute which have already been adopted by the parties.

3. In making recommendations under this Article the Security Council should also take into consideration that legal disputes

should as a general rule be referred by the parties to the International Court of Justice in accordance with the provisions of the Statute of the Court.

Article 37

1. Should the parties to a dispute of the nature referred to in Article 33 fail to settle it by the means indicated in that Article, they shall refer it to the Security Council.

2. If the Security Council deems that the continuance of the dispute is in fact likely to endanger the maintenance of international peace and security, it shall decide whether to take action under Article 36 or to recommend such terms of settlement as it may consider appropriate.

Article 38

Without prejudice to the provisions of Articles 33 to 37, the Security Council may, if all the parties to any dispute so request, make recommendations to the parties with a view to a pacific settlement of the dispute.

CHAPTER VII
ACTION WITH RESPECT TO THREATS TO THE PEACE, BREACHES OF THE PEACE, AND ACTS OF AGGRESSION

Article 39

The Security Council shall determine the existence of any threat to the peace, breach of the peace, or act of aggression and shall make recommendations, or decide what measures shall be taken in accordance with Articles 41 and 42, to maintain or restore international peace and security.

Article 40

In order to prevent an aggravation of the situation, the Security Council may, before making the recommendations or deciding upon the measures provided for in Article 39, call upon the parties concerned to comply with such provisional measures as it deems necessary or desirable. Such provisional measures shall be without prejudice to the rights, claims, or position of the parties concerned. The Security Council shall duly take account of failure to comply with such provisional measures.

Article 41

The Security Council may decide what measures not involving the use of armed force are to be employed to give effect to its decisions, and it may call upon the Members of the United Nations to apply such measures. These may include complete or partial interruption of economic relations and of rail, sea, air, postal, telegraphic, radio, and other means of communication, and the severance of diplomatic relations.

Article 42

Should the Security Council consider that measures provided for in Article 41 would be inadequate or have proved to be inadequate, it may take such action by air, sea, or land forces as may be necessary to maintain or restore international peace and security. Such action may include demonstrations, blockade, and other operations by air, sea, or land forces of Members of the United Nations.

Article 43

1. All Members of the United Nations, in order to contribute to the maintenance of international peace and security, undertake to make available to the Security Council, on its call and in accordance with a special agreement or agreements, armed forces, assistance, and facilities, including rights of passage, necessary for the purpose of maintaining international peace and security.
2. Such agreement or agreements shall govern the numbers and types of forces, their degree of readiness and general location, and the nature of the facilities and assistance to be provided.
3. The agreement or agreements shall be negotiated as soon as possible on the initiative of the Security Council. They shall be concluded between the Security Council and Members or between the Security Council and groups of Members and shall be subject to ratification by the signatory states in accordance with their respective constitutional processes.

Article 44

When the Security Council has decided to use force it shall, before calling upon a Member not represented on it to provide armed forces in fulfillment of the obligations assumed under Article 43, invite that Member, if the Member so desires, to participate in the decisions of the Security Council concerning the employment of contingents of that Member's armed forces.

Article 45

In order to enable the United Nations to take urgent military measures, Members shall hold immediately available national air-force contingents for combined international enforcement action. The strength and degree of readiness of these contingents and plans for their combined action shall be determined, within the limits laid down in the special agreement or agreements referred to in Article 43, by the Security Council with the assistance of the Military Staff Committee.

Article 46

Plans for the application of armed force shall be made by the Security Council with the assistance of the Military Staff Committee.

Article 47

1. There shall be established a Military Staff Committee to advise and assist the Security Council on all questions relating to the Security Council's military requirements for the maintenance of international peace and security, the employment and command of forces placed at its disposal, the regulation of armaments, and possible disarmament.
2. The Military Staff Committee shall consist of the Chiefs of Staff of the permanent members of the Security Council or their representatives. Any Member of the United Nations not permanently represented on the Committee shall be invited by the Committee to be associated with it when the efficient discharge of the Committee's responsibilities requires the participation of that Member in its work.
3. The Military Staff Committee shall be responsible under the Security Council for the strategic direction of any armed forces placed at the disposal of the Security Council. Questions relating to the command of such forces shall be worked out subsequently.
4. The Military Staff Committee, with the authorization of the Security Council and after consultation with appropriate regional agencies, may establish regional subcommittees.

Article 48

1. The action required to carry out the decisions of the Security Council for the maintenance of international peace and security shall be taken by all the Members of the United Nations or by some of them, as the Security Council may determine.

2. Such decisions shall be carried out by the Members of the United Nations directly and through their action in the appropriate international agencies of which they are members.

Article 49

The Members of the United Nations shall join in affording mutual assistance in carrying out the measures decided upon by the Security Council.

Article 50

If preventive or enforcement measures against any state are taken by the Security Council, any other state, whether a Member of the United Nations or not, which finds itself confronted with special economic problems arising from the carrying out of those measures shall have the right to consult the Security Council with regard to a solution of those problems.

Article 51

Nothing in the present Charter shall impair the inherent right of individual or collective self-defense if an armed attack occurs against a Member of the United Nations, until the Security Council has taken measures necessary to maintain international peace and security. Measures taken by Members in the exercise of this right of self-defense shall be immediately reported to the Security Council and shall not in any way affect the authority and responsibility of the Security Council under the present Charter to take at any time such action as it deems necessary in order to maintain or restore international peace and security.

CHAPTER VIII
REGIONAL ARRANGEMENTS

Article 52

1. Nothing in the present Charter precludes the existence of regional arrangements or agencies for dealing with such matters

relating to the maintenance of international peace and security as are appropriate for regional action, provided that such arrangements or agencies and their activities are consistent with the Purposes and Principles of the United Nations.

2. The Members of the United Nations entering into such arrangements or constituting such agencies shall make every effort to achieve pacific settlement of local disputes through such regional arrangements or by such regional agencies before referring them to the Security Council.

3. The Security Council shall encourage the development of pacific settlement of local disputes through such regional arrangements or by such regional agencies either on the initiative of the states concerned or by reference from the Security Council.

4. This Article in no way impairs the application of Articles 34 and 35.

Article 53

1. The Security Council shall, where appropriate, utilize such regional arrangements or agencies for enforcement action under its authority. But no enforcement action shall be taken under regional arrangements or by regional agencies without the authorization of the Security Council, with the exception of measures against any enemy state, as defined in paragraph 2 of this Article, provided for pursuant to Article 107 or in regional arrangements directed against renewal of aggressive policy on the part of any such state, until such time as the Organization may, on request of the Governments concerned, be charged with the responsibility for preventing further aggression by such a state.

2. The term enemy state as used in paragraph 1 of this Article applies to any state which during the Second World War has been an enemy of any signatory of the present Charter.

Article 54

The Security Council shall at all times be kept fully informed of activities undertaken or in contemplation under regional arrangements or by regional agencies for the maintenance of international peace and security.

CHAPTER IX
INTERNATIONAL ECONOMIC AND SOCIAL CO-OPERATION

Article 55

With a view to the creation of conditions of stability and well-being which are necessary for peaceful and friendly relations among nations based on respect for the principle of equal rights and self-determination of peoples, the United Nations shall promote:

a. higher standards of living, full employment, and conditions of economic and social progress and development;

b. solutions of international economic, social, health, and related problems; and international cultural and educational co-operation; and

c. universal respect for, and observance of, human rights and fundamental freedoms for all without distinction as to race, sex, language, or religion.

Article 56

All Members pledge themselves to take joint and separate action in cooperation with the Organization for the achievement of the purposes set forth in Article 55.

Article 57

1. The various specialized agencies, established by intergovernmental agreement and having wide international responsibilities, as defined in their basic instruments, in economic, social, cultural, educational, health, and related fields, shall be brought into relationship with the United Nations in accordance with the provisions of Article 63.

2. Such agencies thus brought into relationship with the United Nations are hereinafter referred to as specialized agencies.

Article 58

The Organization shall make recommendations for the coordination of the policies and activities of the specialized agencies.

Article 59

The Organization shall, where appropriate, initiate negotiations among the states concerned for the creation of any new specialized agencies required for the accomplishment of the purposes set forth in Article 55.

Article 60

Responsibility for the discharge of the functions of the Organization set forth in this Chapter shall be vested in the General Assembly and, under the authority of the General Assembly, in the Economic and Social Council, which shall have for this purpose the powers set forth in Chapter X.

CHAPTER X
THE ECONOMIC AND SOCIAL COUNCIL

Composition

Article 61

1. The Economic and Social Council shall consist of twenty-seven Members of the United Nations elected by the General Assembly.
2. Subject to the provisions of paragraph 3, nine members of the Economic and Social Council shall be elected each year for a term of three years. A retiring member shall be eligible for immediate re-election.
3. At the first election after the increase in the membership of the Economic and Social Council from eighteen to twenty-seven members, in addition to the members elected in place of the six members whose term of office expires at the end of that year, nine additional members shall be elected. Of these nine additional members, the term of office of three members so elected shall expire at the end of one year, and of three other members at the end of two years, in accordance with arrangements made by the General Assembly.
4. Each member of the Economic and Social Council shall have one representative.

Functions and Powers

Article 62

1. The Economic and Social Council may make or initiate studies and reports with respect to international economic, social, cultural, educational, health, and related matters and may make recommendations with respect to any such matters to the General Assembly, to the Members of the United Nations, and to the specialized agencies concerned.

2. It may make recommendations for the purpose of promoting respect for, and observance of, human rights and fundamental freedoms for all.

3. It may prepare draft conventions for submission to the General Assembly, with respect to matters falling within its competence.

4. It may call, in accordance with the rules prescribed by the United Nations, international conferences on matters falling within its competence.

Article 63

1. The Economic and Social Council may enter into agreements with any of the agencies referred to in Article 57, defining the terms on which the agency concerned shall be brought into relationship with the United Nations. Such agreements shall be subject to approval by the General Assembly.

2. It may coordinate the activities of the specialized agencies through consultation with and recommendations to such agencies and through recommendations to the General Assembly and to the Members of the United Nations.

Article 64

1. The Economic and Social Council may take appropriate steps to obtain regular reports from the specialized agencies. It may make arrangements with the Members of the United Nations and with the specialized agencies to obtain reports on the steps taken to give effect to its own recommendations and to recommendations on matters falling within its competence made by the General Assembly.

2. It may communicate its observations on these reports to the General Assembly.

Article 65

The Economic and Social Council may furnish information to the Security Council and shall assist the Security Council upon its request.

Article 66

1. The Economic and Social Council shall perform such functions as fall within its competence in connection with the carrying out of the recommendations of the General Assembly.
2. It may, with the approval of the General Assembly, perform services at the request of Members of the United Nations and at the request of specialized agencies.
3. It shall perform such other functions as are specified elsewhere in the present Charter or as may be assigned to it by the General Assembly.

Voting

Article 67

1. Each member of the Economic and Social Council shall have one vote.
2. Decisions of the Economic and Social Council shall be made by a majority of the members present and voting.

Procedure

Article 68

The Economic and Social Council shall set up commissions in economic and social fields and for the promotion of human rights, and such other commissions as may be required for the performance of its functions.

Article 69

The Economic and Social Council shall invite any Member of the United Nations to participate, without vote, in its deliberations on any matter of particular concern to that Member.

Article 70

The Economic and Social Council may make arrangements for representatives of the specialized agencies to participate, without vote, in its deliberations and in those of the commissions established by it, and for its representatives to participate in the deliberations of the specialized agencies.

Article 71

The Economic and Social Council may make suitable arrangements for consultation with non-governmental organizations which are concerned with matters within its competence. Such arrangements may be made with international organizations and, where appropriate, with national organizations after consultation with the Member of the United Nations concerned.

Article 72

1. The Economic and Social Council shall adopt its own rules of procedure, including the method of selecting its President.
2. The Economic and Social Council shall meet as required in accordance with its rules, which shall include provision for the convening of meetings on the request of a majority of its members.

CHAPTER XI
DECLARATION REGARDING NON-SELF-GOVERNING TERRITORIES

Article 73

Members of the United Nations which have or assume responsibilities for the administration of territories whose peoples have not yet attained a full measure of self-government recognize the principle that the interests of the inhabitants of these territories are paramount, and accept as a sacred trust the obligation to promote to the utmost, within the system of international peace and security established by the present Charter, the well-being of the inhabitants of these territories, and, to this end:

a. to ensure, with due respect for the culture of the peoples concerned, their political, economic, social, and educational advancement, their just treatment, and their protection against abuses;

b. to develop self-government, to take due account of the political aspirations of the peoples, and to assist them in the progressive development of their free political institutions, according to the particular circumstances of each territory and its peoples and their varying stages of advancement;

c. to further international peace and security;

d. to promote constructive measures of development, to encourage research, and to cooperate with one another and, when and where appropriate, with specialized international bodies with a view to the practical achievement of the social, economic, and scientific purposes set forth in this Article; and

e. to transmit regularly to the Secretary-General for information purposes, subject to such limitation as security and constitutional considerations may require, statistical and other information of a technical nature relating to economic, social, and educational conditions in the territories for which they are respectively responsible other than those territories to which Chapter XII and XIII apply.

Article 74

Members of the United Nations also agree that their policy in respect of the territories to which this Chapter applies, no less than in respect of their metropolitan areas, must be based on the general principle of good-neighborliness, due account being taken of the interests and well-being of the rest of the world, in social, economic, and commercial matters.

Chapter XII
INTERNATIONAL TRUSTEESHIP SYSTEM

Article 75

The United Nations shall establish under its authority an international trusteeship system for the administration and supervision of such territories as may be placed thereunder by subsequent individual agreements. These territories are hereinafter referred to as trust territories.

Article 76

The basic objectives of the trusteeship system, in accordance with the Purposes of the United Nations laid down in Article 1 of the present Charter, shall be:

a. to further international peace and security;

b. to promote the political, economic, social, and educational advancement of the inhabitants of the trust territories, and their progressive development towards self-government or independence as may be appropriate to the particular circumstances of each territory and its peoples and the freely expressed wishes of the peoples concerned, and as may be provided by the terms of each trusteeship agreement;

c. to encourage respect for human rights and for fundamental freedoms for all without distinction as to race, sex, language, or religion, and to encourage recognition of the interdependence of the peoples of the world; and

d. to ensure equal treatment in social, economic, and commercial matters for all Members of the United Nations and their nationals, and also equal treatment for the latter in the administration of justice, without prejudice to the attainment of the foregoing objectives and subject to the provisions of Article 80.

Article 77

1. The trusteeship system shall apply to such territories in the following categories as may be placed thereunder by means of trusteeship agreements:

a. territories now held under mandate;

b. territories which may be detached from enemy states as a result of the Second World War; and

c. territories voluntarily placed under the system by states responsible for their administration.

2. It will be a matter for subsequent agreement as to which territories in the foregoing categories will be brought under the trusteeship system and upon what terms.

Article 78

The trusteeship system shall not apply to territories which have become Members of the United Nations, relationship among which shall be based on respect for the principle of sovereign equality.

Article 79

The terms of trusteeship for each territory to be placed under the trusteeship system, including any alteration or amendment, shall be agreed upon by the states directly concerned, including the mandatory power in the case of territories held under mandate by a Member of the United Nations, and shall be approved as provided for in Articles 83 and 85.

Article 80

1. Except as may be agreed upon in individual trusteeship agreements, made under Articles 77, 79, and 81, placing each territory under the trusteeship system, and until such agreements have been concluded, nothing in this Chapter shall be construed in or of itself to alter in any manner the rights whatsoever of any states or any peoples or the terms of existing international instruments to which Members of the United Nations may respectively be parties.

2. Paragraph 1 of this Article shall not be interpreted as giving grounds for delay or postponement of the negotiation and conclusion of agreements for placing mandated and other territories under the trusteeship system as provided for in Article 77.

Article 81

The trusteeship agreement shall in each case include the terms under which the trust territory will be administered and designate the authority which will exercise the administration of the trust territory. Such authority, hereinafter called the administering authority, may be one or more states or the Organization itself.

Article 82

There may be designated, in any trusteeship agreement, a strategic area or areas which may include part or all of the trust territory to which the agreement applies, without prejudice to any special agreement or agreements made under Article 43.

Article 83

1. All functions of the United Nations relating to strategic areas, including the approval of the terms of the trusteeship agreements and of their alteration or amendment, shall be exercised by the Security Council.

2. The basic objectives set forth in Article 76 shall be applicable to the people of each strategic area.

3. The Security Council shall, subject to the provisions of the trusteeship agreements and without prejudice to security considerations, avail itself of the assistance of the Trusteeship Council to perform those functions of the United Nations under the trusteeship system relating to political, economic, social, and educational matters in the strategic areas.

Article 84

It shall be the duty of the administering authority to ensure that the trust territory shall play its part in the maintenance of international peace and security. To this end the administering authority may make use of volunteer forces, facilities, and assistance from the trust territory in carrying out the obligations towards the Security Council undertaken in this regard by the administering authority, as well as for local defense and the maintenance of law and order within the trust territory.

Article 85

1. The functions of the United Nations with regard to trusteeship agreements for all areas not designated as strategic, including the approval of the terms of the trusteeship agreements and of their alteration or amendment, shall be exercised by the General Assembly.

2. The Trusteeship Council, operating under the authority of the General Assembly, shall assist the General Assembly in carrying out these functions.

CHAPTER XIII
THE TRUSTEESHIP COUNCIL

Composition

Article 86

1. The Trusteeship Council shall consist of the following Members of the United Nations:

a. those Members administering trust territories;

b. such of those Members mentioned by name in Article 23 as are not administering trust territories; and

c. as many other Members elected for three-year terms by the General Assembly as may be necessary to ensure that the total number of members of the Trusteeship Council is equally divided between those Members of the United Nations which administer trust territories and those which do not.

2. Each member of the Trusteeship Council shall designate one specially qualified person to represent it therein.

Functions and Powers

Article 87

The General Assembly and, under its authority, the Trusteeship Council, in carrying out their functions, may:

a. consider reports submitted by the administering authority;

b. accept petitions and examine them in consultation with the administering authority;

c. provide for periodic visits to the respective trust territories at times agreed upon with the administering authority; and

d. take these and other actions in conformity with the terms of the trusteeship agreements.

Article 88

The Trusteeship Council shall formulate a questionnaire on the political, economic, social, and educational advancement of the inhabitants of each trust territory, and the administering authority for each trust territory within the competence of the General Assembly shall make an annual report to the General Assembly upon the basis of such questionnaire.

Voting

Article 89

1. Each member of the Trusteeship Council shall have one vote.
2. Decisions of the Trusteeship Council shall be made by a majority of the members present and voting.

Procedure

Article 90

1. The Trusteeship Council shall adopt its own rules of procedure, including the method of selecting its President.
2. The Trusteeship Council shall meet as required in accordance with its rules, which shall include provision for the convening of meetings on the request of a majority of its members.

Article 91

The Trusteeship Council shall, when appropriate, avail itself of the assistance of the Economic and Social Council and of the specialized agencies in regard to matters with which they are respectively concerned.

CHAPTER XIV
THE INTERNATIONAL COURT OF JUSTICE

Article 92

The International Court of Justice shall be the principal judicial organ of the United Nations. It shall function in accordance with the annexed Statute, which is based upon the Statute of the Permanent Court of International Justice and forms an integral part of the present Charter.

Article 93

1. All Members of the United Nations are *ipso facto* parties to the Statute of the International Court of Justice.

2. A state which is not a Member of the United Nations may become a party to the Statute of the International Court of Justice on conditions to be determined in each case by the General Assembly upon the recommendation of the Security Council.

Article 94

1. Each Member of the Untied Nations undertakes to comply with the decision of the International Court of Justice in any case to which it is a party.

2. If any party to a case fails to perform the obligations incumbent upon it under a judgment rendered by the Court, the other party may have recourse to the Security Council, which may, if it deems necessary, make recommendations or decide upon measures to be taken to give effect to the judgment.

Article 95

Nothing in the present Charter shall prevent Members of the United Nations from entrusting the solution of their differences to other tribunals by virtue of agreements already in existence or which may be concluded in the future.

Article 96

1. The General Assembly or the Security Council may request the International Court of Justice to give an advisory opinion on any legal question.

2. Other organs of the United Nations and specialized agencies, which may at any time be so authorized by the General Assembly, may also request advisory opinions of the Court on legal questions arising within the scope of their activities.

CHAPTER XV
THE SECRETARIAT

Article 97

The Secretariat shall comprise a Secretary-General and such staff as the Organization may require. The Secretary-General shall be appointed by the General Assembly upon the recommendation of the Security Council. He shall be the chief administrative officer of the Organization.

Article 98

The Secretary-General shall act in that capacity in all meetings of the General Assembly, of the Security Council, of the Economic and Social Council, and of the Trusteeship Council, and shall perform such other functions as are entrusted to him by these organs. The Secretary-General shall make an annual report to the General Assembly on the work of the Organization.

Article 99

The Secretary-General may bring to the attention of the Security Council any matter which in his opinion may threaten the maintenance of international peace and security.

Article 100

1. In the performance of their duties the Secretary-General and the staff shall not seek or receive instructions from any government or from any other authority external to the Organization. They shall refrain from any action which might reflect on their position as international officials responsible only to the Organization.

2. Each Member of the United Nations undertakes to respect the exclusively international character of the responsibilities of the Secretary-General and the staff and not to seek to influence them in the discharge of their responsibilities.

Article 101

1. The staff shall be appointed by the Secretary-General under regulations established by the General Assembly.

2. Appropriate staffs shall be permanently assigned to the Economic and Social Council, the Trusteeship Council, and, as required, to other organs of the United Nations. These staffs shall form a part of the Secretariat.

3. The paramount consideration in the employment of the staff and in the determination of the conditions of service shall be the necessity of securing the highest standards of efficiency, competence, and integrity. Due regard shall be paid to the importance of recruiting the staff on as wide a geographical basis as possible.

CHAPTER XVI
MISCELLANEOUS PROVISIONS

Article 102

1. Every treaty and every international agreement entered into by any Member of the United Nations after the present Charter comes into force shall as soon as possible be registered with the Secretariat and published by it.

2. No party to any such treaty or international agreement which has not been registered in accordance with the provisions of paragraph 1 of this Article may invoke that treaty or agreement before any organ of the United Nations.

Article 103

In the event of a conflict between the obligations of the Members of the United Nations under the present Charter and their obligations under any other international agreement, their obligations under the present Charter shall prevail.

Article 104

The Organization shall enjoy in the territory of each of its Members such legal capacity as may be necessary for the exercise of its functions and the fulfillment of its purposes.

Article 105

1. The Organization shall enjoy in the territory of each of its Members such privileges and immunities as are necessary for the fulfillment of its purposes.

2. Representatives of the Members of the United Nations and officials of the Organization shall similarly enjoy such privileges and immunities as are necessary for the independent exercise of their functions in connection with the Organization.

3. The General Assembly may make recommendations with a view to determining the details of the application of paragraphs

1 and 2 of this Article or may propose conventions to the Members of the United Nations for this purpose.

CHAPTER XVII
TRANSITIONAL SECURITY ARRANGEMENTS

Article 106

Pending the coming into force of such special agreements referred to in Article 43 as in the opinion of the Security Council enable it to begin the exercise of its responsibilities under Article 42, the parties to the Four-Nation Declaration, signed at Moscow, October 30, 1943, and France, shall, in accordance with the provisions of paragraph 5 of that Declaration, consult with one another and as occasion requires with other Members of the United Nations with a view to such joint action on behalf of the Organization as may be necessary for the purpose of maintaining international peace and security.

Article 107

Nothing in the present Charter shall invalidate or preclude action, in relation to any state which during the Second World War has been an enemy of any signatory to the present Charter, taken or authorized as a result of that war by the Governments having responsibility for such action.

CHAPTER XVIII
AMENDMENTS

Article 108

Amendments to the present Charter shall come into force for all Members of the United Nations when they have been adopted by a vote of two thirds of the members of the General Assembly and ratified in accordance with their respective constitutional processes by two thirds of the Members of the United Nations, including all the permanent members of the Security Council.

Article 109

1. A General Conference of the Members of the United Nations for the purpose of reviewing the present Charter may be held at a date and place to be fixed by a two-thirds vote of the members

of the General Assembly and by a vote of any seven members of the Security Council. Each member of the United Nations shall have one vote in the conference.

2. Any alteration of the present Charter recommended by a two-thirds vote of the conference shall take effect when ratified in accordance with their respective constitutional processes by two thirds of the Members of the United Nations including all the permanent members of the Security Council.

3. If such a conference has not been held before the tenth annual session of the General Assembly following the coming into force of the present Charter, the proposal to call such a conference shall be placed on the agenda of that session of the General Assembly, and the conference shall be held if so decided by a majority vote of the members of the General Assembly and by a vote of any seven members of the Security Council.

CHAPTER XIX
RATIFICATION AND SIGNATURE

Article 110

1. The present Charter shall be ratified by the signatory states in accordance with their respective constitutional processes.

2. The ratifications shall be deposited with the Government of the United States of America, which shall notify all the signatory states of each deposit as well as the Secretary-General of the Organization when he has been appointed.

3. The present Charter shall come into force upon the deposit of ratifications by the Republic of China, France, the Union of Soviet Socialist Republics, the United Kingdom of Great Britain and Northern Ireland, and the United States of America, and by a majority of the other signatory states. A protocol of the ratifications deposited shall thereupon be drawn up by the Government of the United States of America which shall communicate copies thereof to all the signatory states.

4. The states signatory to the present Charter which ratify it after it has come into force will become original Members of the United Nations on the date of the deposit of their respective ratifications.

Article 111

The present Charter, of which the Chinese, French, Russian, English, and Spanish texts are equally authentic, shall remain deposited in the archives of the Government of the United States of America. Duly certified copies thereof shall be transmitted by that Government to the Governments of the other signatory states.

IN FAITH WHEREOF the representatives of the Governments of the United Nations have signed the present Charter.

DONE at the city of San Francisco the twenty-sixth day of June, one thousand nine hundred and forty-five.

STATUTE OF THE INTERNATIONAL COURT OF JUSTICE

Article 1

THE INTERNATIONAL COURT OF JUSTICE established by the Charter of the United Nations as the principal judicial organ of the United Nations shall be constituted and shall function in accordance with the provisions of the present Statute.

CHAPTER I
ORGANIZATION OF THE COURT

Article 2

The Court shall be composed of a body of independent judges, elected regardless of their nationality from among persons of high moral character, who possess the qualifications required in their respective countries for appointment to the highest judicial offices, or are jurisconsults of recognized competence in international law.

Article 3

1. The Court shall consist of fifteen members, no two of whom may be nationals of the same state.

2. A person who for the purposes of membership in the Court could be regarded as a national of more than one state shall be deemed to be a national of the one in which he ordinarily exercises civil and political rights.

Article 4

1. The members of the Court shall be elected by the General Assembly and by the Security Council from a list of persons nominated by the national groups in the Permanent Court of Arbitration, in accordance with the following provisions.

2. In the case of Members of the United Nations not represented in the Permanent Court of Arbitration, candidates shall be nominated by national groups appointed for this purpose by their governments under the same conditions as those prescribed for members of the Permanent Court of Arbitration by Article 44 of the Convention of The Hague of 1907 for the pacific settlement of international disputes.

3. The conditions under which a state which is a party to the present Statute but is not a Member of the United Nations may participate in electing the members of the Court shall, in the absence of a special agreement, be laid down by the General Assembly upon recommendation of the Security Council.

Article 5

1. At least three months before the date of the election, the Secretary-General of the United Nations shall address a written request to the members of the Permanent Court of Arbitration belonging to the states which are parties to the present Statute, and to the members of the national groups appointed under Article 4, paragraph 2, inviting them to undertake, within a given time, by national groups, the nomination of persons in a position to accept the duties of a member of the Court.

2. No group may nominate more than four persons, not more than two of whom shall be of their own nationality. In no case may the number of candidates nominated by a group be more than double the number of seats to be filled.

Article 6

Before making these nominations, each national group is recommended to consult its highest court of justice, its legal faculties and schools of law, and its national academies and national sections of international academies devoted to the study of law.

Article 7

1. The Secretary-General shall prepare a list in alphabetical order of all the persons thus nominated. Save as provided in Article 12, paragraph 2, these shall be the only persons eligible.

2. The Secretary-General shall submit this list to the General Assembly and to the Security Council.

Article 8

The General Assembly and the Security Council shall proceed independently of one another to elect the members of the Court.

Article 9

At every election, the electors shall bear in mind not only that the persons to be elected should individually possess the qualifications required, but also that in the body as a whole the representation of the main forms of civilization and of the principal legal systems of the world should be assured.

Article 10

1. Those candidates who obtain an absolute majority of votes in the General Assembly and in the Security Council shall be considered as elected.

2. Any vote of the Security Council, whether for the election of judges or for the appointment of members of the conference envisaged in Article 12, shall be taken without any distinction between permanent and non-permanent members of the Security Council.

3. In the event of more than one national of the same state obtaining an absolute majority of the votes both of the General Assembly and of the Security Council, the eldest of these only shall be considered as elected.

Article 11

If, after the first meeting held for the purpose of the election, one or more seats remain to be filled, a second and, if necessary, a third meeting shall take place.

Article 12

1. If, after the third meeting, one or more seats still remain unfilled, a joint conference consisting of six members, three ap-

pointed by the General Assembly and three by the Security Council, may be formed at any time at the request of either the General Assembly or the Security Council, for the purpose of choosing by the vote of an absolute majority one name for each seat still vacant, to submit to the General Assembly and the Security Council for their respective acceptance.

2. If the joint conference is unanimously agreed upon any person who fulfills the required conditions, he may be included in its list, even though he was not included in the list of nominations referred to in Article 7.

3. If the joint conference is satisfied that it will not be successful in procuring an election, those members of the Court who have already been elected shall, within a period to be fixed by the Security Council, proceed to fill the vacant seats by selection from among those candidates who have obtained votes either in the General Assembly or in the Security Council.

4. In the event of an equality of votes among the judges, the eldest judge shall have a casting vote.

Article 13

1. The members of the Court shall be elected for nine years and may be re-elected; provided, however, that of the judges elected at the first election, the terms of five judges shall expire at the end of three years and the terms of five more judges shall expire at the end of six years.

2. The judges whose terms are to expire at the end of the above-mentioned initial periods of three and six years shall be chosen by lot to be drawn by the Secretary-General immediately after the first election has been completed.

3. The members of the Court shall continue to discharge their duties until their places have been filled. Though replaced, they shall finish any cases which they may have begun.

4. In the case of the resignation of a member of the Court, the resignation shall be addressed to the President of the Court for transmission to the Secretary-General. This last notification makes the place vacant.

Article 14

Vacancies shall be filled by the same method as that laid down for the first election, subject to the following provision: the Secretary-General shall, within one month of the occurrence of the vacancy, proceed to issue the invitations provided for in Article 5, and the date of the election shall be fixed by the Security Council.

Article 15

A member of the Court elected to replace a member whose term of office has not expired shall hold office for the remainder of his predecessor's term.

Article 16

1. No member of the Court may exercise any political or administrative function, or engage in any other occupation of a professional nature.
2. Any doubt on this point shall be settled by the decision of the Court.

Article 17

1. No member of the Court may act as agent, counsel, or advocate in any case.
2. No member may participate in the decision of any case in which he has previously taken part as agent, counsel, or advocate for one of the parties, or as a member of a national or international court, or of a commission of enquiry, or in any other capacity.
3. Any doubt on this point shall be settled by the decision of the Court.

Article 18

1. No member of the Court can be dismissed unless, in the unanimous opinion of the other members, he has ceased to fulfill the required conditions.
2. Formal notification thereof shall be made to the Secretary-General by the Registrar.
3. This notification makes the place vacant.

Article 19

The members of the Court, when engaged on the business of the Court, shall enjoy diplomatic privileges and immunities.

Article 20

Every member of the Court shall, before taking up his duties, make a solemn declaration in open court that he will exercise his powers impartially and conscientiously.

Article 21

1. The Court shall elect its President and Vice-President for three years; they may be re-elected.

2. The Court shall appoint its Registrar and may provide for the appointment of such other officers as may be necessary.

Article 22

1. The seat of the Court shall be established at The Hague. This, however, shall not prevent the Court from sitting and exercising its functions elsewhere whenever the Court considers it desirable.

2. The President and the Registrar shall reside at the seat of the Court.

Article 23

1. The Court shall remain permanently in session, except during the judicial vacations, the dates and duration of which shall be fixed by the Court.

2. Members of the Court are entitled to periodic leave, the dates and duration of which shall be fixed by the Court, having in mind the distance between The Hague and the home of each judge.

3. Members of the Court shall be bound, unless they are on leave or prevented from attending by illness or other serious reasons duly explained to the President, to hold themselves permanently at the disposal of the Court.

Article 24

1. If, for some special reason, a member of the Court considers that he should not take part in the decision of a particular case, he shall so inform the President.

2. If the President considers that for some special reason one of the members of the Court should not sit in a particular case, he shall give him notice accordingly.

3. If in any such case the member of the Court and President disagree, the matter shall be settled by the decision of the Court.

Article 25

1. The full Court shall sit except when it is expressly provided otherwise in the present Statute.

2. Subject to the condition that the number of judges available to constitute the Court is not thereby reduced below eleven, the

Rules of the Court may provide for allowing one or more judges, according to circumstances and in rotation, to be dispensed from sitting.

3. A quorum of nine judges shall suffice to constitute the Court.

Article 26

1. The Court may from time to time form one or more chambers, composed of three or more judges as the Court may determine, for dealing with particular categories of cases; for example, labor cases and cases relating to transit and communications.

2. The Court may at any time form a chamber for dealing with a particular case. The number of judges to constitute such a chamber shall be determined by the Court with the approval of the parties.

3. Cases shall be heard and determined by the chambers provided for in this Article if the parties so request.

Article 27

A judgment given by any of the chambers provided for in Articles 26 and 29 shall be considered as rendered by the Court.

Article 28

The chambers provided for in Articles 26 and 29 may, with the consent of the parties, sit and exercise their functions elsewhere than at The Hague.

Article 29

With a view to the speedy dispatch of business, the Court shall form annually a chamber composed of five judges which, at the request of the parties, may hear and determine cases by summary procedure. In addition, two judges shall be selected for the purpose of replacing judges who find it impossible to sit.

Article 30

1. The Court shall frame rules for carrying out its functions. In particular, it shall lay down rules of procedure.

2. The Rules of the Court may provide for assessors to sit with the Court or with any of its chambers, without the right to vote.

Article 31

1. Judges of the nationality of each of the parties shall retain their right to sit in the case before the Court.

2. If the Court includes upon the Bench a judge of the nationality of one of the parties, any other party may choose a person to sit as judge. Such person shall be chosen preferably from among those persons who have been nominated as candidates as provided in Articles 4 and 5.

3. If the Court includes upon the Bench no judge of the nationality of the parties, each of these parties may proceed to choose a judge as provided in paragraph 2 of this Article.

4. The provisions of this Article shall apply to the case of Articles 26 and 29. In such cases, the President shall request one or, if necessary, two of the members of the Court forming the chamber to give place to the members of the Court of the nationality of the parties concerned, and, failing such, or if they are unable to be present, to the judges specially chosen by the parties.

5. Should there be several parties in the same interest, they shall, for the purpose of the preceeding provisions, be reckoned as one party only. Any doubt upon this point shall be settled by the decision of the Court.

6. Judges chosen as laid down in paragraphs 2, 3, and 4 of this Article shall fulfill the conditions required by Articles 2, 17 (paragraph 2), 20, and 24 of the present Statute. They shall take part in the decision on terms of complete equality with their colleagues.

Article 32

1. Each member of the Court shall receive an annual salary.

2. The President shall receive a special annual allowance.

3. The Vice-President shall receive a special allowance for every day on which he acts as President.

4. The judges chosen under Article 31, other than members of the Court, shall receive compensation for each day on which they exercise their functions.

5. These salaries, allowances, and compensation shall be fixed by the General Assembly. They may not be decreased during the term of office.

6. The salary of the Registrar shall be fixed by the General Assembly on the proposal of the Court.

7. Regulations made by the General Assembly shall fix the conditions under which retirement pensions may be given to members of the Court and to the Registrar, and the conditions under which members of the Court and the Registrar shall have their traveling expenses refunded.

8. The above salaries, allowances, and compensation shall be free of all taxation.

Article 33

The expenses of the Court shall be borne by the United Nations in such a manner as shall be decided by the General Assembly.

Chapter II
COMPETENCE OF THE COURT

Article 34

1. Only states may be parties in cases before the Court.

2. The Court, subject to and in conformity with its Rules, may request of public international organizations information relevant to cases before it, and shall receive such information presented by such organizations on their own initiative.

3. Whenever the construction of the constituent instrument of a public international organization or of an international convention adopted thereunder is in question in a case before the Court, the Registrar shall so notify the public international organization concerned and shall communicate to it copies of all the written proceedings.

Article 35

1. The Court shall be open to the states parties to the present Statute.

2. The conditions under which the Court shall be open to other states shall, subject to the special provisions contained in treaties in force, be laid down by the Security Council, but in no case shall such conditions place the parties in a position of inequality before the Court.

3. When a state which is not a Member of the United Nations is a party to a case, the Court shall fix the amount which that party is to contribute towards the expenses of the Court. This provision shall not apply if such state is bearing a share of the expenses of the Court.

Article 36

1. The jurisdiction of the Court comprises all cases which the parties refer to it and all matters specially provided for in the

Charter of the United Nations or in treaties and conventions in force.

2. The states parties to the present Statute may at any time declare that they recognize as compulsory *ipso facto* and without special agreement, in relation to any other state accepting the same obligation, the jurisdiction of the Court in all legal disputes concerning:

a. the interpretation of a treaty;

b. any question of international law;

c. the existence of any fact which, if established, would constitute a breach of an international obligation;

d. the nature or extent of the reparation to be made for the breach of an international obligation.

3. The declarations referred to above may be made unconditionally or on condition of reciprocity on the part of several or certain states, or for a certain time.

4. Such declarations shall be deposited with the Secretary-General of the United Nations, who shall transmit copies thereof to the parties to the Statute and to the Registrar of the Court.

5. Declarations made under Article 36 of the Statute of the Permanent Court of International Justice and which are still in force shall be deemed, as between the parties to the present Statute, to be acceptances of the compulsory jurisdiction of the International Court of Justice for the period which they still have to run and in accordance with their terms.

6. In the event of a dispute as to whether the Court has jurisdiction, the matter shall be settled by the decision of the Court.

Article 37

Whenever a treaty or convention in force provides for reference of a matter to a tribunal to have been instituted by the League of Nations, or to the Permanent Court of International Justice, the matter shall, as between the parties to the present Statute, be referred to the International Court of Justice.

Article 38

1. The Court, whose function is to decide in accordance with international law such disputes as are submitted to it, shall apply:

a. international conventions, whether general or particular, establishing rules expressly recognized by the contesting states;

b. international custom, as evidence of a general practice accepted as law;

c. the general principles of law recognized by civilized nations;

d. subject to the provisions of Article 59, judicial decisions and the teachings of the most highly qualified publicists of the various nations, as subsidiary means for the determination of rules of law.

2. This provision shall not prejudice the power of the Court to decide a case *ex aequo et bono*, if the parties agree thereto.

Chapter III
PROCEDURE

Article 39

1. The official languages of the Court shall be French and English. If the parties agree that the case shall be conducted in French, the judgment shall be delivered in French. If the parties agree that the case shall be conducted in English, the judgment shall be delivered in English.

2. In the absence of an agreement as to which language shall be employed, each party may, in the pleadings, use the language which it prefers; the decision of the Court shall be given in French and English. In this case the Court shall at the same time determine which of the two texts shall be considered as authoritative.

3. The Court shall, at the request of any party, authorize a language other than French or English to be used by that party.

Article 40

1. Cases are brought before the Court, as the case may be, either by the notification of the special agreement or by a written application addressed to the Registrar. In either case the subject of the dispute and the parties shall be indicated.

2. The Registrar shall forthwith communicate the application to all concerned.

3. He shall also notify the Members of the United Nations through the Secretary-General, and also any other states entitled to appear before the Court.

Article 41

1. The Court shall have the power to indicate, if it considers that circumstances so require, any provisional measures which ought to be taken to preserve the respective rights of either party.

2. Pending the final decision, notice of the measures suggested shall forthwith be given to the parties and to the Security Council.

Article 42

1. The parties shall be represented by agents.

2. They may have the assistance of counsel or advocates before the Court.

3. The agents, counsel, and advocates of parties before the Court shall enjoy the privileges and immunities necessary to the independent exercise of their duties.

Article 43

1. The procedure shall consist of two parts: written and oral.

2. The written proceedings shall consist of the communication to the Court and to the parties of memorials, counter-memorials and, if necessary, replies; also all papers and documents in support.

3. These communications shall be made through the Registrar, in the order and within the time fixed by the Court.

4. A certified copy of every document produced by one party shall be communicated to the other party.

5. The oral proceedings shall consist of the hearing by the Court of witnesses, experts, agents, counsel, and advocates.

Article 44

1. For the service of all notices upon persons other than the agents, counsel, and advocates, the Court shall apply direct to the government of the state upon whose territory the notice has to be served.

2. The same provision shall apply whenever steps are to be taken to procure evidence on the spot.

Article 45

The hearing shall be under the control of the President or, if he is unable to preside, of the Vice-President; if neither is able to preside, the senior judge present shall preside.

Article 46

The hearing in Court shall be public, unless the Court shall decide otherwise, or unless the parties demand that the public be not admitted.

Article 47

1. Minutes shall be made at each hearing and signed by the Registrar and the President.
2. These minutes alone shall be authentic.

Article 48

The Court shall make orders for the conduct of the case, shall decide the form and time in which each party must conclude its arguments, and make all arrangements connected with the taking of evidence.

Article 49

The Court may, even before the hearing begins, call upon the agents to produce any document or to supply any explanations. Formal note shall be taken of any refusal.

Article 50

The Court may, at any time, entrust any individual, body, bureau, commission, or other organization that it may select, with the task of carrying out an enquiry or giving an expert opinion.

Article 51

During the hearing any relevant questions are to be put to the witnesses and experts under the conditions laid down by the Court in the rules of procedure referred to in Article 30.

Article 52

After the Court has received the proofs and evidence within the time specified for the purpose, it may refuse to accept any further oral or written evidence that one party may desire to present unless the other side consents.

Article 53

1. Whenever one of the parties does not appear before the Court, or fails to defend its case, the other party may call upon the Court to decide in favor of its claim.

2. The Court must, before doing so, satisfy itself, not only that it has jurisdiction in accordance with Articles 36 and 37, but also that the claim is well founded in fact and law.

Article 54

1. When, subject to the control of the Court, the agents, counsel, and advocates have completed their presentation of the case, the President shall declare the hearing closed.

2. The Court shall withdraw to consider the judgment.

3. The deliberations of the Court shall take place in private and remain secret.

Article 55

1. All questions shall be decided by a majority of the judges present.

2. In the event of an equality of votes, the President or the judge who acts in his place shall have a casting vote.

Article 56

1. The judgment shall state the reasons on which it is based.

2. It shall contain the names of the judges who have taken part in the decision.

Article 57

If the judgment does not represent in whole or in part the unanimous opinion of the judges, any judge shall be entitled to deliver a separate opinion.

Article 58

The judgment shall be signed by the President and by the Registrar. It shall be read in open court, due notice having been given to the agents.

Article 59

The decision of the Court has no binding force except between the parties and in respect of that particular case.

Article 60

The judgment is final and without appeal. In the event of dispute as to the meaning or scope of the judgment, the Court shall construe it upon the request of any party.

Article 61

1. An application for revision of a judgment may be made only when it is based upon the discovery of some fact of such a nature as to be a decisive factor, which fact was, when the judgment was given, unknown to the Court and also to the party claiming revision, always provided that such ignorance was not due to negligence.
2. The proceedings for revision shall be opened by a judgment of the Court expressly recording the existence of the new fact, recognizing that it has such a character as to lay the case open to revision, and declaring the application admissible on this ground.
3. The Court may require previous compliance with the terms of the judgment before it admits proceedings in revision.
4. The application for revision must be made at latest within six months of the discovery of the new fact.
5. No application for revision may be made after the lapse of ten years from the date of the judgment.

Article 62

1. Should a state consider that it has an interest of a legal nature which may be affected by the decision in the case, it may submit a request to the Court to be permitted to intervene.
2. It shall be for the Court to decide upon this request.

Article 63

1. Whenever the construction of a convention to which states other than those concerned in the case are parties is in question, the Registrar shall notify all such states forthwith.
2. Every state so notified has the right to intervene in the proceedings; but if it uses this right, the construction given by the judgment will be equally binding upon it.

Article 64

Unless otherwise decided by the Court, each party shall bear its own costs.

CHAPTER IV
ADVISORY OPINIONS

Article 65

1. The Court may give an advisory opinion on any legal question at the request of whatever body may be authorized by or in accordance with the Charter of the United Nations to make such a request.

2. Questions upon which the advisory opinion of the Court is asked shall be laid before the Court by means of a written request containing an exact statement of the question upon which an opinion is required, and accompanied by all documents likely to throw light upon the question.

Article 66

1. The Registrar shall forthwith give notice of the request for an advisory opinion to all states entitled to appear before the Court.

2. The Registrar shall also, by means of a special and direct communication, notify any state entitled to appear before the Court or international organization considered by the Court, or, should it not be sitting, by the President, as likely to be able to furnish information on the question, that the Court will be prepared to receive, within a time limit to be fixed by the President, written statements, or to hear, at a public sitting to be held for the purpose, oral statements relating to the question.

3. Should any such state entitled to appear before the Court have failed to receive the special communication referred to in paragraph 2 of this Article, such state may express a desire to submit a written statement or to be heard; and the Court will decide.

4. States and organizations having presented written or oral statements or both shall be permitted to comment on the statements made by other states or organizations in the form, to the extent, and within the time limits which the Court, or, should it not be sitting, the President, shall decide in each particular case. Accordingly, the Registrar shall in due time communicate any such written statements to states and organizations having submitted similar statements.

Article 67

The Court shall deliver its advisory opinions in open court, notice having been given to the Secretary-General and to the representatives of Members of the United Nations, of other states and of international organizations immediately concerned.

Article 68

In the exercise of its advisory functions the Court shall further be guided by the provisions of the present Statute which apply in contentious cases to the extent to which it recognizes them to be applicable.

CHAPTER V
AMENDMENT

Article 69

Amendments to the present Statute shall be effected by the same procedure as is provided by the Charter of the United Nations for amendments to that Charter, subject, however, to any provisions which the General Assembly upon recommendation of the Security Council may adopt concerning the participation of states which are parties to the present Statute but are not Members of the United Nations.

Article 70

The Court shall have power to propose such amendments to the present Statute as it may deem necessary, through written communications to the Secretary-General, for consideration in conformity with the provisions of Article 69.

UNIVERSAL DECLARATION OF HUMAN RIGHTS

Preamble

Whereas recognition of the inherent dignity and of the equal and inalienable rights of all members of the human family is the foundation of freedom, justice and peace in the world,

Whereas disregard and contempt for human rights have resulted in barbarous acts which have outraged the conscience of mankind, and the advent of a world in which human beings shall enjoy freedom of speech and belief and freedom from fear and want has been proclaimed as the highest aspiration of the common people,

Whereas it is essential, if man is not to be compelled to have recourse, as a last resort, to rebellion against tyranny and oppression, that human rights should be protected by the rule of law,

Whereas it is essential to promote the development of friendly relations between nations,

Whereas the peoples of the United Nations have in the Charter reaffirmed their faith in fundamental human rights, in the dignity and worth of the human person and in the equal rights of men and women and have determined to promote social progress and better standards of life in larger freedom,

Whereas Member States have pledged themselves to achieve, in co-operation with the United Nations, the promotion of universal respect for and observance of human rights and fundamental freedoms,

Whereas a common understanding of these rights and freedoms is of the greatest importance for the full realization of this pledge,

Now, Therefore,

THE GENERAL ASSEMBLY

proclaims

THIS UNIVERSAL DECLARATION OF HUMAN RIGHTS as a common standard of achievement for all peoples and all nations, to the end that every individual and every organ of society, keeping this Declaration constantly in mind, shall strive by teaching and education to promote respect for these rights and freedoms and by progressive measures, national and international, to secure their universal and effective recognition and observance, both among the peoples of Member States themselves and among the peoples of territories under their jurisdiction.

Article 1

All human beings are born free and equal in dignity and rights. They are endowed with reason and conscience and should act towards one another in a spirit of brotherhood.

Article 2

Everyone is entitled to all the rights and freedoms set forth in this Declaration, without distinction of any kind, such as race, colour, sex, language, religion, political or other opinion, national or social origin, property, birth or other status. Furthermore, no distinction shall be made on the basis of the political, jurisdictional or international status of the country or territory to which a person belongs, whether it be independent, trust, non-self-governing or under any other limitation of sovereignty.

Article 3

Everyone has the right to life, liberty and security of person.

Article 4

No one shall be held in slavery or servitude; slavery and the slave trade shall be prohibited in all their forms.

Article 5

No one shall be subjected to torture or to cruel, inhuman or degrading treatment or punishment.

Article 6

Everyone has the right to recognition everywhere as a person before the law.

Article 7

All are equal before the law and are entitled without any discrimination to equal protection of the law. All are entitled to equal protection against any discrimination in violation of this Declaration and against any incitement to such discrimination.

Article 8

Everyone has the right to an effective remedy by the competent national tribunals for acts violating the fundamental rights granted him by the constitution or by law.

Article 9

No one shall be subjected to arbitrary arrest, detention or exile.

Article 10

Everyone is entitled in full equality to a fair and public hearing by an independent and impartial tribunal, in the determination of his rights and obligations and of any criminal charge against him.

Article 11

1. Everyone charged with a penal offence has the right to be presumed innocent until proved guilty according to law in a public trial at which he has had all the guarantees necessary for his defence.
2. No one shall be held guilty of any penal offence on account of any act or omission which did not constitute a penal offence, under national or international law, at the time when it was committed. Nor shall a heavier penalty be imposed than the one that was applicable at the time the penal offence was committed.

Article 12

No one shall be subjected to arbitrary interference with his privacy, family, home or correspondence, nor to attacks upon his honour and reputation. Everyone has the right to the protection of the law against such interference or attacks.

Article 13

1. Everyone has the right to freedom of movement and residence within the borders of each state.
2. Everyone has the right to leave any country, including his own, and to return to his country.

Article 14

1. Everyone has the right to seek and to enjoy in other countries asylum from persecution.

2. This right may not be invoked in the case of prosecutions genuinely arising from non-political crimes or from acts contrary to the purposes and principles of the United Nations.

Article 15

1. Everyone has the right to a nationality.

2. No one shall be arbitrarily deprived of his nationality nor denied the right to change his nationality.

Article 16

1. Men and women of full age, without any limitation due to race, nationality or religion, have the right to marry and to found a family. They are entitled to equal rights as to marriage, during marriage and at its dissolution.

2. Marriage shall be entered into only with the free and full consent of the intending spouses.

3. The family is the natural and fundamental group unit of society and is entitled to protection by society and the State.

Article 17

1. Everyone has the right to own property alone as well as in association with others.

2. No one shall be arbitrarily deprived of his property.

Article 18

Everyone has the right to freedom of thought, conscience and religion; this right includes freedom to change his religion or belief, and freedom, either alone or in community with others and in public or private, to manifest his religion or belief in teaching, practice, worship and observance.

Article 19

Everyone has the right to freedom of opinion and expression; this right includes freedom to hold opinions without interference and to seek, receive and impart information and ideas through any media and regardless of frontiers.

Article 20

1. Everyone has the right to freedom of peaceful assembly and association.

2. No one may be compelled to belong to an association.

Article 21

1. Everyone has the right to take part in the government of his country, directly or through freely chosen representatives.

2. Everyone has the right of equal access to public service in his country.

3. The will of the people shall be the basis of the authority of government; this will shall be expressed in periodic and genuine elections which shall be by universal and equal suffrage and shall be held by secret vote or by equivalent free voting procedures.

Article 22

Everyone, as a member of society, has the right to social security and is entitled to realization, through national effort and international co-operation and in accordance with the organization and resources of each State, of the economic, social and cultural rights indispensable for his dignity and the free development of his personality.

Article 23

1. Everyone has the right to work, to free choice of employment, to just and favourable conditions of work and to protection against unemployment.

2. Everyone, without any discrimination, has the right to equal pay for equal work.

3. Everyone who works has the right to just and favourable remuneration ensuring for himself and his family an existence worthy of human dignity, and supplemented, if necessary, by other means of social protection.

4. Everyone has the right to form and to join trade unions for the protection of his interests.

Article 24

Everyone has the right to rest and leisure, including reasonable limitation of working hours and periodic holidays with pay.

Article 25

1. Everyone has the right to a standard of living adequate for the health and well-being of himself and of his family, including food, clothing, housing and medical care and necessary social services, and the right to security in the event of unemployment, sickness, disability, widowhood, old age or other lack of livelihood in circumstances beyond his control.

2. Motherhood and childhood are entitled to special care and assistance. All children, whether born in or out of wedlock, shall enjoy the same social protection.

Article 26

1. Everyone has the right to education. Education shall be free, at least in the elementary and fundamental stages. Elementary education shall be compulsory. Technical and professional education shall be made generally available and higher education shall be equally accessible to all on the basis of merit.

2. Education shall be directed to the full development of the human personality and to the strengthening of respect for human rights and fundamental freedoms. It shall promote understanding, tolerance and friendship among all nations, racial or religious groups, and shall further the activities of the United Nations for the maintenance of peace.

3. Parents have a prior right to choose the kind of education that shall be given to their children.

Article 27

1. Everyone has the right freely to participate in the cultural life of the community, to enjoy the arts and to share in scientific advancement and its benefits.

2. Everyone has the right to the protection of the moral and material interests resulting from any scientific, literary or artistic production of which he is the author.

Article 28

Everyone is entitled to a social and international order in which the rights and freedoms set forth in this Declaration can be fully realized.

Article 29

1. Everyone has duties to the community in which alone the free and full development of his personality is possible.

2. In the exercise of his rights and freedoms, everyone shall be subject only to such limitations as are determined by law solely for the purpose of securing due recognition and respect for the rights and freedoms of others and of meeting the just requirements of morality, public order and the general welfare in a democratic society.

3. These rights and freedoms may in no case be exercised contrary to the purposes and principles of the United Nations.

Article 30

Nothing in this Declaration may be interpreted as implying for any State, group or person any right to engage in any activity or to perform any act aimed at the destruction of any of the rights and freedoms set forth herein.

—18—

ESSENTIAL ELEMENTS OF LASTING PEACE

Harry S Truman

June 11, 1949

When President Franklin D. Roosevelt died in April, 1945, few political observers thought his Vice President—a machine politician from Kansas City, Missouri—would prove up to the job. In fact, Harry S Truman emerged as a forceful president. After successfully concluding the Second World War, Truman grew concerned about the advance of communism in China and signs of aggressive behavior by Stalin's Soviet Union. In 1947, he laid the foundations of America's foreign policy for the next forty years by announcing the Truman Doctrine. At the time, communist guerrillas were fighting to overthrow the pro-Western government of Greece, and the republic of Turkey felt threatened by its looming neighbor, the U.S.S.R. In response to the crisis, Truman announced a major military and economic aid program to both countries; under the Truman Doctrine, he committed the United States to aiding any country in the world threatened by communist forces. In the following speech, delivered in Little Rock, Arkansas, in 1949, Truman delivered one of the clearest statements ever made of America's strategy for fighting the Cold War under his famous Doctrine: to secure prosperity for America and the Western world, and to prevent the spread of communism.

ESSENTIAL ELEMENTS OF LASTING PEACE

We are here to dedicate this beautiful park to the memory of the dead of two World Wars.

The brave men who lost their lives in those wars would approve of the way you have chosen to honor them. This park will be a place of rest and recreation. It is fitting that a war memorial should be something that can be used and enjoyed by the people. Nothing could be more appropriate than to devote a war memorial to those values of human life which our soldiers died to preserve—the values of freedom and peace.

We are not a militaristic country. We do not glorify the military way of life. Some nations have taken greater pride in their military victories than in any other national achievements, but it has never been so with us. When we think of war, it is with a prayer that the sacrifices our dead have made will never have to be repeated.

After every war we have solemnly resolved to prevent future wars. We have learned, however, that it is not enough to make resolutions. It is not enough to utter them in speeches or to engrave them on monuments. We have learned that we must devote the best efforts of our whole nation to make those resolutions come true.

We entered the first World War to restore peace and to preserve human freedom; but when that war was finished, we turned aside from the task we had begun. We turned our backs upon the League of Nations—the international organization which was established to maintain peace. We ignored the economic problems of the world, and adopted a tariff policy which only made them worse. We let our domestic affairs fall into the hands of selfish interests.

We failed to join with others to take the steps which might have prevented a second world war.

This time we are fully aware of the mistakes that were made in the past. We are on guard against the indifference and isolationism which can only lead to the tragedy of war. This time we will not let our decisions be made for us by a little group of men who are concerned only with their own special interests.

This time we have taken vigorous and far-seeing measures to preserve peace and restore prosperity throughout the world. We have assumed the responsibility that I believe God intended this great republic to assume after the first World War. We have shouldered the enormous responsibilities that go with our tremendous strength.

We have been fortunate in having many public servants of ability and vision who have devoted themselves to the problems of foreign affairs and national defense. We have able leaders in the Congress, who have mastered the complex details of our relations with other nations. They have made themselves familiar with the effects of our policies in all parts of the globe. They have labored painstakingly to enact a body of legislation to carry out the responsibilities we have assumed.

Most significant of all, the people of this country understand the supreme importance of our foreign policy and the great objectives toward which we are moving. Public debate has threshed out the basic questions of our foreign policy. The people have made up their minds. They have supported, and will continue to support, the measures necessary to maintain peace.

We have had to work for peace in the face of troubled conditions and against Communist pressures. But because we have been united in our determination to use our strength and our substance, we have already turned the tide in favor of freedom and peace. The disintegration of the democracies of Europe has been halted. Free peoples in many parts of the world have been given new hope and new confidence. The restoration of a system of world trade has begun. And all this has been accomplished without closing the door to peaceful negotiation of the differences between the free nations and the Soviet Union.

But we are only midway in carrying out our policy. We have a long way to go before we can make the free world secure against the social and political evils on which Communism thrives. The cause of peace and freedom is still threatened.

Yet there are some who have grown weary of the effort we are making. There are voices which claim that because our policy has been successful so far, we can now afford to relax. There are some who want to slash the aid we are giving to the economic recovery of other nations; there are some who want to reject the measures that are necessary for defense against aggression; there are some who wish to abandon our efforts toward the revival of world trade. These are the same voices that misled us in the 1920's. They are misguided by short-run considerations. They refuse to face the plain facts. They try to convince us that we cannot afford to pay the price of peace.

But the people of the United States will not be misled a second time. We know that the shortsighted course, the easy way, is not the path to peace. The path is difficult and requires firm determination and steadfast effort.

We know that if we are to build a lasting peace in the world we must achieve three essential conditions.

First, this nation must be strong and prosperous.

Second, other nations devoted to the cause of peace and freedom must also be strong and prosperous.

Third, there must be an international structure capable of adjusting international differences and maintaining peace.

The first condition is our own strength and prosperity.

It is unusual for this nation to maintain substantial armed forces in time of peace. Yet, so long as there is a threat to the principles of peace—the principles on which the United Nations is founded—we must maintain strong armed forces. Any uncertainty as to the ability or the willingness of the free nations of the world to defend themselves is an invitation to aggression. We have seen the truth of this statement in the outbreak of two World Wars.

Our national strength is not, however, simply a matter of weapons and trained men. Even more important are our economic growth and continued prosperity.

Our economy is the center of a world economy. The hope of economic revival throughout the world depends in large measure upon the prosperity of the United States. If our production and purchasing power are badly impaired, if the buying and selling and investing that we do in other parts of the world are cut off, other nations will be plunged into chaos and despair.

It is a prime belief of the Communist philosophy that our kind of economy is doomed to failure. The Communists predict that our prosperity will collapse—bringing the rest of the free world down with it. But they are wrong—wrong as they can be.

We know more today about keeping our economy strong than we have ever known before. We know how to strengthen our economy through the expansion of production and purchasing power and the improvement of standards of living. We understand that constantly rising national output, increasing real wages, and a fair income for farmers are basic elements of our economic strength.

To maintain these elements of prosperity, it is not sufficient to drift with the tide. We must take advantage of the new opportunities, the increased demands which result from the natural growth of our population. We must develop our natural resources and restore those we have depleted or wasted. We must establish a fair distribution of business opportunity; we must have a free labor movement able to hold its own at the bargaining table; we must protect the purchasing power of Americans against the hazards and misfortunes of life.

These steps are necessary if we are to continue strong and prosperous. That is why our domestic programs for the development of resources, for protection against economic hazards, for the improvement of social conditions, are fundamental to our national effort for peace.

The second condition essential to peace is that other nations, as well as our own, must be strong and prosperous.

We need other nations as our allies in the cause of human freedom. We have seen free nations lost to the democratic way of life because of economic disaster. We know that despair over economic conditions will turn men away from freedom and into the hands of dictators.

It is to our interest, therefore, to aid other nations to restore and maintain their economic health. Our aim is not only to help other nations to help themselves, but also to encourage economic cooperation among them.

We have taken the lead in cooperating with other nations to restore a mutually beneficial system of world trade. No nation today can achieve prosperity in isolation. Only through participation in the trade of the world can a country raise its own standards of living and contribute to the welfare of other nations.

For years before the war, world trade was crippled by high tariffs, import quotas, exchange manipulation, and other artificial devices for securing commercial advantage. These practices were a symptom of international anarchy. They resulted, ultimately, in idle ships, idle men, and economic chaos.

We have come a long way toward correcting these evils. Since 1934, we have worked out a multitude of agreements with other countries to reduce specific tariff barriers. In the General Agreement on Tariffs and Trade of 1948, we struck a world-wide blow at these obstacles to trade.

But this work is not yet finished. If we are to succeed it is vital that the authority to negotiate reciprocal-trade agreements be extended. We should then go on to establish a permanent international trade organization to apply standards of fair dealing in the commerce among nations.

The same cooperative principle has been applied in our great undertaking to restore the economies of the Western European nations to a self-sustaining basis. The food, fuel, and equipment which we have sent to Europe have been matched by the efforts which these nations have made to restore their own economies and to cooperate with one another in increasing their production and raising their standards of living.

It is fair to say that the European Recovery Program has halted the social and economic disintegration which threatened the countries of Western Europe with Communism and civil strife.

Nevertheless, the European Recovery Program is still in its early stages. At the outset it was estimated that it would take four years before these countries could again become independent of special economic aid. Only a little more than one year has passed since we began.

If we were to falter now and cut down our aid, the momentum of recovery would be destroyed. The people of these countries would be thrown into confusion, and their advance toward economic self-reliance would be blocked. A slash in the funds available for European recovery at this time would be the worst kind of false economy. It would cancel the hopes and the plans of the Western European nations. It would be a great gain for Communism.

I am confident we shall not make this mistake.

Our concern with the economic health of the world also extends to its underdeveloped regions. The prospects for peace will be immeasurably brighter if we can offer a future of hope and a better life to the people of these regions. In these areas there are millions who for centuries have known nothing but exploitation and poverty, and whose economic life is still primitive.

I have offered a program for bringing these people the benefits of our modern civilization. It is not a program of relief. While it is intended ultimately to bring about a great movement of capital through the channels of private investment for the development of these poverty-stricken regions, it is not a program of imperialism. The development of these areas offers enormous potential benefits to a growing world economy.

We have to lay the foundations for this program with care. I expect shortly to send to the Congress recommendations for initial legislation. This will be but the first step of many that we shall take, over the years to come, in this cooperative effort to better the living standards and to unlock the human skills and the natural resources of the underdeveloped parts of the globe.

The third condition essential for peace is an international structure capable of suppressing international violence. However well conceived our economic programs may be, they cannot succeed unless there is some assurance against the outbreak of aggression. Neither our own prosperity nor the prosperity of other nations can survive unless we can protect the operations of economic life from the threat of war.

Such protection depends on two factors. First, there must be constant efforts by all nations to adjust their differences peacefully. Second, there must be an agreement among nations to employ overwhelming force against armed aggression.

The United Nations is a valuable instrument for accomplishing these ends. It has already achieved the peaceful settlement of difficult issues. It has stopped hostilities in the Near East and in Indonesia. It has done a great deal to explore and find solutions for many of the economic and social problems which afflict the world.

Much remains to be done, however, to carry out the principles of the United Nations. Within the terms of the United Nations Charter, we and certain other countries have undertaken to provide greater assurance against the danger of armed conflict. That is the purpose of the North Atlantic Treaty. The idea behind this treaty—the association of democratic nations for mutual defense—is well understood in this country. Perhaps we do not understand, however, the importance of this pact in the eyes of the other democratic nations which are parties to it. They have been greatly weakened by the war. They have been haunted by the fear of again becoming the scene of conflict. By assuring them of our support the pact goes a long way to dispel their fears.

I have been greatly heartened by the unanimous report of the Foreign Relations Committee of the Senate this past week in favor of the North Atlantic Treaty. I believe that it will soon be passed by an overwhelming majority in the Senate. The effect of this action will be immediate and far-reaching in allaying the fears which have retarded economic recovery in Europe.

It is of vital importance that the Atlantic pact be followed by a program of military aid to increase the effective strength of the free nations against aggression. This military assistance program—based upon mutual help—will give additional confidence to the people of those nations as they continue to rebuild their economies.

These measures will bring a stability to the democratic nations of Europe, which has not existed since the end of the war. They will at the same time contribute directly to the security of the United States.

I have discussed the three essential elements of lasting peace—a strong and prosperous United States; a strong and prosperous community of free nations; an international organization capable of preventing aggression.

We have given greatly of our effort and our strength to build a firm and enduring foreign policy upon these essentials. The burdens we have had to assume in this enterprise have been unusual. The size of the national budget shows that we are engaged in an undertaking without parallel in the history of our country or of the world.

But the goal we seek is a great one, and worth the price. Never has a nation had the opportunity which we have today to do so much for the peace and prosperity of mankind. Never has a nation had a better chance of reaching this high goal.

We must not falter now.

We must not defeat our own efforts by doing only half the job that lies before us.

The brave men, whose memory we honor here, did all that was required of them. They did not fail us. We must not fail them in our efforts to reach the goal for which they died.

We must press on in the confidence that we will succeed in the mission a divine Providence has assigned to us.

—19—

FAREWELL ADDRESS

Dwight D. Eisenhower

January 17, 1961

In January, 1961, President Dwight D. Eisenhower spoke to the American people on television and radio as he prepared to retire after forty-six years of public service. After serving as Supreme Commander of the Allied forces in Western Europe during World War II, military commander of NATO, and president of Columbia University, he spent two terms as one of the most popular presidents in American history. But in his Farewell Address, Eisenhower warned about the growing power of the "military-industrial complex."

During most of America's history, the government spent little money on defense; the army was usually kept quite small, and most soldiers spent their time on the frontier, fighting or guarding against Indians. Even the First World War required a crash mobilization, and the army was reduced to a token force with the onset of peace. The Second World War, followed by the Cold War, marked a dramatic break with this past. The United States took over a leading role in almost every area of world affairs, from the international economic system to the battle against communism, which required a substantial military. Technological advances, too, brought a large increase in the investment required for weapons. Jets, missiles, and nuclear submarines became standard equipment for the Pentagon, fostering the birth of the modern defense industry. The Manhattan Project, which built the atomic bomb, gave birth to a massive nuclear weapons program. Eisenhower's administration also witnessed the beginning of the space race, as the Soviets put the first artificial satellite in orbit. As a thoughtful military man, Eisenhower recognized the dangers these developments posed for a democratic society. His Farewell Address immediately became a touchstone for Americans worried by the influence of the powerful defense establishment.

FAREWELL ADDRESS

My fellow Americans:

Three days from now, after half a century in the service of our country, I shall lay down the responsibilities of office as, in traditional and solemn ceremony, the authority of the Presidency is vested in my successor.

This evening I come to you with a message of leave-taking and farewell, and to share a few final thoughts with you, my countrymen.

Like every other citizen, I wish the new President, and all who will labor with him, Godspeed. I pray that the coming years will be blessed with peace and prosperity for all.

Our people expect their President and the Congress to find essential agreement on issues of great moment, the wise resolution of which will better shape the future of the Nation.

My own relations with the Congress, which began on a remote and tenuous basis when, long ago, a member of the Senate appointed me to West Point, have since ranged to the intimate during the war and immediate post-war period, and, finally, to the mutually interdependent during these past eight years.

In this final relationship, the Congress and the Administration have, on most vital issues, cooperated well, to serve the national good rather than mere partisanship, and so have assured that the business of the Nation should go forward. So, my official relationship with the Congress ends in a feeling, on my part, of gratitude that we have been able to do so much together.

II.

We now stand ten years past the midpoint of a century that has witnessed four major wars among great nations. Three of these involved our own country. Despite these holocausts America is today the strongest, the most influential and most productive nation in the world. Understandably proud of this pre-eminence, we yet realize that America's leadership and prestige depend, not merely upon our unmatched material progress, riches and military strength, but on how we use our power in the interests of world peace and human betterment.

III.

Throughout America's adventure in free government, our basic purposes have been to keep the peace; to foster progress in human achievement, and to enhance liberty, dignity and integrity among people and among nations. To strive for less would be unworthy of a free and religious people. Any failure traceable to arrogance, or our lack of comprehension or readiness to sacrifice would inflict upon us grievous hurt both at home and abroad.

Progress toward these noble goals is persistently threatened by the conflict now engulfing the world. It commands our whole attention, absorbs our very beings. We face a hostile ideology—global in scope, atheistic in character, ruthless in purpose, and insidious in method. Unhappily the danger it poses promises to be of indefinite duration. To meet it successfully, there is called for, not so much the emotional and transitory sacrifices of crisis, but rather those which enable us to carry forward steadily, surely, and without complaint the burdens of a prolonged and complex struggle—with liberty the stake. Only thus shall we remain, despite every provocation, on our charted course toward permanent peace and human betterment.

Crises there will continue to be. In meeting them, whether foreign or domestic, great or small, there is a recurring temptation to feel that some spectacular and costly action could become the miraculous solution to all current difficulties. A huge increase in newer elements of our defense; development of unrealistic programs to cure every ill in agriculture; a dramatic expansion in basic and applied research—these and many other possibilities, each possibly promising in itself, may be suggested as the only way to the road we wish to travel.

But each proposal must be weighed in the light of a broader consideration: the need to maintain balance in and among national programs—balance between the private and the public economy, balance between cost and hoped for advantage—balance between the clearly necessary and the comfortably desirable; balance between our essential requirements as a nation and the duties imposed by the nation upon the individual; balance between actions of the moment and the national welfare of the future. Good judgment seeks balance and progress; lack of it eventually finds imbalance and frustration.

The record of many decades stands as proof that our people and their government have, in the main, understood these truths and have responded to them well, in the face of stress and threat. But threats, new in kind or degree, constantly arise. I mention two only.

IV.

A vital element in keeping the peace is our military establishment. Our arms must be mighty, ready for instant action, so that no potential aggressor may be tempted to risk his own destruction.

Our military organization today bears little relation to that known by any of my predecessors in peacetime, or indeed by the fighting men of World War II or Korea.

Until the latest of our world conflicts, the United States had no armaments industry. American makers of plowshares could, with time and as required, make swords as well. But now we can no longer risk emergency improvisation of national defense; we have been compelled to create a permanent armaments industry of vast proportions. Added to this, three and a half million men and women are directly engaged in the defense establishment. We annually spend on military security more than the net income of all United States corporations.

This conjunction of an immense military establishment and a large arms industry is new in the American experience. The total influence—economic, political, even spiritual—is felt in every city, every State house, every office of the Federal government. We recognize the imperative need for this development. Yet we must not fail to comprehend its grave implications. Our toil, resources and livelihood are all involved; so is the very structure of our society.

In the councils of government, we must guard against the acquisition of unwarranted influence, whether sought or unsought, by the military-industrial complex. The potential for the disastrous rise of misplaced power exists and will persist.

We must never let the weight of this combination endanger our liberties or democratic processes. We should take nothing for granted. Only an alert and knowledgeable citizenry can compel the proper meshing of the huge industrial and military machinery of defense with our peaceful methods and goals, so that security and liberty may prosper together.

Akin to, and largely responsible for the sweeping changes in our industrial-military posture, has been the technological revolution during recent decades.

In this revolution, research has become central; it also becomes more formalized, complex, and costly. A steadily increasing share is conducted for, by, or at the direction of, the Federal government.

Today, the solitary inventor, tinkering in his shop, has been overshadowed by task forces of scientists in laboratories and testing fields. In the same fashion, the free university, historically the fountainhead of free ideas and scientific discovery, has experienced a revolution in the conduct of research. Partly because of the huge costs involved, a government contract becomes virtually a substitute for intellectual curiosity. For every old blackboard there are now hundreds of new electronic computers.

The prospect of domination of the nation's scholars by Federal employment, project allocations, and the power of money is ever present—and is gravely to be regarded.

Yet, in holding scientific research and discovery in respect, as we should, we must also be alert to the equal and opposite danger that public policy could itself become the captive of a scientific-technological elite.

It is the task of statesmanship to mold, to balance, and to integrate these and other forces, new and old, within the principles of our democratic system—ever aiming toward the supreme goals of our free society.

V.

Another factor in maintaining balance involves the element of time. As we peer into society's future, we—you and I, and our government—must avoid the impulse to live only for today, plundering, for our own ease and convenience, the precious resources of tomorrow. We cannot mortgage the material assets of our grandchildren without risking the loss also of their political and spiritual heritage. We want democracy to survive for all generations to come, not to become the insolvent phantom of tomorrow.

VI.

Down the long lane of the history yet to be written America knows that this world of ours, ever growing smaller, must avoid becoming a community of dreadful fear and hate, and be, instead, a proud confederation of mutual trust and respect.

Such a confederation must be one of equals. The weakest must come to the conference table with the same confidence as do we, protected as we are by our moral, economic, and military strength. That table, though scarred by many past frustrations, cannot be abandoned for the certain agony of the battlefield.

Disarmament, with mutual honor and confidence, is a continuing imperative. Together we must learn how to compose differences, not with arms, but with intellect and decent purpose. Because this need is so sharp and apparent I confess that I lay down my official responsibilities in this field with a definite sense of disappointment. As one who has witnessed the horror and the lingering sadness of war—as one who knows that another war could utterly destroy this civilization which has been so slowly and painfully built over thousands of years—I wish I could say tonight that a lasting peace is in sight.

Happily, I can say that war has been avoided. Steady progress toward our ultimate goal has been made. But, so much remains to be done. As a private citizen, I shall never cease to do what little I can to help the world advance along that road.

VII.

So—in this my last good night to you as your President—I thank you for the many opportunities you have given me for public service in war and peace. I trust that in that service you find some things worthy; as for the rest of it, I know you will find ways to improve performance in the future.

You and I—my fellow citizens—need to be strong in our faith that all nations, under God, will reach the goal of peace with justice. May we be ever unswerving in devotion to principle, confident but humble with power, diligent in pursuit of the Nation's great goals.

To all the peoples of the world, I once more give expression to America's prayerful and continuing aspiration:

We pray that peoples of all faiths, all races, all nations, may have their great human needs satisfied; that those now denied opportunity shall come to enjoy it to the full; that all who yearn for freedom may experience its spiritual blessings; that those who have freedom will understand, also, its heavy responsibilities; that all who are insensitive to the needs of others will learn charity; that the scourges of poverty, disease and ignorance will be made to disappear from the earth, and that, in the goodness of time, all peoples will come to live together in a peace guaranteed by the binding force of mutual respect and love.

—20—

INAUGURAL ADDRESS

John F. Kennedy

January, 1961

Many Americans remember President John F. Kennedy's administration almost as a golden age in twentieth century American history. Kennedy was the youngest man ever elected president of the United States, and he brought tremendous energy and optimism to the office. His administration, falling between the long presidency of Eisenhower and the American entrance into the Vietnam War, seemed to capture the nation at its most powerful and idealistic; his triumphs included the Cuban Missile Crisis, the Nuclear Test-Ban Treaty, and the creation of the Peace Corps. President Kennedy's inaugural address captured the spirit of his administration. In this speech, he set out a powerful vision of America's mission in the world, calling for a new era of public-spirited idealism. President Kennedy was assassinated in November, 1963.

INAUGURAL ADDRESS

Vice President Johnson, Mr. Speaker, Mr. Chief Justice, President Eisenhower, Vice President Nixon, President Truman, Reverend Clergy, Fellow Citizens: We observe today not a victory of a party but a celebration of freedom—symbolizing an end as well as a beginning—signifying renewal as well as change. For I have sworn before you and Almighty God the same solemn oath our forebears prescribed nearly a century and three quarters ago.

The world is very different now. For man holds in his mortal hands the power to abolish all forms of human poverty and all forms of human life. And yet the same revolutionary beliefs for which our forebears fought are still at issue around the globe—the belief that the rights of man come not from the generosity of the state but from the hand of God.

We dare not forget today that we are the heirs of that first revolution. Let the word go forth from this time and place, to friend and foe alike, that the torch has been passed to a new generation of Americans—born in this century, tempered by war, disciplined by a hard and bitter peace, proud of our ancient heritage—and unwilling to witness or permit the slow undoing of those human rights to which this Nation has always been committed, and to which we are committed today at home and around the world.

Let every nation know, whether it wishes us well or ill, that we shall pay any price, bear any burden, meet any hardship, support any friend, oppose any foe to assure the survival and success of liberty.

This much we pledge—and more.

To those old allies whose cultural and spiritual origins we share, we pledge the loyalty of faithful friends. United, there is little we cannot do in a host of cooperative ventures. Divided, there is little we can do—for we dare not meet a powerful challenge at odds and split asunder.

To those new states whom we welcome to the ranks of the free, we pledge our word that one form of colonial control shall not have passed away merely to be replaced by a far more iron tyranny. We shall not always expect to find them supporting our view. But we shall always hope to find them strongly supporting their own freedom—and to remember that, in the past, those who foolishly sought power by riding the back of the tiger ended up inside.

To those peoples in the huts and villages of half the globe struggling to break the bonds of mass misery, we pledge our best efforts to help them help themselves, for whatever period is required—not because the Communists may be doing it, not because we seek their votes, but because it is right. If a free society cannot help the many who are poor, it cannot save the few who are rich.

To our sister republics south of our border, we offer a special pledge—to convert our good words into good deeds—in a new alliance for progress—to assist free men and free governments in casting off the chains of poverty. But this peaceful revolution of hope cannot become the prey of hostile powers. Let all our neighbors know that we shall join with them to oppose aggression or subversion anywhere in the Americas. And let every other power know that this hemisphere intends to remain the master of its own house.

To that world assembly of sovereign states, the United Nations, our last best hope in an age where the instruments of war have far outpaced the instruments of peace, we renew our pledge of support—to prevent it from becoming merely a forum for invective—to strengthen its shield of the new and the weak—and to enlarge the area in which its writ may run.

Finally, to those nations who would make themselves our adversary, we offer not a pledge but a request: that both sides begin anew the quest for peace, before the dark powers of destruction unleashed by science engulf all humanity in planned or accidental self-destruction.

We dare not tempt them with weakness. For only when our arms are sufficient beyond doubt can we be certain beyond doubt that they will never be employed.

But neither can two great and powerful groups of nations take comfort from our present course—both sides overburdened by the cost of modern weapons, both rightly alarmed by the steady spread of the deadly atom, yet both racing to alter that uncertain balance of terror that stays the hand of mankind's final war.

So let us begin anew—remembering on both sides that civility is not a sign of weakness, and sincerity is always subject to proof. Let us never negotiate out of fear. But let us never fear to negotiate.

Let both sides explore what problems unite us instead of belaboring those problems which divide us. Let both sides, for the first time, formulate serious and precise proposals for the inspection and control of arms—and bring the absolute power to destroy other nations under the absolute control of all nations.

Let both sides seek to invoke the wonders of science instead of its terrors. Together let us explore the stars, conquer the deserts, eradicate disease, tap the ocean depths and encourage the arts and commerce.

Let both sides unite to heed in all corners of the earth the command of Isaiah—to "undo the heavy burdens and to let the oppressed go free."

And if a beach-head of cooperation may push back the jungle of suspicion, let both sides join in a new endeavor; not a new balance of power, but a new world of law, where the strong are just and the weak secure and the peace preserved.

All this will not be finished in the first one hundred days. Nor will it be finished in the first one thousand days, nor in the life of this Administration, nor even perhaps in our lifetime on this planet. But let us begin.

In your hands, my fellow citizens, more than mine, will rest the final success or failure of our course. Since this country was founded, each generation of Americans has been summoned to give testimony to its national loyalty. The graves of young Americans who answered the call to service surround the globe.

Now the trumpet summons us again—not as a call to bear arms, though arms we need—not as a call to battle, though embattled we are—but a call to bear the burden of a long twilight struggle, year in and year out, "rejoicing in hope, patient in tribulation"—a struggle against the common enemies of man: tyranny, poverty, disease and war itself.

Can we forge against these enemies a grand and global alliance, North and South, East and West, that can assure a more fruitful life for all mankind? Will you join in that historic effort?

In the long history of the world, only a few generations have been granted the role of defending freedom in its hour of maximum danger. I do not shrink from this responsibility—I welcome it. I do not believe that any of us would exchange places with any other people or any other generation. The energy, the faith, the devotion which we bring to this endeavor will light our country and all who serve it—and the glow from that fire can truly light the world.

And so, my fellow Americans: Ask not what your country can do for you—ask what you can do for your country.

My fellow citizens of the world: Ask not what America will do for you, but what together we can do for the freedom of man.

Finally, whether you are citizens of America or citizens of the world, ask of us here the same high standards of strength and sacrifice which we ask of you. With a good conscience our only sure reward, with history the final judge of our deeds, let us go forth to lead the land we love, asking His blessing and His help, but knowing that here on earth God's work must truly be our own.

—21—

I HAVE A DREAM

Martin Luther King, Jr.

August 8, 1963

On August 8, 1963, Reverend Martin Luther King, Jr., addressed a massive crowd at the Lincoln Memorial, a crowd that had come to Washington as a part of the March on Washington protest for civil rights for African-Americans. Reverend King was already the foremost civil rights leader of his day. Following the examples of nonviolent resistance to injustice set by Henry David Thoreau and Mohandas Gandhi, he led massive demonstrations against discrimination and segregation laws in the South. Through his eloquence, personal courage, and nonviolent philosophy, he achieved a moral stature unequaled by almost any other American leader in the twentieth century. He commanded worldwide respect, and in 1964 he was awarded the Nobel Prize for Peace. But Reverend King never spoke more eloquently than he did on August 8, 1963. The speech he delivered that day has been burned into the American consciousness as our greatest expression of the vision of liberty and equality for all. Martin Luther King, Jr., was assassinated on April 4, 1968.

I HAVE A DREAM

I am happy to join with you today in what will go down in history as the greatest demonstration for freedom in the history of our nation.

Fivescore years ago, a great American, in whose symbolic shadow we stand today, signed the Emancipation Proclamation. This momentous decree came as a great beacon light of hope to millions of Negro slaves who had been seared in the flames of withering injustice. It came as a joyous daybreak to end the long night of their captivity.

But one hundred years later, the Negro still is not free; one hundred years later, the life of the Negro is still sadly crippled by the manacles of segregation and the chains of discrimination; one hundred years later, the Negro lives on a lonely island of poverty in the midst of a vast ocean of material prosperity; one hundred years later, the Negro is still languished in the corners of American society and finds himself in exile in his own land.

So we've come here today to dramatize a shameful condition. In a sense we've come to our nation's capital to cash a check. When the architects of our republic wrote the magnificent words of the Constitution and the Declaration of Independence, they were signing a promissory note to which every American was to fall heir. This note was the promise that all men, yes, black men as well as white men, would be guaranteed the unalienable rights of life, liberty, and the pursuit of happiness.

It is obvious today that America has defaulted on this promissory note in so far as her citizens of color are concerned. Instead of honoring this sacred obligation, America has given the Negro people a bad check; a check which has come back marked "insufficient funds." We refuse to believe that there are insufficient funds in the great vaults of opportunity of this nation. And so we've come to cash this check, a check that will give us upon demand the riches of freedom and the security of justice.

We have also come to this hallowed spot to remind America of the fierce urgency of now. This is no time to engage in the luxury of cooling off or to take the tranquilizing drug of gradualism. Now is the time to make real the promises of democracy; now is the time to rise from the dark and desolate valley of segregation to the sunlit path of racial justice; now is the time to lift our nation from the quicksands of racial injustice to the solid rock of brotherhood; now is the time to make justice a reality for all God's children. It would be fatal for the nation to overlook the urgency of the moment. This sweltering summer of the Negro's legitimate discontent will not pass until there is an invigorating autumn of freedom and equality.

Nineteen sixty-three is not an end, but a beginning. And those who hope that the Negro needed to blow off steam and will now be content, will have a rude awakening if the nation returns to business as usual.

There will be neither rest nor tranquility in America until the Negro is granted his citizenship rights. The whirlwinds of revolt will continue to shake the foundations of our nation until the bright day of justice emerges.

But there is something that I must say to my people who stand on the warm threshold which leads into the palace of justice. In the process of gaining our rightful place we must not be guilty of wrongful deeds.

Let us not seek to satisfy our thirst for freedom by drinking from the cup of bitterness and hatred. We must forever conduct our struggle on the high plane of dignity and discipline. We must not allow our creative protest to degenerate into physical violence. Again and again we must rise to the majestic heights of meeting physical force with soul force.

The marvelous new militancy which has engulfed the Negro community must not lead us to a distrust of all white people, for many of our white brothers, as evidenced by their presence here today, have come to realize that their destiny is tied up with our destiny and they have come to realize that their freedom is inextricably bound to our freedom. This offense we share mounted to storm the battlements of injustice must be carried forth by a biracial army. We cannot walk alone.

And as we walk, we must make the pledge that we shall always march ahead. We cannot turn back. There are those who are asking the devotees of civil rights, "When will you be satisfied?" We can never be satisfied as long as the Negro is the victim of the unspeakable horrors of police brutality.

We can never be satisfied as long as our bodies, heavy with fatigue of travel, cannot gain lodging in the motels of the highways and the hotels of the cities. We cannot be satisfied as long as the Negro's basic mobility is from a smaller ghetto to a larger one.

We can never be satisfied as long as our children are stripped of their selfhood and robbed of their dignity by signs stating "for whites only." We cannot be satisfied as long as a Negro in Mississippi cannot vote and a Negro in New York believes he has nothing for which to vote. No, we are not satisfied, and we will not be satisfied until justice rolls down like waters and righteousness like a mighty stream.

I am not unmindful that some of you have come here out of excessive trials and tribulation. Some of you have come fresh from narrow jail cells. Some of you have come from areas where your quest for freedom left you battered by the storms of persecution and staggered by the winds of police brutality. You have been the veterans of creative suffering. Continue to work with the faith that unearned suffering is redemptive.

Go back to Mississippi; go back to Alabama; go back to South Carolina; go back to Georgia; go back to Louisiana; go back to the slums and ghettos of the northern cities, knowing that somehow this situation can, and will be changed. Let us not wallow in the valley of despair.

So I say to you, my friends, that even though we must face the difficulties of today and tomorrow, I still have a dream. It is a dream deeply rooted in the American dream that one day this nation will rise up and live out the true meaning of its creed—we hold these truths to be self-evident, that all men are created equal.

I have a dream that one day on the red hills of Georgia, sons of former slaves and sons of former slave-owners will be able to sit down together at the table of brotherhood.

I have a dream that one day, even the state of Mississippi, a state sweltering with the heat of injustice, sweltering with the heat of oppression, will be transformed into an oasis of freedom and justice.

I have a dream my four little children will one day live in a nation where they will not be judged by the color of their skin but by content of their character. I have a dream today!

I have a dream that one day, down in Alabama, with its vicious racists, with its governor having his lips dripping with the words of interposition and nullification, that one day, right there in Alabama, little black boys and black girls will be able to join hands with little white boys and white girls as sisters and brothers. I have a dream today!

I have a dream that one day every valley shall be exalted, every hill and mountain shall be made low, the rough places shall be made plain, and the crooked places shall be made straight and the glory of the Lord will be revealed and all flesh shall see it together.

This is our hope. This is the faith that I go back to the South with.

With this faith we will be able to hear out of the mountain of despair a stone of hope. With this faith we will be able to transform the jangling discords of our nation into a beautiful symphony of brotherhood.

With this faith we will be able to work together, to pray together, to struggle together, to go to jail together, to stand up for freedom together, knowing that we will be free one day. This will be the day when all of God's children will be able to sing with new meaning—"my country 'tis of thee; sweet land of liberty; of thee I sing; land where my fathers died, land of the pilgrim's pride; from every mountain side, let freedom ring"—and if America is to be a great nation, this must become true.

So let freedom ring from the prodigious hilltops of New Hampshire.

Let freedom ring from the mighty mountains of New York.

Let freedom ring from the heightening Alleghenies of Pennsylvania.

Let freedom ring from the snow-capped Rockies of Colorado.

Let freedom ring from the curvaceous slopes of California.

But not only that.

Let freedom ring from Stone Mountain of Georgia.

Let freedom ring from Lookout Mountain of Tennessee.

Let freedom ring from every hill and molehill of Mississippi, from every mountainside, let freedom ring.

And when we allow freedom to ring, when we let it ring from every village and hamlet, from every state and city, we will be able to speed up that day when all of God's children—black men and white men, Jews and Gentiles, Catholics and Protestants—will be able to join hands and to sing in the words of the old Negro spiritual, "Free at last, free at last; thank God Almighty, we are free at last."

—22—

SPECIAL MESSAGE TO THE CONGRESS: THE AMERICAN PROMISE—"WE SHALL OVERCOME" SPEECH

Lyndon B. Johnson

March 15, 1965

The first Federal attempts at enforcing civil rights for African Americans took place during the years of Reconstruction, beginning with the Civil Rights Act of 1866. A conservative Supreme Court, however, later ruled that many Reconstruction-era laws were unconstitutional because they infringed on states' rights. As Reconstruction drew to a close, traditional Democrats in the South (known as "Redeemers") swept back into control of state governments. In the last decades of the nineteenth century, Southern states passed a series of segregation acts known as Jim Crow laws. For most of a century after the end of Reconstruction, blacks suffered severe restrictions on their access to public facilities, public office, education, and voting, in addition to the terror of lynching and violence by the Ku Klux Klan. This history was challenged by the civil rights movement of the 1950s and 1960s.

Led by Martin Luther King, Jr., and many others, African Americans held mass protests that forced the nation to confront the problem of widespread discrimination and segregation. For the first time since Reconstruction, the Federal government responded to the problem with a series of Civil Rights acts, beginning in the 1950s. But the most powerful and important legislations were the Civil Rights Act of 1964 and the Voting Rights Act of 1965. These laws gave Federal agencies the power to enforce civil rights for African Americans, making civil rights the permanent concern of the Federal government. In the speech that follows, President Lyndon Johnson—an old Southern politician himself—firmly committed the national government to the cause of civil rights, and marked the triumph of the civil rights movement over the resistance of conservative Southern states.

SPECIAL MESSAGE TO THE CONGRESS: THE AMERICAN PROMISE

Mr. Speaker, Mr. President, Members of the Congress:

I speak tonight for the dignity of man and the destiny of democracy.

I urge every member of both parties, Americans of all religions and of all colors, from every section of this country, to join me in that cause.

At times history and fate meet at a single time in a single place to shape a turning point in man's unending search for freedom. So it was at Lexington and Concord. So it was a century ago at Appomattox. So it was last week in Selma, Alabama.

There, long-suffering men and women peacefully protested the denial of their rights as Americans. Many were brutally assaulted. One good man, a man of God, was killed.

There is no cause for pride in what has happened in Selma. There is no cause for self-satisfaction in the long denial of equal rights of millions of Americans. But there is cause for hope and for faith in our democracy in what is happening here tonight.

For the cries of pain and the hymns and protests of oppressed people have summoned into convocation all the majesty of this great Government—the Government of the greatest Nation on earth.

Our mission is at once the oldest and the most basic of this country: to right wrong, to do justice, to serve man.

In our time we have come to live with moments of great crisis. Our lives have been marked with debate about great issues; issues of war and peace, issues of prosperity and depression. But rarely in any time does an issue lay bare the secret heart of America itself. Rarely are we met with a challenge, not to our growth or abundance, our welfare or our security, but rather to the values and the purposes and the meaning of our beloved Nation.

The issue of equal rights for American Negroes is such an issue. And should we defeat every enemy, should we double our wealth and conquer the stars, and still be unequal to this issue, then we will have failed as a people and as a nation.

For with a country as with a person, "What is a man profited, if he shall gain the whole world, and lose his own soul?"

There is no Negro problem. There is no Southern problem. There is no Northern problem. There is only an American problem. And we are met here tonight as Americans—not as Democrats or Republicans—we are met here as Americans to solve that problem.

This was the first nation in the history of the world to be founded with a purpose. The great phrases of that purpose still sound in every American heart, North and South: "All men are created equal"—"government by consent of the governed"—"give me liberty or give me death." Well, those are not just clever words, or those are not just empty theories. In their name Americans have fought and died for two centuries, and tonight around the world they stand there as guardians of our liberty, risking their lives.

Those words are a promise to every citizen that he shall share in the dignity of man. This dignity cannot be found in a man's possessions; it cannot be found in his power, or in his position. It really rests on his right to be treated as a man equal in opportunity to all others. It says that he shall share in freedom, he shall choose his leaders, educate his children, and provide for his family according to his ability and his merits as a human being.

To apply any other test—to deny a man his hopes because of his color or race, his religion or the place of his birth—is not only to do injustice, it is to deny America and to dishonor the dead who gave their lives for American freedom.

THE RIGHT TO VOTE

Our fathers believed that if this noble view of the rights of man was to flourish, it must be rooted in democracy. The most basic right of all was the right to choose your own leaders. The history of this country, in large measure, is the history of the expansion of that right to all of our people.

Many of the issues of civil rights are very complex and most difficult. But about this there can and should be no argument. Every American citizen must have an equal right to vote. There is no reason which can excuse the denial of that right. There is no duty which weighs more heavily on us than the duty we have to ensure that right.

Yet the harsh fact is that in many places in this country men and women are kept from voting simply because they are Negroes.

Every device of which human ingenuity is capable has been used to deny this right. The Negro citizen may go to register only to be told that the day is wrong, or the hour is late, or the official in charge is absent. And if he persists, and if he manages to present himself to the registrar, he may be disqualified because he did not spell out his middle name or because he abbreviated a word on the application.

And if he manages to fill out an application he is given a test. The registrar is the sole judge of whether he passes this test. He may be asked to recite the entire Constitution, or explain the most complex provisions of State law. And even a college degree cannot be used to prove that he can read and write.

For the fact is that the only way to pass these barriers is to show a white skin.

Experience has clearly shown that the existing process of law cannot overcome systematic and ingenious discrimination. No law that we now have on the books—and I have helped to put three of them there—can ensure the right to vote when local officials are determined to deny it.

In such a case our duty must be clear to all of us. The Constitution says that no person shall be kept from voting because of his race or his color. We have all sworn an oath before God to support and to defend that Constitution. We must now act in obedience to that oath.

GUARANTEEING THE RIGHT TO VOTE

Wednesday I will send to Congress a law designed to eliminate illegal barriers to the right to vote.

The broad principles of that bill will be in the hands of the

Democratic and Republican leaders tomorrow. After they have reviewed it, it will come here formally as a bill. I am grateful for this opportunity to come here tonight at the invitation of the leadership to reason with my friends, to give them my views, and to visit with my former colleagues.

I have had prepared a more comprehensive analysis of the legislation which I had intended to transmit to the clerk tomorrow but which I will submit to the clerks tonight. But I want to really discuss with you now briefly the main proposals of this legislation.

This bill will strike down restrictions to voting in all elections—Federal, State, and local—which have been used to deny Negroes the right to vote.

This bill will establish a simple, uniform standard which cannot be used, however ingenious the effort, to flout our Constitution.

It will provide for citizens to be registered by officials of the United States Government if the State officials refuse to register them.

It will eliminate tedious, unnecessary lawsuits which delay the right to vote.

Finally, this legislation will ensure that properly registered individuals are not prohibited from voting.

I will welcome the suggestions from all of the Members of Congress—I have no doubt that I will get some—on ways and means to strengthen this law and to make it effective. But experience has plainly shown that this is the only path to carry out the command of the Constitution.

To those who seek to avoid action by their National Government in their own communities; who want to and who seek to maintain purely local control over elections, the answer is simple:

Open your polling places to all your people.

Allow men and women to register and vote whatever the color of their skin.

Extend the rights of citizenship to every citizen of this land.

THE NEED FOR ACTION

There is no constitutional issue here. The command of the Constitution is plain.

There is no moral issue. It is wrong—deadly wrong—to deny

any of your fellow Americans the right to vote in this country.

There is no issue of States rights or national rights. There is only the struggle for human rights.

I have not the slightest doubt what will be your answer.

The last time a President sent a civil rights bill to the Congress it contained a provision to protect voting rights in Federal elections. That civil rights bill was passed after 8 long months of debate. And when that bill came to my desk from the Congress for my signature, the heart of the voting provision had been eliminated.

This time, on this issue, there must be no delay, no hesitation and no compromise with our purpose.

We cannot, we must not, refuse to protect the right of every American to vote in every election that he may desire to participate in. And we ought not and we cannot and we must not wait another 8 months before we get a bill. We have already waited a hundred years and more, and the time for waiting is gone.

So I ask you to join me in working long hours—nights and weekends, if necessary—to pass this bill. And I don't make that request lightly. For from the window where I sit with the problems of our country I recognize that outside this chamber is the outraged conscience of a nation, the grave concern of many nations, and the harsh judgment of history on our acts.

WE SHALL OVERCOME

But even if we pass this bill, the battle will not be over. What happened in Selma is part of a far larger movement which reaches into every section and State of America. It is the effort of American Negroes to secure for themselves the full blessings of American life.

Their cause must be our cause too. Because it is not just Negroes, but really it is all of us, who must overcome the crippling legacy of bigotry and injustice.

And we shall overcome.

As a man whose roots go deeply into Southern soil I know how agonizing racial feelings are. I know how difficult it is to reshape the attitudes and the structure of our society.

But a century has passed, more than a hundred years, since the

Negro was freed. And he is not fully free tonight.

It was more than a hundred years ago that Abraham Lincoln, a great President of another party, signed the Emancipation Proclamation, but emancipation is a proclamation and not a fact.

A century has passed, more than a hundred years, since equality was promised. And yet the Negro is not equal.

A century has passed since the day of promise. And the promise is unkept.

The time of justice has now come. I tell you that I believe sincerely that no force can hold it back. It is right in the eyes of man and God that it should come. And when it does, I think that day will brighten the lives of every American.

For Negroes are not the only victims. How many white children have gone uneducated, how many white families have lived in stark poverty, how many white lives have been scarred by fear, because we have wasted our energy and our substance to maintain the barriers of hatred and terror?

So I say to all of you here, and to all in the Nation tonight, that those who appeal to you to hold on to the past do so at the cost of denying you your future.

This great, rich, restless country can offer opportunity and education and hope to all: black and white, North and South, sharecropper and city dweller. These are the enemies: poverty, ignorance, disease. They are the enemies and not our fellow man, not our neighbor. And these enemies too, poverty, disease and ignorance, we shall overcome.

AN AMERICAN PROBLEM

Now let none of us in any sections look with prideful righteousness on the troubles in another section, or on the problems of our neighbors. There is really no part of America where the promise of equality has been fully kept. In Buffalo as well as in Birmingham, in Philadelphia as well as in Selma, Americans are struggling for the fruits of freedom.

This is one Nation. What happens in Selma or in Cincinnati is a matter of legitimate concern to every American. But let each of us look within our own hearts and our own communities, and let each of us put our shoulder to the wheel to root out injustice wherever it exists.

As we meet here in this peaceful, historic chamber tonight, men from the South, some of whom were at Iwo Jima, men from the North who have carried Old Glory to far corners of the world and brought it back without a stain on it, men from the East and from the West, are all fighting together without regard to religion, or color, or region, in Viet-Nam. Men from every region fought for us across the world 20 years ago.

And in these common dangers and these common sacrifices the South made its contribution of honor and gallantry no less than any other region of the great Republic—and in some instances, a great many of them, more.

And I have not the slightest doubt that good men from everywhere in this country, from the Great Lakes to the Gulf of Mexico, from the Golden Gate to the harbors along the Atlantic, will rally together now in this cause to vindicate the freedom of all Americans. For all of us owe this duty; and I believe that all of us will respond to it.

Your President makes that request of every American.

PROGRESS THROUGH THE DEMOCRATIC PROCESS

The real hero of this struggle is the American Negro. His actions and protests, his courage to risk safety and even to risk his life, have awakened the conscience of this Nation. His demonstrations have been designed to call attention to injustice, designed to provoke change, designed to stir reform.

He has called upon us to make good the promise of America. And who among us can say that we would have made the same progress were it not for his persistent bravery, and his faith in American democracy.

For at the real heart of battle for equality is a deep-seated belief in the democratic process. Equality depends not on the force of arms or tear gas but upon the force of moral right; not on recourse to violence but on respect for law and order.

There have been many pressures upon your President and there will be others as the days come and go. But I pledge you tonight that we intend to fight this battle where it should be fought: in the courts, and in the Congress, and in the hearts of men.

We must preserve the right of free speech and the right of free assembly. But the right of free speech does not carry with it, as has been said, the right to holler fire in a crowded theater. We must preserve the right to free assembly, but free assembly does not carry with it the right to block public thoroughfares to traffic.

We do have a right to protest, and a right to march under conditions that do not infringe the constitutional rights of our neighbors. And I intend to protect all those rights as long as I am permitted to serve in this office.

We will guard against violence, knowing it strikes from our hands the very weapons which we seek—progress, obedience to law, and belief in American values.

In Selma as elsewhere we seek and pray for peace. We seek order. We seek unity. But we will not accept the peace of stifled rights, or the order imposed by fear, or the unity that stifles protest. For peace cannot be purchased at the cost of liberty.

In Selma tonight, as in every—and we had a good day there—as in every city, we are working for just and peaceful settlement. We must all remember that after this speech I am making tonight, after the police and the FBI and the Marshals have all gone, and after you have promptly passed this bill, the people of Selma and the other cities of the Nation must still live and work together. And when the attention of the Nation has gone elsewhere they must try to heal the wounds and to build a new community.

This cannot be easily done on a battleground of violence, as the history of the South itself shows. It is in recognition of this that men of both races have shown such an outstandingly impressive responsibility in recent days—last Tuesday, again today.

RIGHTS MUST BE OPPORTUNITIES

The bill that I am presenting to you will be known as a civil rights bill. But, in a larger sense, most of the program I am recommending is a civil rights program. Its object is to open the city of hope to all people of all races.

Because all Americans just must have the right to vote. And we are going to give them that right.

All Americans must have the privileges of citizenship regardless of race. And they are going to have those privileges of citizenship regardless of race.

But I would like to caution you and remind you that to exercise these privileges takes much more than just legal right. It requires a trained mind and a healthy body. It requires a decent home, and the chance to find a job, and the opportunity to escape from the clutches of poverty.

Of course, people cannot contribute to the Nation if they are never taught to read or write, if their bodies are stunted from hunger, if their sickness goes untended, if their life is spent in hopeless poverty just drawing a welfare check.

So we want to open the gates to opportunity. But we are also going to give all our people, black and white, the help that they need to walk through those gates.

THE PURPOSE OF THIS GOVERNMENT

My first job after college was as a teacher in Cotulla, Tex., in a small Mexican-American school. Few of them could speak English, and I couldn't speak much Spanish. My students were poor and they often came to class without breakfast, hungry. They knew even in their youth the pain of prejudice. They never seemed to know why people disliked them. But they knew it was so, because I saw it in their eyes. I often walked home late in the afternoon, after the classes were finished, wishing there was more that I could do. But all I knew was to teach them the little that I knew, hoping that it might help them against the hardships that lay ahead.

Somehow you never forget what poverty and hatred can do when you see its scars on the hopeful face of a young child.

I never thought then, in 1928, that I would be standing here in 1965. It never even occurred to me in my fondest dreams that I might have the chance to help the sons and daughters of those students and to help people like them all over this country.

But now I do have that chance—and I'll let you in on a secret—I mean to use it. And I hope that you will use it with me.

This is the richest and most powerful country which ever occupied the globe. The might of past empires is little compared to ours. But I do not want to be the President who built empires, or sought grandeur, or extended dominion.

I want to be the President who educated young children to the wonders of their world. I want to be the President who helped to feed the hungry and to prepare them to be taxpayers instead of taxeaters.

I want to be the President who helped the poor to find their own way and who protected the right of every citizen to vote in every election.

I want to be the President who helped to end hatred among his fellow men and who promoted love among the people of all races and all regions and all parties.

I want to be the President who helped to end war among the brothers of this earth.

And so at the request of your beloved Speaker and the Senator from Montana; the majority leader, the Senator from Illinois; the minority leader, Mr. McCullosh, and other Members of both parties, I came here tonight—not as President Roosevelt came down one time in person to veto a bonus bill, not as President Truman came down one time to urge the passage of a railroad bill—but I came down here to ask you to share this task with me and to share it with the people that we both work for. I want this to be the Congress, Republicans and Democrats alike, which did all these things for all these people.

Beyond this great chamber, out yonder in 50 States, are the people that we serve. Who can tell what deep and unspoken hopes are in their hearts tonight as they sit there and listen. We all can guess, from our own lives, how difficult they often find their own pursuit of happiness, how many problems each little family has. They look most of all to themselves for their futures. But I think that they also look to each of us.

Above the pyramid on the great seal of the United States it says—in Latin—"God has favored our undertaking."

God will not favor everything that we do. It is rather our duty to divine His will. But I cannot help believing that He truly understands and that He really favors the undertaking that we begin here tonight.